The Church of North India
A Historical and Systematic Theological Inquiry
into an Ecumenical Ecclesiology

STUDIEN ZUR INTERKULTURELLEN GESCHICHTE DES CHRISTENTUMS
ETUDES D´HISTOIRE INTERCULTURELLE DU CHRISTIANISME
STUDIES IN THE INTERCULTURAL HISTORY OF CHRISTIANITY

begründet von/fondé par/founded by
Hans Jochen Margull †, Hamburg

herausgegeben von/édité par/edited by

Richard Friedli   Walter J. Hollenweger   Theo Sundermeier
Université de Fribourg   University of Birmingham   Universität Heidelberg

Jan A. B. Jongeneel
Rijksuniversiteit Utrecht

Band 88

PETER LANG

Frankfurt am Main · Berlin · Bern · New York · Paris · Wien

Dhirendra Kumar Sahu

The Church of North India

A Historical and Systematic Theological Inquiry into an Ecumenical Ecclesiology

PETER LANG
Europäischer Verlag der Wissenschaften

Die Deutsche Bibliothek - CIP-Einheitsaufnahme

Sahu, Dhirendra Kumar:

The Church of North India : a historical and systematic
theological inquiry into an ecumenical ecclesiology / Dhirendra
Kumar Sahu. - Frankfurt am Main ; Berlin ; Bern ; New York ;
Paris ; Wien : Lang, 1994
  (Studien zur interkulturellen Geschichte des Christentums ;
  Bd. 88)
  Zugl.: Birmingham, Univ., Diss., 1992
  ISBN 3-631-46908-X

NE: GT

ISSN 0170-9240
ISBN 3-631-46908-X
© Peter Lang GmbH
Europäischer Verlag der Wissenschaften
Frankfurt am Main 1994
All rights reserved.

Printed in Germany 1 2 3 5 6 7

TO
MY WIFE MANJU
THE BOYS BIBHU AND ASHIS

ACKNOWLEDGEMENTS

I express my thanks to my supervisor, Professor David Ford, for the patient and scholarly way in which he has enabled me to bring this thesis to completion, and his willingness to continue supervision even after becoming the Regius Professor of Divinity at Cambridge. I value his constant encouragement to pursue this research, and his willingness, so often, to go the 'second mile'. His friendship and deep commitment as a Christian theologian is something that I shall always appreciate. I am also grateful to Dr Hugh McLeod for his initial support and willingness to supervise during the sabbatical term of Prof. David Ford in 1989.

I express my thanks to the Baptist Missionary Society for providing the financial assistance for this research. This is the second time that the Society has supported me with a family scholarship, the first one being from 1979-82 to enable me read theology at the University of Oxford. My family and I are deeply indebted to Dr Barrie White, the former Principal of Regent's Park College, Oxford, for the many ways in which he supported us during our four years of residence in Oxford for this research. My gratitude also to Dr Mathew P. John, Serampore College, India for the initial suggestion to pursue this subject which arose during our working together on the Theological Commission of the Church of North India. I am indebted to Edna Outlaw, Deborah Rooke, Alan McCormack, Christine Joynes, Margaret Okole, John Greenwood and Robin Rees for all their help. Publication of this thesis was made possible by financial support from

The Pollock Memorial Missionary Trust, the Bethune-Baker Fund and Prof. David and Mrs. Deborah Ford for which I am grateful. I am also grateful to many friends in near and distant places for prayerful support in this research.

To my two sons, Bibhu and Ashis, for bearing with their father for so long, and last but not least, to my wife, Manju, for companionship and constant support during the period of graduate studies, 'Thank you' is not enough.

FOREWORD

Christianity has spread by a constantly renewed history of fresh embodiments in different contexts. There has been immense variety in forms of community, worship, political commitment, cultural expression, theology and other aspects of its life. Indeed, it might be said that in order to be true to its origins it must be constantly open to being realised through new groups of people in diverse contexts. Yet one obvious major issue in this is how it is to remain true to its identity. What are the marks of continuity with its origins in the midst of all the changes? And as it responds to new contexts, what sort of community should it try to become? More pointedly, how can such questions be worked through in a specific situation taking into account the complexities of that place?

Dr. Sahu has produced a remarkable work of historical and theological insight into the Christian Church in North India. He has shown the ways in which Indian Christians have answered those basic questions. He has done detailed historical work on one of Christianity's main ecumenical achievements, the formation of the Church of North India. Above all, he has faced with an eye to the future the theological questions of Christian identity, the nature of the church, the appropriate forms of Christianity in India and the agenda that needs to be born in mind as the next millennium draws near. He has drawn deeply on many sources but has always made them his own, serving the overall task of discerning what the Church of North India has been, what it is now and what it is called to be.

This is a work of fine scholarship and thoughtful theology, but it deserves to be read too at another level, as an offering of wisdom not only to India but also to the wider world. As the world and its religions undergo massive transformations it is crucial that there be high quality thinking at the leading edge of each community. Here we have a good example of such thought, deeply acquainted with the origins and development of Christianity in East and West, attentive to the contemporary situation, drawing on some of the best in recent Christian theology and daring to trace the lines along which a particular community of Christians might enter the future.

David F. Ford

Regius Professor of Divinity

University of Cambridge

CONTENTS

DEDICATION   v

ACKNOWLEDGEMENTS   vii

FOREWORD   ix

CONTENTS   xi

INTRODUCTION   1

CHAPTER I MISSION AND CHRISTIAN IDENTITY   9

    The Establishment of Missions   11

    Missionary Methods   20

    Missionary Cooperation and Tension   26

    Missionary Attitudes   35

    Conclusion   59

CHAPTER II NATIONALISM AND CHRISTIAN IDENTITY   65

    Indian Nationalism   68

    Mission and Independence   80

    Conclusion   101

CHAPTER III THE STORY OF THE NEGOTIATIONS   104

    First Phase: 1929-51   107

    Second Phase: 1951-65   120

    Third Phase: 1965-70   131

    Post Union Phase   138

CHAPTER IV THE THEOLOGY OF THE UNION   143

    Basis of Union   146

    The Statement of Faith   156

    Conclusion   176

xii

CHAPTER V   THE NATURE OF IDENTITY   179
    Ecclesial Identity   180
    An Assessment   199
    Social and Religious Identity   208
    Conclusion   222
CHAPTER VI   A UNITING ECCLESIOLOGY   225
    Categories of Ecclesiology   227
    Performative Identity of Koinonia   293
    Conclusion   312
CONCLUSION   316
ABBREVIATIONS   323
APPENDIX I   The Doctrines of the Church   324
APPENDIX II An Affirmation of Faith and Commitment   326
APPENDIX III Statistics   329
APPENDIX IV A Map of the CNI   330
BIBLIOGRAPHY   331
INDEX   348

INTRODUCTION

The creation of the British Empire in India, the establishment of the Christian mission, the cultural renaissance in Indian society, the emergence of Indian nationalism and the final achievement of independence have all made important contributions to the development of unity among the Churches in India. Not the least of these contributions has been the effect of focusing attention on the question of the identity of Indian Christianity. The question of identity is important because there is a sense of foreignness attached to being Christian in India and the Church has been trying its best to be Indian as well as Christian.

Basic to the search for Christian identity is the ability to identify the forces that shape it. One of the tasks of ecclesiology is to express the identity of a believing community and to help the community deal with the social change that comes upon it. At the heart of the matter are two questions. The first is about what gives distinctiveness to the community, because any group forms its identity by marking its boundaries. Once the boundaries are set up then the second question is how they can be sustained and justified in the context of a world view. They need to be justified because the received notions of what it means to be a Christian may be called into question by the emergence of new circumstances or ideas or by new awareness of social relationships.

The growth of twentieth century ecumenism is one aspect of the search for Christian identity. Even those who look on ecumenism with suspicion can scarcely fail to acknowledge that it has renewed the vision of the Church. Ecumenism (oikoumene) refers in this thesis to the movement which has come into being in this century to overcome the division within the Church and to restore its unity. The general impression might be that once a covenant is signed, uniting churches live happily ever after. If this were true, this thesis would be of purely historical interest. However, the fact of coming together often causes tensions to be felt more severely than they are felt in separation. The integration of local worshipping groups may prove more difficult than the unification of confessions, particularly when union is based on the principle of freedom of conscience. The concern in the union is to manifest the universality as well as the particularity of the Church, expressing its identity as the people of God. This concern has occupied an important place in the history of Christianity in India.[1]

The theological rediscovery of a vision of a united Church within the ecumenical movement in north India arose from the experience of long years of debate, from the way the theological and non-theological factors functioned during the negotiation, and from the pain of the last minute withdrawal of a major negotiating church, namely the Methodist Church in Southern Asia (now the Methodist Church in India). The vision was

---

[1] VISSER'T HOOFT, W.A. The Word 'Ecumenical' - Its History and Use. In ROUSE, Ruth and NEILL, Stephen eds. A History of the Ecumenical Movement 1517-1948. WCC, Geneva, 1986, Vol.1, p735. There are seven meanings of the word ecumenical:
i.   pertaining to or representing the whole (inhabited) Earth.
ii.   pertaining to or representing the whole of the (Roman) Empire.
iii.   pertaining to or representing the whole of the Church.
iv.   that which has universal ecclesiastical validity;
v.   pertaining to the world-wide missionary outreach of the Church;
vi.   pertaining to the relations between and unity of two or more churches (or of Christians of various confessions);
vii.   that quality or attitude which expresses the consciousness of and desire for Christian unity.

realized in the joyful reunion of six major denominations - the Church of India, Pakistan, Burma and Ceylon, the United Church of North India (merger of Presbyterian and Congregation2al), the Methodist Church (British and Australian Conference), the Church of the Brethren, the Church of the Disciples of Christ, and the churches connected with the Council of the Baptist Churches in Northern India - to form the Church of North India (hereafter the CNI).

The union of churches in north India marked a transition from denominational identity to a corporate identity. But the question of ecclesial identity is not an isolated phenomenon when considered in a particular historical context like that of India. At any given time the Church as a particular expression of Christianity is the outcome of a historical process of development, and therefore takes differing forms in the course of history. Thus the uniting churches adopted the ideal of organic union as a contemporary expression of the identity of the Church. This means that within the union, each uniting church was required to see its own identity as being not the whole but a part of a common identity. The strength of this new identity lies in the discovery of the richness of various traditions, along with the way in which groups of people in different regions make their own contribution to the witness and service of the Church.

While the union is a partial victory of north Indian Christianity over the divisions brought by western missions, and no doubt a remarkable achievement, the union has also brought in its wake a series of new problems, the response to which is vital in the search for an Indian Christian identity. One strength of the union lies in its potential for constructing an identity that will witness to the reconciling power of the

Gospel. However the united Church has also become the repository of considerable and varied resources. Adherents of diverse persuasions were brought face to face within a single corporate body. The challenge has been to reconcile different convictions, castes, regions and language groups in a unified Church with one structure. Therefore such union is vulnerable to internal power politics.

My intention is to identify some factors related to the Christian missions, Indian nationalism, Indian Christians and wider Hindu communities which undermined the rigidity of denominational barriers and to show the subtle ways in which the Church could be complacent after the dissolution of its various denominational identities. It is considerations of this kind that have prompted the present study. The aim is not to work out a systematic ecclesiology but to analyse the historical developments in the formation of the CNI, and to propose a provisional ecumenical ecclesiology as a possible framework for the CNI.

The great strength and toughness of family, caste and community in India ensure that the individual has an assurance of acceptance by a group. However, becoming a Christian demands some separation from the ties of one's former identity. Generally one's identity is defined in terms of the social group to which one belongs, with its traditions and privileges, and which like all human groups tends to seek its own corporate advancement. Therefore it is natural for any community to be defensive. The Church, however, is called to be a new humanity which must try to transcend the narrow identities that are opposed to development of a full humanity. It must also be able to see sin within itself and change when change is called for. Not surprisingly, this strategy involves a complex of issues concerning the nature of ecclesial identity, both social and religious. These matters will be explored and will constantly recur in the thesis.

The first part of the thesis will set the context by identifying the factors which weakened the rigidity of denominational barriers. The first chapter will contain an outline of the history of the Christian missions, highlighting the missionary methods, co-operation, tension and attitudes. The overlap between the modern missionary movement and colonialism provides the problematic starting point for the process of defining the identity of the Church in India. The link between mission and ecumenism is evident in the concern to overcome the divisions between Christians. However with the growing recognition of nationalism, the statement of such a link is complex. Therefore the second chapter will contain an introduction to Indian nationalism and the early indigenous Christian movements which were Christian associations arising from the protest of a few Christian elites against the paternalism of the missionaries. It was no coincidence that their protest, both individual and institutional, came together with the national awakening. Therefore it will be helpful to assess their views as inspired and modified by the national movement. The object is to understand the complementarity of both the missionary movement and Indian nationalism in the formation and growth of a united Church, and to respond creatively to the demand to transcend natural cultural constraints in the search for koinonia in a particular locality.

The second part of the thesis will narrate the debate. The third chapter will contain a survey of the story of the negotiations and the fourth chapter will discuss the theology of the union in north India. The achievement of the union of churches is through an intricate network of many different and sometimes seemingly contradictory endeavours. There are different points of conviction and different impulses for union, but the transition was from denominational identity to an ecumenical identity through the relationship of theological and non-theological factors. This has ranged over matters to do with both faith and order within the Church. The questions of faith and order have converged during the discussion but sometimes the question of order took priority over faith. It is important to identify their relationship as the uniting partners of the CNI did through a definite plan of union. It is through this web of convictions, opinions and diverse emphases that finally the way was found for union.

In the light of the descriptive part of the thesis, the third part will deal with its application. A systematic inquiry will be made in order to suggest an ecumenical identity of the ecclesia. The fifth chapter will discuss the nature of identity, aiming to describe the issues involved in the search for an appropriate ecclesial identity in the social and religious context of India. It will also contain four models of ecclesiology which will be used to portray the Christian responses concerning the identity of an Indian Church. The sixth chapter will outline a provisional ecumenical ecclesiology in the light of the above discussion.

The movement for union in north India would never have developed through a mere theological relativism. Enthusiasm for mission and consciousness of being an Indian were two major factors of the church union movement in north India. It is necessary for the CNI to reappropriate that which is intrinsic to its own identity as a koinonia in history. However, the CNI self-consciously admits plurality which implies the rationale for the vision of a Church where discipleship includes the irreducible diversity of human social existence. It would be wrong on the part of the CNI to assume that church unity was an end in itself. The ideal is to be an indigenous fellowship for worship, mission and service. Therefore the Church must be aware of the subtle ways in which the influence of certain factors can change its direction. The CNI has brought together six denominational churches and people of different caste, class, tribe, and language groups forming homogeneous as well as heterogeneous congregations. These congregations are scattered over north India in a pluralistic society with a cultural milieu thoroughly permeated by Hinduism. The CNI's conviction is that the Church being the first fruit and instrument of God's election must live in obedience to His call as congregations among communities of diverse religious convictions.

The self-understanding of the CNI is influenced both by inherited Christian traditions and the socio-religious character of Indian society. In the light of these twin dimensions of identity formation, an attempt is made in this thesis to propose a provisional ecclesiology as a way of defining a critical self-awareness of faith for Indian Christians. The object is to interrelate the sense of identity both as an Indian and as a Christian in the corporate life and thought of a united Church. During the past, there have been several attempts to define the nature of the relation between the two identities in the life and thought of Indian Christians. Theologians have spoken of adoption and adaptation of one or more features of Hindu heritage for use in theological reflection in the form of 'indigenization' or 'contextualization' or 'inculturation' of the Christian faith. These ideas are evidence of how complex and intricate a task it is to describe adequately the dynamic nature of an identity that must be Indian as well as Christian.

In proposing an ecumenical ecclesiology, it is suggested that the CNI needs to be aware how dynamic the conjunction of the Indian and Christian identities can be, and needs to draw attention to worship through the Lord's Supper as a focal point for construing ecclesial identity. The identity construed in such a way is important, as no expression of identity is as fundamental as the community gathered for worship. The community so construed would reveal itself in the capacity to read the signs of the times, and to discern the action of God in history and to respond to it as the people of God. Such an identity is not over against or superior to the identity of other religious communities, but consists in the mediatory and servant rôle of a community witnessing to the reconciling power of the Gospel. Only such a community could claim to be the avant garde of the new age in the kingdom of God.

PART I

CONTEXT

CHAPTER ONE

MISSION AND CHRISTIAN IDENTITY

The coming of modern mission to India was the founding of a new community in the pluralistic Indian society. This community embraced a faith which arrived with a colonial power and was dependent on finance from the West. It was made up of people drawn from various other religious communities and caste backgrounds, the majority of whom came from lower castes and the economically backward classes. The challenge therefore was to integrate these different identities in one community. But, in the course of history, the visible Christian community in India as elsewhere has often failed to express the fruits of new life in Christ in a sense of renewal, freedom and dignity. Caste or class still persists in the Indian Christian community in some form or other. It is right to admit this more openly than has perhaps been done previously.

Any serious consideration of the Church as a new community must take into account the story of early Christianity in India, that is, the story of the Syrian Christians. The story goes that the foundation of the Church in India was laid by St. Thomas, or St. Thomas and St. Bartholomew, the Apostles, or that the arrival of Christianity in India was due to the enterprise of merchants and missionaries of the East Syrian or Persian Church. There is insufficient documentary evidence to arrive at any precise knowledge and little evidence in western tradition to supplement the local tradition. But there is no doubt that the history of Christianity in India goes back to an early period.

It is almost certain that there were well established churches in parts of south India not later than the beginning of the sixth century and perhaps from a considerably earlier date, but it is probable that these were at least in part churches of foreigners, worshipping in Syriac and cared for by foreign priests and bishops.[1]

The nucleus of the Indian Christian community in the pre-sixteenth century period lay chiefly in what is now central Kerala and this was unquestionably the first Christian community in India. This community at the extreme corner of south India was very much dependent on the Persian church.

The relation between the Church of India and the East Syrian church which started in the third and fourth century grew to such a proportion that the former in course of time, became so dependent on the latter that everything ecclesiastical in India was practically east Syrian....Perhaps the community of the Thomas Christians was able to maintain a strong tradition on account of dependence... This dependence further prevented the Church of India from developing an Indian Christian culture, especially in the sphere of theology, liturgy, church law and custom.[2]

The history of the Syrian Christians from the earliest times till the latter half of the sixteenth century was that of a single denomination. They were called Syrian Christians because of their relationship with the Eastern

---

[1] NEILL, Stephen C. The History of Christianity in India. CUP, Cambridge, 1984, p48.

[2] MUNDADAN, Mathias A. History of Christianity in India: From the beginning to the Middle of Sixteenth Century. Vol.I, Theological Publications in India, Bangalore, 1984, p115.

Syrian churches and their liturgy in the Syrian language. They were assimilated with Indian society by conforming to the pattern and practices of Indian society. In the following centuries the Syrian Christians were divided into three main groups: those who accepted the authority of the Pope while retaining their Eastern rites and customs; those who recognized the leadership of the Patriarch of Antioch; and the Mar Thoma Christians who were separated from the major group during the earlier part of the nxineteenth century due to the impact of the Church Missionary Society.

The Establishment of Missions

Modern missions arose from a 'Christendom' situation in the West, which started with the reign of Constantine when Christianity became the official religion of the state. With the present recognition that Christendom as such has passed away, there is need to reassess the case for mission and this obviously has great significance for the Church in India. A detailed history of the Syrian, the Roman Catholic and the Protestant Churches would be ideal for this purpose, but for the purpose of my thesis I will limit myself to a brief outline of the establishment of modern missions in India and select those issues relating to the missionary movement which were important for the founding of the Christian community in India.   India was conquered from time to time during the course of her long history. The long reign of Hindu states had been broken at the end of the twelfth century by the foreign rule of Muslim Turks. For two centuries the Delhi empire controlled the north and at times the centre of the country. In 1526 Babur from Afghanistan defeated the rival powers in a great battle at Panipat and his dynasty was entitled the Mogul dynasty. This was the beginning of Mogul dominion in India. One of the great Mogul monarchs was Akabar who ruled India from 1556-1605. The Mogul empire became a political fact over half of India and a factor in the life of India which has influenced her ever since.[3]

The coming of the Portuguese at the end of the fifteenth century marked the beginning of the Western colonial period in India. European colonialism in India was a period covering four hundred and fifty years and included an encounter between East and West. The Roman Catholic and Protestant missions followed the colonial flag. The extent and nature of this relationship between missions and colonialism varied from one colonial power to another. Nevertheless the Christian missions appeared as outposts of western imperialism, and the Church was identified with western imperialism.

The story began with the Portuguese. Pope Nicholas V on 18 June 1452 granted to the king of Portugal the power to conquer the kingdoms of the pagans and to possess their temporal goods. That also included the right to found and support churches and monasteries, and the sole right of the Crown to appoint bishops with territorial jurisdiction. With the discovery of the sea route to India by Vasco da Gama when he came to Calicut in 1498, the Portuguese laid claim to ecclesiastical as well as political sovereignty over India and invoked the Papal charter to this effect. The Franciscans took Goa, Calicut, Cochin and Malabar coast as their mission field in 1517. Pope Paul III designated Goa as the seat of a future bishopric

---

[3] SPEAR, Percival. <u>A History of India</u>. Vol.II, Penguin Books, Harmonds-worth, 1968, pp15-39.

and later of an Archbishopric with wide jurisdiction on 3rd November 1534. In 1557, Goa became an archbishopric. By the end of the sixteenth century, the efforts of Archbishop Alexis de Menezes had brought the Syrian Christians to an acknowledgement of the authority of the Pope. But the changes and methods which he employed roused bitter opposition among the Syrians, and in 1653 they gathered in indignation at the Koonen Cross in the churchyard at Mattancheri and swore an oath to expel the Jesuits and to accept no ecclesiastical authority other than that of their own archdeacon, until they should receive a bishop from the eastern church.

When Portugal began to find it difficult to fulfil her commitments because of the decline of her power and resources, Pope Gregory XV took action and on 6th January 1622 brought into being the Sacred Congregation for the Propagation of the Faith, often referred to as the Propaganda. It was the first serious attempt to view the missionary work of the Church of Rome as a unity. Everything was expected to be done exactly as was done in Rome. The aim was to bring the mission under the direct control of the Pope. Different nationalities of missionaries and different religious orders were enlisted and sent to India. This brought the Holy See into a conflict with the Portuguese which lasted for more than two centuries.[4]

In the beginning the Roman Church had worked with and through the Portuguese power. But the conflict about the rights of Portugal, tension

---

[4] MUNDADAN, Mathias A. History of Christianity in India.Vol.I, Theological Publications in India, Bangalore, 1984, pp 233-82. THEKKE-DATH, Joseph. History of Christianity in India. Vol.II, Theological Publications in India, Bangalore, 1982, pp414-420. NEILL, Stephen. A History of Christianity in India.CUP, Cambridge, 1984, p333.

between the representatives of different religious orders and between the missionaries from different nations together with the suppression of the Jesuit order first in Portugal and then elsewhere, seriously weakened the work. Nevertheless one thing worth highlighting is that under Portuguese power the identity of the Church and state was complete. Christianization was a means of strengthening the Portuguese political power, although their effort was mainly confined to small areas of India where they held political power.

The coming of the East India Company in the seventeenth century inaugurated the first phase in the history of Protestant mission in India. The Company was formed on 31st December 1600. The completion of the British conquest in the nineteenth century was to protect the East India Company's trading posts with no thought of dominating all India. But once one territory had been acquired, wars and further annexations became inevitable. Most of India was brought under British control, some directly by the East India Company and some by princes who had allied with the British by the middle of the nineteenth century.[5]

Initially there was a handicap to the spread of Christianity as the East India Company refused missionaries passage on its ships and forbade them to carry on their labours in its territories. This was the situation in the 1790's and early 1800's. However at the renewal of the Company's charter in 1813, the evangelicals had obtained modifications and with the act of 1833 the other restrictions were withdrawn. The formal permission to reside

---

[5] LATOURETTE, Kenneth Scott. <u>A History of the Expansion of Christianity</u>. Vol.VI, 1943, pp65-74.

was no longer necessary except in the territories of semi-independent rulers.

> It was necessary, first to break down the Mohammedan power, extending over most of the country, secondly, to break down the Brahminical power resting upon caste and having the sanction of ages, and thirdly when the East India Company had answered its purpose, it was needful to bring that great selfish corporation to an end. India was not fully prepared for the outcome of the gospel, until these results were all substantially attained.[6]

The arrival of William Carey on 11 November 1793 is usually marked as the beginning of modern missions. Although Carey stood in a succession of many other pioneers, he is generally known as 'the father of modern missions'. His work was a turning point, marking the entry of the English speaking world on a large scale into missionary enterprise. The situation on his arrival was not favourable for the foundation of a mission, as the East India Company was suspicious of missionaries and hostile to their entrance. Therefore Carey had to spend some years in Mudanbati to superintend an indigo factory belonging to George Udny. While living there, he made preaching tours, learnt Bengali and translated the New Testament into Bengali. With the arrival of Joshua Marshman (1768-1837) and William Ward (1769-1823) in 1799, the situation changed. They realized that the best way to ensure their safety was to settle at Serampore, the Danish colony sixteen miles from Calcutta. William Carey was persuaded to come and join them at Serampore and there was laid the foundation of one of the most

---

[6] ANDERSON, Rufus. Foreign Missions & their Relations & Claims. New York, 1869, p2. Anderson was the Foreign Secretary of the American Board of Commission for Foreign Missions.

famous partnerships in the whole history of mission.[7]

The evangelical awakening in Britain was the cause of the development of the British missionary societie.[8] It is true that this was not without

---

[7] CAREY, William was born in 1761, and worked as a shoemaker and schoolmaster before becoming the pastor of the Baptist Church at Moulton, Northamptonshire in 1785. He moved to Harvey Lane Church, Leicester in 1789. In 1792 he persuaded a group of fellow ministers to form the Particular Baptist Missionary Society. MARSHMAN, Joshua was born in 1768, in 1794 accepted a teaching post at Bristol, was baptized and began attending courses at Bristol Academy. He answered the call of BMS for missionaries. Hannah Marshman's Girls' School in Serampore was one of the most important schools. WARD, William was born in 1769, became an apprentice to a printer in Derby and spent six years as editor, first of the Derby Mercury and then of the Hull Advertiser. He was baptized in 1796, began training for the ministry and later responded to a BMS call for missionaries. He spent most of his time printing and cutting type for a wide variety of Oriental languages. See MARSHMAN, John Clark. The Life and Times of Carey, Marshman, and Ward Embracing the history of the Serampore Mission, 2 Vols. London, 1859; and The Life and Labours of Carey, Marshman and Ward, London, 1873. DREWERY, Mary. William Carey. Hodder & Stoughton, London, 1978.

[8] The societies that were committed in the mission in India were:
1698 The Society for Promoting Christian Knowledge.
1701 The Society for Propagating the Gospel.
1792 The Baptist (Particular) Missionary Society.
1795 The London Missionary Society.
1799 The Church Missionary Society.
1799 The Religious Tract Society.
1804 The British and Foreign Bible Society.
1817 The Wesleyan Methodist Missionary Society.
1818 The General Baptist Missionary Society.
 Amalgamated with the Baptist Missionary Society in 1891.
1826 The Mission of SPCK was transferred to SPG.
1822 Scottish Missionary Society.
 Taken over by the Church of Scotland in 1835.

its difficulties since the spirit of rivalry and mutual criticism soon began to make its influence felt. But the different missionary societies, in spite of varying traditions of church order, did have the one common object of communicating the Gospel, which in the early days was presupposed in the establishment of missionary societies. The founders of the London Missionary Society had resolved in their founding principle not to send Presbyterianism, Independency, Episcopacy or any other form of church order and government but to preach the eternal Gospel to the heathen.[9] While the Anglicans did not deny so much of their heritage and founded the CMS in 1799, the same men were cooperating with Non-conformists in the foundation of the Religious Tract Society in 1799 and the British and Foreign Bible Society in 1804.

The Continental Missionary Societies had grown out of the pietist movement of the seventeenth century.[10] The Pietists had opened their university at Halle in 1694 which became an educational centre of pietism and the source of the missionary enterprise of the eighteenth century. Out of this University grew the first Protestant mission - the Danish Halle Mission. Its initial impetus originated in Denmark, hence the name. In 1620

---

[9] LOVETT, Richard. The History of LMS. 1795-1895. Vol.I, London, 1899, p49.

[10] 1824 The Berlin Missionary Society. 1815 The Basel Evangelical Missionary Society. The Basel Mission started work in India in 1834. 1836 The Gossner Mission. 1836 The Leipzig Mission Society. See RICHTER, Julius. A History of Missions in India. Translated by Moore, Sydney H., Oliphant Anderson and Ferrier, 1908, Edinburgh and London, p192-201. The Basel Mission was from the start ecumenically minded, drawing support from several countries - S. Germany, Switzerland, Austria, Alsace and the churches of both Lutheran and Reformed confession.

Denmark had established its first trading colony at Tranquebar on the east coast of India and ministers were sent out to serve the needs of the colonists. Missionary work among the indigenous population started with Bartholomew Ziegenbalg and Heinrich Plutschau from 1706.

In many areas of Germany, the pietistic awakening was parallelled by a churchly and confessional movement of renewal. From this second movement arose the Leipzig Lutheran Mission in 1836 and others. The so-called confessional missions from the beginning regarded themselves as representatives of their churches, unlike the former group of societies in which the relationship to specific churches was ill defined. Stephen Neill says that it was perhaps in consequence of this lack of clear church connection that the German missions developed those two formidable characters - the mission director and mission inspector.[11]

During the last quarter of the eighteenth century while individuals were trying to convince Christians of their duty to propagate the gospel,[12]

---

[11] NEILL, Stephen C. A History of Christianity in India: 1707-1858, CUP, Cambridge, 1985, p409.

[12] a. CAREY, William. An Enquiry into the Obligation of Christians to use Means for the Conversion of the Heathens, May 1792. New Facsimile Edition 1961. Reprinted 1991. Baptist Missionary Society. Carey's arguments were addressed primarily to those who justified their inaction on behalf of the spiritual condition of non-Christian people by the claim that the Great Commission of Mt.28:18-20 did not apply to them. He persuaded a group at Kettering to accept the idea of forming a voluntary society among Particular (Calvinistic) Baptists to spread the Gospel.
b. BUCHANAN, Claudius's famous sermon, 'The Star in the East', 1809 was preached at the Parish Church of St. James, Bristol for the benefit of the CMS. The object of this sermon was to detail some of the more prominent proofs that the day had at length begun to dawn and the day-star to rise on

the United States of America was passing through 'The Great Awakening'.[13] The first missionaries sent out by the American Board of Commission for Foreign Mission in 1812 were Adoniram Judson, Samuel Newell and Samuel Nott with their wives, and Gordon Hall andB Luther Rice.[14] Adoniram Judson, his wife and Luther Rice changed their view on baptism on arrival ibn Calcutta and were baptized by William Ward, one of Carey's colleagues at Serampore. Judson resigned from the ABCFM and proceeded to Rangoon in Burma while Luther Rice returned to America to lay before the denomination the wants of the heathen world. This led later to the formation of the American Baptist Foreign Mission in 1814 and Judson

the inhabitants of Asia to diffuse Christianity in the East. Buchanan's sermon had appeared in <u>Massachusetts Baptist Missionary Magazine</u>, September 1809. See PEARSON, H. <u>The Memoirs of Rev Dr Claudius Buchanan</u>. Vol I & II, 1819. London.

[13] The evangelicalism out of which the American missions grew had an intellectual heritage in the works of Americans like Jonathan Edwards and Samuel Hopkins. Samuel Hopkins' address before the Providence Society for Abolishing the Slave Trade, on 17th May 1793, was based on MT 28:19-20. It should be ranked alongside the great Sermon of William Carey a few months earlier. His conviction was that the Good News should be published through the whole world, and the offer of Christ's salvation be made to all mankind. It illustrates the convictions that motivated a large number of people who manned the protestant missionary effort.

[14] The object of the board was defined in their meeting on 27 June 27 1810 'to devise, adopt and prosecute ways and means for propagating the Gospel among those who are destitute of any knowledge of Christianity'. American Board, First Ten Annual Reports, p35-36, cited in PATHAK, S.M. <u>American Missionaries and Hinduism</u>. 1813-1910, Munshiram Manoharlal, Delhi, 1967, p34-35.

became the first missionary of this society to Burma.[15]

The establishment of missions began the founding of the identity of the Indian Christian community. The loyalty of the Indian Christians was to the mission and this was naturally identified with the missionaries, with their way of doing things, and with their attitudes. Therefore it will be appropriate to examine missionary methods, cooperation, tensions and attitudes to evangelizing India, before discussing the emergence of Indian nationalism.

Missionary Methods
a. Evangelism
The common object of all was to evangelize India. First and foremost was the preaching of the Gospel in the streets of the city, under the village tree where the gathering might consist of half a dozen men, or in the vicinity of some popular temple on days of festival when many thousands

---

[15] a. The American Societies that were committed in India were:
1813 The American Board of Commission for Foreign Mission (Congre)
1814 The American Baptist Foreign Mission Society
1834 The American Presbyterian Mission
1856 The Missionary Society of the Methodist Episcopal Church.

b. The mission work of William Carey in India excited considerable interest in American church circles, especially in New York, Connecticut, Massachusetts, Philadelphia. Dr Carey had received nearly $6000 from American Christians between 1806-07 and again in 1810, a sum of $4,650 for translation work from the Boston Baptist Association. See PATHAK, S.M., American Missionaries and Hinduism, p32.

might be assembled. But as the years passed it was found as a matter of experience that preaching was more successful when it was attempted in a room and at regular intervals.[16] In the initial stage, all the missionaries had adopted very much a common method. As people accepted the Gospel, they were instructed in the element of Christianity, baptized and organized into congregations. The missionary would select the brighter young men, give them some measure of education and training and put them in charge of their congregation under his supervision.[17]

One outstanding achievement was in making available the word of God as a means for the propagation of the Gospel. Ziegenbalg as a first Protestant missionary had engaged himself in the study of the Tamil language and was able to publish a translation of the New Testament into Tamil in 1714, the first in an Indian language. William Carey was the other pioneer Protestant missionary translator. His initial years were full of adversity and constraint. With his refuge in Serampore under the Danish flag and the support of his colleagues Joshua Marshman and William Ward, a large part of the time and energy of the Serampore group was devoted to literary work especially the translation of the Bible into Indian languages.

---

[16] FINDLAY, G.G. & HOLDSWORTH, W.W. History of the Wesleyan Missionary Society. Vol.V Part 11. Methodist Missions in India, Epworth Press, 1924, p151.

[17] Newbigin comments that in most committees and councils it is often taken for granted that the Church is controlled through these paid agents. This becomes very clear whenever a proposal for voluntary Presbyter is considered. The question is always asked 'How will you be able to control them?' Behind that question lies a whole picture of the church which needs to be brought out into the open and criticized. See NEWBIGIN, Lesslie J.E. The Ministry of the Church. Edinburgh House Press, undated.

It was a gigantic task. Translation of the Bible as well as the New Testament alone and separate Bible portions was completed and edited into thirty seven languages of which twenty-nine were done by Carey.[18]

b. Social Reform

The missionaries had their own conception of Christian conduct. It was obvious that they were the products of their own background and their own social, educational, economic and political environment. Although there were some exceptions, they often assumed that they came to bring the blessing of civilization, identified with Christianity, to a backward people.

> All things being now ready, there began to spring up in the bosom of the British churches a wide and simultaneous sense of the solemn responsibility under which they had been laid by the providence, to avail themselves of so favourable an opening for the diffusion of the Gospel throughout the western world. Men qualified to undertake the high commission must be sent across the ocean.[19]

But one outstanding achievement of the missionaries in the first half of the nineteenth century was to bring about a social reform in Indian

---

[18] See for the details of the languages, CHATTERJEE, Sunil K. William Carey and Serampore. Ghosh Publishing Concern, Calcutta, 1984, p.vi. See also Historical Catalogue of Printed Christian Scriptures in the Languages of the Indian Sub-Continent. British and Foreign Bible Society, 1977.
MARTYN, Henry was perhaps one of the ablest chaplains. His contribution was the introduction of new expertise into the art of Bible translation in Asia. He felt himself to be drawn to Muslims and devoted himself to the production of a completely new translation of the New Testament in Hindustani, Persian and Arabic.

[19] DUFF, Alexander, India and India Missions, Edinburgh, 1839, p27.

society. They tried their best to emancipate individuals from superstitions. The Serampore missionaries carried a long campaign against 'Sati', the burning of a Hindu widow on the pyre of her husband, and 'Meriä', a form of sacrificial infanticide practised among the Konds of Orissa which was of great significance politically in cementing alliance between clans as well as being a regular, cyclical ritual. The victims of sacrifice were called 'Meriäs'; most of them were children kidnapped from distant Konds or other castes.

Through the columns of Samāchar Darpana and Friend of India,[20] the missionaries campaigned to pressurise the government to abolish such inhuman practices. The Baptists continued over the years to draw attention to them, demanding government patronage for their warfare against 'sati', infanticide, and the plights of widows. When Lord William Bentinck took up office as Governor-General in 1828, he turned his attention to social reform and in 1829 declared the practice of 'sati' illegal and criminal. The issue of Friend of India for 1 July 1841 said, 'We are confident that it needs only be known to the government which extinguished 'Sati' that such enormities exist, to call forth its benevolent and energetic interference'. Thirteen years later the custom was almost suppressed.[21]

---

[20] The Serampore trio founded in 1818 a Bengali newspaper: 'Samachar Darpan' and an English magazine: 'The Friend of India'. The Friend of India was a most influential organ in the fight against evil practices of the society.

[21] 'Murder of Children by the Khunds'. Friend of India, 1 July 1841, p 401-2. For a full discussion about the Konds in Orissa, see BOAL, Barbara M. The Konds: Human Sacrifice and Religious Change. Warminster: Aris and Phillips, 1982. PADEL, Felix J. 'British Rule and the Konds of Orissa: A Study of Tribal administration and its Legitimacy Discourse'. D.Phil Thesis, Oxford, 1987.

Education was part of the Protestant missionary activity from the very beginning. The early missionaries were primarily preachers but church and school in the Protestant fields went hand in hand. In the beginning it was the mud and thatched elementary school in the village. Then it was the question of College. The majority of the missionaries were sceptical of the value of higher education as an evangelistic method. They believed that it would result only in replacing ignorant unbelievers by well educated and aggressive unbelievers. But higher education gave the work of the Church of Scotland its first great impetus when Alexander Duff (1806-1878) commenced his pioneering educational work at Calcutta. Duff was in favour of English education, and he arrived in Calcutta on 27th May 1830 determined to introduce a form of Christian higher education in English. This was used not merely as a means of producing an educated Christian population, but also to bring the Gospel to that intellectual elite which can hardly be reached by any other method. Duff laid the foundation for the use of higher education by Protestants as a means for reaching the youth of India. Commenting on the Scottish mission in India, Miller said that:

> Scottish Missions were not, in the most literal sense, the first to work through an English education.... still I believe that the Scottish Missions were the first to make education the leading and controlling feature of their work. That in point of fact it was Scottish Missions that practically gave the impulse to all English education in India, and that it was their example that practically made the educational element bulk so largely as it does now in the work of all the missionary bodies.[22]

---

[22] MILLER, William. Scottish Missions in India: Two Lectures. Madras, 1868, p20.

One of Duff's converts was Krishna Mohan Banerjee, one of the most distinguished Indian Christians in Bengal. Banerjee was deeply respected by all classes and was a pioneer in his attempt to make Christianity genuinely Indian by drawing on the resources of the ancient Hindu culture. The appeal of Duff was always to the reasonableness of Christianity as contrasted with the irrationality of much in non-Christian religions. Another Indian who was influenced by Duff was Lal Behari Day, a student of Duff in 1834. He admired Duff's teaching as thoroughly intellectual and lively. The contribution of Banerjee and Day will be discussed in the next chapter.[23]

After the revolt of 1857, the leadership of reform of Indian religions and society went into the hands of the Indian intellectuals. The social activities of the missionaries were mainly concentrated on philanthropic activities such as the building of hospitals, orphanages and vocational training institutions. Part of the reason was their disappointment with the small number of converts made through educational institutions. Medical work came to occupy an outstanding position in the missionary agenda. The inadequacy of medical facilities in India induced Christian agencies to start hospitals and dispensaries both in cities and villages.

---

[23] Duff's method having proved successful, it was not surprising that it led to the foundation of a college by John Wilson in 1832, Bombay, later to become Wilson College, followed by the institutions founded by Anderson and Braithwaite in Madras in 1837, the ancestor of the Madras Christian College, and in 1844 by Stephen Hislop in Nagpur, later to become Hislop College. NEILL, Stephen C. A History of Christian Missions. Revised by Owen Chadwick, Penguin Books, London, 1987, p234.

Missionary Cooperation and Tension

The missionaries experienced the benefits of cooperation in many ways. The first two missionaries of the Danish-Halle mission, Bartholomaus Ziegenbalg and Heinrich Plutschau, arrived at Tranquebar on the Coromondal coast on 9th July 1706, south of Madras. They were both German Lutherans of the pietist tradition with which the University of Halle was associated, but the responsibility for this mission was accepted by the Church of England through the SPCK. All Anglican missionary work in south India was carried out by Lutheran missionaries for many years. They were not episcopally ordained. Englishmen in Anglican orders did not come to south India as missionaries until the evangelical revival. Even after the foundation of CMS, the society found itself for many years obliged to employ a proportion of ministers from the continent of Europe.

A growing sense of mutual cooperation found expression in missionary conferences. One example in north India was the Calcutta Missionary Conference. The missionaries of the various societies in the city used to meet monthly for prayer and consultation. The local missionary conferences grew in the major cities of India. They reduced friction among missionaries, promoted cooperation and became a powerful forum of missionary opinion which significantly influenced mission policies, leading to the discussion of common problems.[24] They were small gatherings which had the common object of serving the same Master and one faith, and they found advantage in bringing together their common wants and experience. The cause of

---

[24] SINGH, D.V. The Calcutta Missionary Conference. <u>Indian Church History Review</u>.
Vol.XIII, No I, June, 1979, p8f.

cooperation may be claimed to be the inevitable result of evangelistic zeal. When Christians burned with eagerness to win others for Christ, they found themselves at one with members of other churches!

This kind of prayer and consultation in fact prepared the way to organize a General Conference of Protestant Missionaries in Bengal. The General Christian Conference at Calcutta in 1855 was attended by six missionary societies and it was first of a series of similar gatherings held at different places in the East of which seventeen are recorded between 1855-1906. The enthusiasm on a smaller scale was taken up in the wider circle. The centenary conference of Protestant missions of the world was held from 9-19th June 1888 in the Exeter Hall, London. Cooperation was one of the great concerns of the gathering. The truth was that wherever missionaries of the Cross of Christ were inspired by supreme love of their Saviour, they found ways to some kind of closer fellowship even where actual union, or particularly organic union was impracticable.[25]

> The relation between different missionary societies constitutes a problem which may be difficult in theory, but which very seldom comparatively speaking, has been found difficult in practice. It does not of course necessarily follow that because there has been very little difficulty in the past, there will be none in the future. One cause of the hitherto prevailing absence of friction has been the fact that, at least until a somewhat recent period, almost all non-Roman missionaries have held

---

[25] At Exeter Hall, had assembled 1316 members representing 53 societies in Great Britain and Ireland, 189 delegates from USA representing 57 societies, 30 delegates from Canada representing 9 societies, 41 delegates from the Continent of Europe representing 18 societies, 3 delegates from Colonies representing 2 societies. HERKLOTS, H.G.G. Milestones in Missionary Cooperation to 1910. p14, undated.

very firmly and definitely those particular doctrines known as 'Evangelical'.[26]

The World Missionary Conference which met in Edinburgh in 1910 was the outgrowth and climax of earlier gatherings through which Protestants expressed their purpose to give the Gospel to the world. The unitive tendency in the mission was expressed quite early in the system of mutual adjustment known as comity. Non-interference in one another's affairs, respect for each other's discipline, adoption of a common standard and procedure were essential features of this system. Comity involved active cooperation from the beginning. The aim was that fellowship might exist and should manifest itself among the different denominations.

Beaver argues that territorial comity was intended first of all to sponsor responsible evangelistic cooperation everywhere and then to be a preliminary step toward a united, independent church in every land. The process should have brought about one church with great diversity within it. It is Beaver's assertion that comity was an expression of unity. 'If the missionary enterprise could, more than a century ago in an era of intense denominationalism, achieve the unity that was expressed in its system of comity and cooperation, what greater and truer expression of spiritual unity ought not to emerge in an ecumenical age!'[27]

Comity in principle was obviously concerned with cooperation in

---

[26] Fenn, C.C., Secretary of CMS, Missionary Comity, cited In JOHNSTON, J. ed. Report of Centenary Conference on Protestant World Mission. 1888, p471.

[27] BEAVER, R. Pierce. The Ecumenical Beginnings in Protestant World Mission. 1962, p327.

mission. It was based on a pragmatic approach for the sake of evangelistic efficiency. To prevent duplication and overlapping of effort, the arrangement of 'comity' was a great advantage for the evangelistic task. While the challenge of the common task tended to draw some of the missionaries together because the division among Christians seemed to be a scandal and denial of faith, and they felt keenly the tragedy of division in the field, not all the missionaries shared that conviction.

> Many, perhaps the majority, held firmly to their inherited denominational patterns. Some, indeed, stimulated by contact with representatives of other denominations, felt strong advocacy of their confessional convictions to be a solemn duty and on occasion and in some regions keen interdenominational rivalries were witnessed.[28]

On occasions the comity agreements were repudiated. For example the Anglican bishops in the provincial synod of India, Burma and Ceylon in 1900 in view of the difficulties that arose from territorial agreement between different missionary bodies, held that all members of the Church of England whether European or Indian, wherever they may be, have a right to the ministries of the Church to which they belong. So the Synod, while commending the spirit of the policy of comity to avoid collision, deprecated any territorial agreement in the future.[29]

Many took Anglican repudiation of comity to be a denial of any real and practical desire for unity and thus it became a stumbling block to negotiations towards union. The strengthened confessionalism in other

---

[28] LATOURETTE, K.S. Ecumenical Bearing of the Missionary Movement and the International Missionary Council. In ROUSE and NEILL ed. A History Of Ecumenical Movement. Vol.1, 1986, p354.

[29] Pan-Anglican Congress. 1908, Vol.V, p162.

communions also gave justification for unilateral expression of the Anglican position. Although the sense of evangelistic urgency reinforced powerfully the movement for fellowship, the story of cooperation and understanding was rather in practical affairs than in steady progress towards ecclesiastical unity.

Cooperation in mission did not exclude tensions. Danes had been at Tranquebar since 1620, and the establishment in their Indian outposts included two resident chaplains who held no permanent appointment. However the missionaries at Tranquebar were Germans who claimed to have a special commission from the King of Denmark. The Danish chaplains inevitably regarded the status of the missionaries as highly questionable. Their own position was not open to question because they had been ordained to the service of the Church of Denmark and temporary absence in India would not hamper their right as ordained ministers; whereas the missionaries, although ordained, were not ordained to any ministry recognized by the Church of Denmark.

The tension was about the relation between mission and church. In most cases Protestant missions had been undertaken as the personal effort of devoted Christians and not as the responsibility of the churches as a whole. A missionary was ordained not by the Church but by the missionary society to the office of 'missionary'. Theoretically the Anglican missionaries should have been free from such complexities. But their situation was less different from that of their colleagues than might have been supposed, because the pioneer missionaries were sent without the direction of a bishop and were responsible to a missionary society in the West. When bishops were provided, the results were sometimes disturbing. For example the first bishop for Asia was Thomas Fenshaw Middleton, who arrived in Calcutta on 25th November 1814.[30] One of his difficulties was his relationship with the CMS. The missionaries of CMS had been in Bengal before the arrival of the bishop but had not been sent by the Church. They were sent to preach to non-Christians with a view to their conversion. They were also ministering to the English inhabitants at a number of places where there were no chaplains. The issue was that the missionaries of CMS were not licensed by the bishop and therefore he did not allow them to preach in the Cathedral or other churches built with Government money. Middleton's intention was to keep the missionary and the chaplain distinct.[31]

The issue with the missionaries reached another phase with the arrival

---

[30] The renewal of the Charter in 1793 had failed to incorporate the appointment of missionaries as brought forward by Wilberforce. But by 1813, there were missionary societies in existence. With the renewal of Charter in 1813, the door was opened for the entry of missionaries and the provision for an Anglican ecclesiastical establishment of a bishop, three archdeacons, and for missionaries to live and work in the territories controlled by the company.

[31] He did not live to carry the matter any further, but it seems that he would soon have licensed the CMS missionaries in Anglican orders upon which the same conditions as his successor did. The difficulty was cleared up by an act of Parliament on ordination for the colonies in 1819. This enabled the Archbishops of Canterbury and York and the Bishop of London to ordain men especially for the colonies and foreign possessions of U.K. GIBBS, M.E. The Anglican Church in India. ISPCK, Delhi, 1972, p74.

of Bishop Wilson, consecrated on 29th April 1832.[32] The question at issue was regarding the exact limit of the Bishop's authority over the missionaries, particularly the clerical missionaries who received the Bishop's licence. The Society claimed their part to be analogous to that of the lay patron in England, presenting a clerk in holy orders to the Bishop for induction into a benefice. The Bishop pointed out that the missionary was more like a stipendiary curate appointed and paid by a beneficed clergyman, or a school or hospital chaplain. Wilson claimed that granting or withholding a licence was entirely within the bishop's discretion and the licence would include a mention of the sphere within which the recipient was to act. The missionary society feared that this would interfere with its authority to locate its missionaries as it liked. Eventually there was an agreement in 1836 which put an end to Wilson's differences with the parent society but the tension had reached a pitch which could be inferred from the following. Fowell Buxton, a member of the Parent Committee, wrote to Wilson from England,

> For God's sake and for the sake of the poor heathen do not let your love of the church obstruct the diffusion of Christianity.

Wilson wrote in reply,

---

[32] One important development was that from now on India was treated as a unity and episcopal organisation was used as a suitable method for the churches in India. The episcopate of the 19th century was very closely connected with the imperial system in India and financially dependent upon it. The Anglican episcopate in India was led to an increasing insistence on the observance of every detail of church life as carried on in England. Bishop Daniel Wilson had been a devoted friend of the CMS but he could not accept the claims to a measure of independence by the CMS.

For God's sake, do not let your dread of the church obstruct the diffusion of Christianity.[33]

In the beginning the missionaries enjoyed almost complete freedom of action. They used to make decisions in the light of the situation as they saw it. But in the course of time they had to refer matters to their home boards. The Boards and the Committees in the West sometimes used to make decisions based on theories rather than a clear appreciation of the facts, and they expected these decisions to be put into operation. At times the decisions were contrary to the direct experience of the missionaries.

The so-called Serampore Controversy is an example of this. William Carey had worked out a plan under which the team had formed a close community based on common ideals. Each family had its own modest establishment for the maintenance of which a small sum as pocket money was distributed, but meals were taken in common. Everything earned by the member of the community was paid into the common fund and was used for the work of the mission. They accounted for every penny sent from England for specified work to the society at home, but they did not give account of their own income. However their control over mission property and work was considered too absolute by the new committee after the death of Fuller in 1815.

The issue was the question of authority from overseas. The trio at Serampore were not willing for the work's sake to succumb to stricter control by the new committee than the old committee had ever expected. Criticism was levelled against the manner of life, the successes and the

---

[33] GIBBS, M.E. The Anglican Church in India, 1600-1970 ISPCK, Delhi, 1972, p122.

character of the three great men. There ensued a hateful literary feud extending over a period of more than fifteen years. Today it can be read as annals of strife but one lesson is that the trio showed their greatness to the very end by making their own society sole heir to their entire work. Eventually after years of painful and wearisome controversy, a separation was agreed upon. Only the missions centred in Calcutta were managed by the Society at home. The breach with Serampore was finally healed in 1854 when the Committee of BMS agreed to take over Serampore College as its missionary and education training centre.[34]

In the beginning confessionalism might not have been in the forefront of missionary problems but it would be wrong to deny its presence. Some were high churchmen who were in favour of the new type of Anglican high church doctrine introduced by Keble, Newman, Pusey and others in the Tractarian movement, and they had also taken a low view of the Noncon-formists and their ways. One can imagine the horror of Bishop Wilson when he returned to Calcutta in April 1841 to find that Tractarianism had secured a firm foothold in Bishop's College, because appointment to the staff of the College at that time was made by SPG in London and they had sent Professor A.W. Street who came with a testimonial from Newman himself. Inevitably the Anglican Church in India reflected the controversy between High Church and Low Church, not only among the Government

[34] MYERS, J.B. ed. Centenary Volume of BMS. 1792-1892, London, 1892, p71.

appointed chaplains, but also between the two great missionary societies, SPG and CMS.[35]

It is not surprising that missionaries were the first to feel the tragedy of division among the churches in foreign missions. It is well known that William Carey had proposed to Andrew Fuller, Secretary of BMS, that a meeting of all denominations of Christians should be summoned at the Cape of Good Hope in 1810 to be followed by another such conference somewhere every ten years. It was turned down by Fuller.[36] Likewise Alexander Duff, who noticed the urgency of international missionary cooperation, had proposed in 1853 to appoint a committee composed of members of different denominations throughout the country to consider the best way of carrying out the object of the immediate task. The missionary and ecumenical history might have taken a different shape if these suggestions had been carried out then; instead the way was paved for the union of churches through the missionary conferences in the mission field, the comity arrangement, and the World Missionary Conference at Edinburgh in 1910.

Missionary Attitudes

a. The Church

The pioneer generation of the Baptists probably came nearer than any other body to the ideal of a truly independent Indian church. One of their

---

[35] CLARK, Ian D. The Tractarian Movement in the Anglican Church in India in 19th century. Indian Church History Review. Vol.XI, No3, 1972, p182.

[36] ROUSE, Ruth. Carey's Pleasing Dream. International Review of Mission. April, 1949, p181-92 where she has worked out what might have flowed from Carey's imaginative proposal if it had been accepted and acted on.

first acts was to form themselves into a church on the Baptist model and to elect a pastor. When converts came, they were baptized and joined the fellowship and from this point the group was independent as a local church. Church and mission from the beginning formed an integrated whole.

A great achievement of the Serampore trio was the founding of Serampore College in 1818, for training pastors and teachers as well as the education of Asiatic youth in Eastern Literature and European Science. In 1827 the King of Denmark gave the College a charter with the power to grant the degrees of Bachelor of Arts and Bachelor of Divinity. The noble building, which still stands, is eloquent testimony to the vision of Carey who had insisted on the need for competent and well trained Indian fellow-workers. A church cannot become genuinely independent unless it has local leaders capable of replacing the missionary to continue the work of mission.

There was at least a theoretical commitment to the goal of an independent Indian church. Analysing the 1872, 1882 and 1892 All India Decennial Missionary Conferences, J.C.B. Webster draws the conclusion that there was an early commitment at least in theory to the goal of an independent Indian Church - the missionary equivalent of the liberal imperialist goal. But what they had in mind was an ecclesiastical equivalent of the moderate Congress programme - local self-government, and gradual transfer of power within existing ecclesiastical structures.

The best possible result for the Indian Christians was to be as closely adapted as possible to what the missionaries had brought with them. What they represented was the best and purest form of Christian faith and organization.[37] Self-government was linked with self-support. The churches were dependent on money from overseas and the missionaries argued that the Indian Church must first create a solid economic base before it could be given independence.

By the 1830's missions came to be generally approved by serious churchmen. There was a wide range of churchmanship which found expression in the mission field. On the one hand there was a theory of episcopacy which was believed to be of apostolic origin but to some too often seemed to be compromised at home. The mission field offered an opportunity to demonstrate this aspect of the essential nature of the church. On the other hand, some found the mission field to offer a good opportunity for experimenting with new patterns. The basic object of world mission was never questioned but it was rethought from time to time in the light of the changing cultural context.

The general secretary of CMS, Henry Venn, in a memorandum in 1851 had defined the ultimate object of mission as being its own euthanasia. 'The euthanasia of a mission takes place when a missionary, surrounded by a well trained native congregations under native pastors, is able to resign all pastoral work into their hands.... so the mission passes into a settled Christian community. Then the missionary and all missionary agencies shall

---

[37] WEBSTER, J.C.B. British Missions in India. In. CHRISTENSEN, T. & HUTCHINSON, W.R. eds. Missionary Ideologies in the Imperialist Era 1880-1920. Denmark, 1982, p42.

be transferred to the region beyond.'[38] The missionary circle for many years paid lip service to Venn's principles. The implication of Venn's statement was that true missionary work is where mission and church are conceived of as not being coexistent but as being consecutive entities. The aim of the mission was to bring into existence a self-governing, self-supporting and self-propagating church.

The other person who had such a vision was Rufus Anderson. He was the first American to recognize the decisive importance of the founding of a wholly indigenous church and the shaping of policies towards that goal.[39] His vision was that the foreign missions must have a limited objective, namely to establish a church which would itself take over responsibility for mission in its area. The missionary should not try to be a leader but should train the future indigenous leaders. Anderson was also opposed to the development of mission schools. In 1854 Anderson's emphasis was to close down mission schools and to concentrate on preaching. In fact he believed that some were necessary for the training of

---

[38] HOEKENDIJK, J.C. The Church in Missionary Thinking.International Review of Missions. July, 1952, p326.

[39] Neill comments that it might have been expected that with the strong democratic tradition of the USA, the American missions would have been organized on a basis of greater freedom than those from Britain and Continent of Europe. In certain cases this might have been true but it did not seem to have been the general rule. This he contends from the example of Rufus Anderson as the chief member of the American Board of Foreign Mission in 1855. He carried things with a high hand, both in south India and in the Bombay Presidency, and little weight seems to have been given to the views of the missionaries on the spot. NEILL, Stephen. A History of Christianity in India 1707-1858. CUP, Cambridge, 1985, p409.

Christian leaders but was opposed to the support of any effort to establish schools as a means for the introduction of Christianity. He was convinced of it being an ineffective method, and that to provide English education is to denationalize people. But his philosophy of schools failed to be decisive in later thought in American Missions.[40]

The Church in the mission field occupied a prominent position in the discussion of mission questions. Missionary work was conceived to be a continual struggle with heathenism. The church in the mission field came to be regarded not as a by-product of mission work but the most efficient element in the Christian propaganda. In presenting the report to the World Missionary Conference in 1910, the Commission presented two features of the Christian community in the mission field where the church had been planted within the last two centuries,

> It may be found rather in two features which are common to every part of the 'the church in the mission field'. On the one hand it is surrounded by a non-Christian community whom it is its function to subdue for the kingdom, and on the other, it is in close relation with an older Christian community from which it at first received the truth which stands to it in a

---

[40] FORMAN, Charles W. A History of Foreign Mission Theory in America. In BEAVER, R.P. ed. American Mission in Bicentennial Perspective. Papers presented at 4th Annual Meeting of American Society of Missiology, Illinois, June 1976. William Carey Library, California, 1977. Forman's history surveys the field of American Mission from 1810-1952, dividing into four parts. His major criticism is that it has been conceived as an individualistic and fragmented discipline and there has been very little in the way of interchange of ideas between the generations. His plea is for a collegial approach to missiology.

parental relation and still offers to it such help, leadership and even control, as may seem appropriate to the present stage.[41]

The majority of the missionaries might have declared that their objective in mission was the emergence of an Indian Church and that their rôle could not be more than transitory. They would all have been agreed in saying that an Indian Church must take root, thrive and survive. But if the missionaries had been asked in what way they understood the meaning of an Indian Church, there would have been different opinions.[42]

b. The Religions

The conservative missionaries were children of one or other of the pietist revivals. In general their outlook was determined by biblical orthodoxy as understood by the pietist movements. They accepted without question the total inspiration of Scriptures, the reality of original sin and its outcome in the perverted will of every single human being. Idolatry was

---

[41] Report of the Commission-II, London, p5.

[42] One person in missionary circles who was ahead of his time was Roland Allen. The heart of Allen's understanding is that the Church lives by faith in Christ. At every level the Church is empowered by Christ to be itself, from the almost illiterate congregation in a village to the Vatican Council itself. He pleaded that the Church be placed on its own feet, that is, for an indigenous Christianity. 'If he has the spirit of St Paul he can in a very real sense practise the method of St Paul in its nature, if not in its form. He can not undo the past, but he can amend the present. He can keep before his mind the truth that he is there to prepare the way for the retirement of the foreign missionary. He can live his life amongst his people and deal with them as though he should have no successor'. ALLEN, Roland. Missionary Methods: St Paul's or Ours? World Dominion Press, 1960, p153.

one of the worst sins. Conversion meant man's total repudiation of all merit of his own and an acceptance of the merits of Christ as the only ground of his salvation. It was an acceptance of the exclusive claims of Christian faith that was expected from the converts, and the religions of the heathen were delusions of the devil. For example Ziegenbalg, when he arrived in India, shared the general view that Indians were a barbarous people and their religion a degenerate superstition. But as slowly he began to understand the culture and people, and as he penetrated more deeply into the classical writings, he discovered the depth of moral insights and the admirable style in which their wisdom was expressed. One of his contributions was the work 'Genealogy of the Malabarian Gods', 1713. It was sent to Halle to be printed and circulated in Europe but the director of the mission, A.H. Francke, wrote back to him saying that the missionaries were sent out to extirpate heathenism and not spread heathenism in Europe. The manuscript remained unread for more than a century before being published.

The missionaries began to become conscious of a growing consensus among the Hindus in distinguishing between Christ and Christianity. For example, Ram Mohan Roy, Keshab Chandra Sen, Swami Vivekananda and others had opposed Christianity but had great reverence for Christ as a great personality and an ethical teacher. Some missionaries began to make a serious attempt to apply liberal theology to encourage Hindus to accept Christ. For example, E.P. Rice, a missionary of the LMS, read a paper at the Bangalore Missionary Conference on 3rd August 1908. In his paper he noted that the main reason why intellectual Hindus rejected the Christian religion was to be found in the growth of rational thinking. The need was to discard the metaphysical doctrines and to emphasize the character of Christ and the ideal quality of his teaching.

We missionaries are concerned with kernel. We have come to India not to preach a theology, although we must have a theology, but to proclaim an evangel. And what is the evangel? Certainly not a bundle of debatable historical and metaphysical evidence, and only the learned can appreciate their value.....in fact it is not so much knowledge that man needs at all, as inspiration to live according to that knowledge which every man already 42has in his moral consciousness.[43]

In advocating this new theology, Rice had approved the distinction between the religion of Christ and Christianity. This liberal thought continued in the line of the fulfilment theory, represented chiefly by J.N. Farquhar. His ideas were expressed in his book, The Crown of Hinduism, 1914.

When we say that Christianity is the fulfilment of Hinduism, we do not mean Christianity as it is lived in any nation, nor Christianity as it is defined and elaborated in detail in the creed, preaching, liturgy and discipline of any single church, but Christianity as it springs living and creative from Christ himself.[44]

The idea of fulfilment was based on the idea that Hinduism would be replaced by Christianity. Not unlike the fulfilment theory of Farquhar was the view of Alfred George Hogg (1857-1954). He was at Madras Christian College from 1903-1939. In the preface to his book Karma and Redemption, he said that 'the innermost faith of all religions which are still, at any time,

---

[43] RICE, E.P. New Theology and missionary Work. Harvest Field. Vol IX, October,1908, p36.

[44] FARQUHAR, J.N. The Crown of Hinduism. Oxford, 1919, p58. See also the review of 'Crown of Hinduism', In HOGG, Alfred G, International Review of Mission. January, 1914, Vol.iii, No.9, p171.

worthy of the name must be one and the same'. Underlying the diversity of belief was the oneness of faith - the absolute and unquestioning trust in a God who reveals himself. Genuine faith exists in other religions. The divergences between the intellectual beliefs by which men seek to preserve the common spirit of faith is nevertheless an immensely important matter. His point of difference from Farquhar was his opposition to the view that Christianity fulfils Hinduism. He identified that Hindu faith must find a new point of reference rather than a merely smooth organic or evolutionary transition into Christianity.[45]

There was also a view of a theory of fulfilment through a development of all higher religions including Christianity into a world religion with Christ at the centre. William Miller, the Principal of Madras Christian College and Bernard Lucas, representing this later group, thought of Hinduism and Christianity as developing alongside each other towards the same goal. They thought that it is not a historical Christianity which is to be the fulfilment of Hinduism and other religions. Rather the fulfilment lies in the evolutionary process brought about by the reciprocal influence of the religions ending in the emergence of a world religion with Christ at the centre.

As a westerner he may be keenly interested in the theological

---

[45] HOGG, Alfred, G. Karma and Redemption. Christian Literature Society, Madras, 1909. reprinted 1923 (p5) & 1970. The Christian Message to the Hindu. SCM, London, 1947. COX, James L., Faith and Faiths: The Significance of A.G.Hogg's Missionary Thought for a theology of Dialogue. Scottish Journal of Theology. Vol.32, No.3, 1979, p241-256. SHARPE, Eric J. The Legacy of A.G. Hogg. International Bulletin of Missionary Research. Vol.6, No.2, April, 1982, p65-69.

and ecclesiastical mould into which Christianity had been cast but as a missionary his chief concern is with the pure gold of religion itself...His gospel is not a scheme of salvation or a body of theological dogmas, but the good news of the possibility of richer and fuller life. His success is not the number of accessions he is able to record in statistical tables but in the spiritual influence he is able to exert. [46]

A true missionary was to appreciate that the western understanding and interpretation of Christ is not the full truth but only the measure of the westerner's capacity for receiving and appropriating the religious thought and feeling of that abundant life which Christ gave. The emphasis of liberal theology upon the historic Jesus had an impact on several Indians. It led some to believe in Jesus but not to accept baptism and join the organized Church.[47]

c. Caste

In the beginning mission work was consolidated in large cities like Calcutta, Madras, Delhi, Trichinapoly, Agra, Tanjore, Lucknow, Benares, Bombay and Poona. This policy was dominant in some quarters between 1857 and 1907. Colleges and schools were established for the education of the higher castes. The city populations were on the whole highly resistant to the Gospel[48]. The educated really admired the outstanding contribution

---

[46] LUCAS, Bernard. Our Task in India. Macmillan, London, 1914, p15-16.

[47] BAAGO, Kaj. Pioneers of Indigenous Christianity. CLS, Madras, 1969, p71f.

[48] It appears from the record for the year 1851 that at that time there were no more than 91,092 registered Protestants including Anglicans in India, 14,661 being communicants. There were no more than 21 ordained

of the missionaries in the field of education, health and social work, but the structure of Indian society made it difficult when the question of changing from one religion to another arose. The strategy of mission was to educate and convert the higher castes and then Christian faith would naturally spread to the villages and lower strata of the Hindu society. One pioneer missionary to apply this strategy was Robert de Nobili.[49] Nobili observed that in eleven years of the work of Fr. Gonzalo Fernandes, not a single high caste Hindu was converted, so he set himself to find out why. The list of reasons was endless: Christians wear leather shoes, eat with knife and fork, drink wine and eat beef. The missionaries had attempted to persuade their converts to adopt Portuguese ways, thereby imposing a fatal barrier on the progress of Christianity. Fernandes's own conviction for example was that all Europeans were superior to all Indians and the

---

Indian ministers. 'During the last five years, the Oxford mission in Calcutta have hardly made six converts, and it is stated in the last report of the Cambridge mission to Delhi, there is not a single case of baptism to show as the result of twenty five years of College work, while in Madras the converts that can be traced, directly or indirectly, during the last forty years to the Christian College, the finest missionary College in India, manned by a splendid staff of able and devoted missionaries and dominated since its foundation by the strong and inspiring personality of Dr Miller, are a mere handful'. WHITEHEAD, H. Our Mission policy in India. SPCK, London, 1907, p61.

[49] Robert de Nobili (1577-1656), the Italian Jesuit. He arrived on 20th, May 1605 and founded the Madura mission. He attempted to focus attention on Brahmins. His first appointment was to the Fisher Coast. He acquired in seven months reasonable fluency in the Tamil language. Then he was appointed to Madurai, a great centre of Tamil culture and education.

Portuguese were superior to all other Europeans! Therefore he had accepted the identity of the Portuguese with 'Pārangi' - the name by which foreigners were known in India of that day - and 'Pārangi' with Christians. In the baptism service he used to put the question to the candidate, 'Do you wish to enter the Pārangi Kulān (family, community)?'[50]

So Nobili thought how to win these Brahmins and tried his best to adopt the life style of a Brahmin. The mission started as an unofficial venture and Pope Gregory XV formally sanctioned De Nobili's method in 1623. However later it was followed by sad years of controversy and the declining health of Nobili. His last years were spent as a missionary traveller and were marked with suffering. The Jesuit Fathers who followed him conformed to the Indian ideas of ascetic life. They pushed the cultures of Christian Brahminism to such a pitch that they refused communion to Pariahs - the outcastes - but the number of higher caste conversions was small.

There was a tolerant attitude to caste by the missionaries in the beginning. The coming of William Carey marked a different phase. The English Baptists began to send back to England highly hostile accounts of caste and identified it as one of the greatest obstacles to the spread of Christianity.

> The Caste is the great obstacle to improvement of knowledge for whatsoever employment the fathers followed that is the employment of their children from generation to generation nor can they get out of it to any other on which account very few can read or write that being the employment of the Brahmins

---

[50] NEILL, Stephen. A History of Christianity in India. CUP, Cambridge, 1984, p280.

and castes and very few others knowing anything of it.[51]

The missionaries at Serampore were not in support of the caste system. William Carey's view was that by eating with the missionaries, the candidates must show outwardly their repudiation of caste and the sincerity of their desire to be adopted into the Christian family. 'Krishna and Gokul sat down to eat with the missionaries in public, by which act caste was abandoned. The servants and all who witnessed it were astonished'.[52] Krishna Pal remained faithful in the service of the mission till his death in 1822. The first Christian marriage at Serampore was between Krishna's daughter and a brahmin convert, Krishna Prasad. When a convert Gokul died on 7th October 1803, the dead body was carried to the grave by Bhaireb - a brahmin, Peeru - a Muslim convert, Marshman and Felix Carey. The people by becoming Christian were rejected by Hindu society and were treated as outcastes. The inevitable result was that they turned to the missionaries for help and support.

The Anglican societies became anxious to discover the attitude of their own agents in south India because the SPCK and SPG gave financial support to the Danish mission at Tranquebar. This mission was still almost entirely staffed by Germans in Lutheran orders. It was the uniform practice of the missionaries from the commencement of the mission along the coast to instruct the converts in the truth of Christianity, to insist upon their living a holy life so showing that they were Christians, but never did they

---

[51] Letter of William Carey, Madanbatty, 12.3.1795 to Richard Brewin, Leicester.

[52] The First Hindoo Convert: A Memoir of Krishna Pal, 1852, p12.

insist that any person who wished to embrace Christianity must renounce his caste. These missionaries had continued a tradition of tolerance to caste in the 19th century. The old SPCK mission in the 18th century was open to criticism for its tolerance of caste. The controversy arose in the matter of an ordination in 1739 about Rajanaiken, who was a man of low caste.

> The supporters of the mission in Europe thought of Rajanaiken, of whom they had been receiving excellent reports, but the missionaries wrote to Francke at Halle, Rajanaiken is very useful and successful as a catechist...but we should hesitate to have the Lord's supper administered by him, lest it should diminish the respect of the Christians of the higher castes for that sacrament itself.[53]

The attitude of the dissenters to caste was also fully shared by evangelical Anglican chaplains and civilians in the north. The congregations in the south continued to be deeply divided on the issue but there was at least the commencement of consolidation of feeling and practice in the Anglican mission by the 1850's. When the Indian episcopate was established in Calcutta, the successive bishops found themselves needing to enforce some kind of uniformity of discipline among all the churches under their jurisdiction. Daniel Wilson, bishop of Calcutta, a prominent evangelical, wrote in his pastoral letter of July 1833,

> These castes are still retained; customs in the public worship of the Almighty God, and even in the approach to the altar of the Lord, are derived from them; ... The distinction of castes, then, must be abandoned, decidedly, immediately, finally; and those who profess to belong to Christ must give this proof of their having really 'put off', concerning the former conversation, 'the

---

[53] GIBBS, M.E., The Anglican Church in India 1600-1970. ISPCK, Delhi, p20-21.

old, and having put on the new man', in Jesus Christ. [54]

Caste was viewed as inconsistent with fundamental principles of Christian brotherhood and fellowship. The Bishop of Madras in his pastoral letter dated 11 July 1894 urged the churches to strive to eradicate such unworthy notions and to promote a spirit of love and Christian brotherhood based on the Christian principle that God has made of one blood all nations of men to dwell on the face of the earth.[55] The majority of the missionaries believed that Hinduism provided the religious sanction and the religious legitimation for caste, and by the 1850's virtually all Protestant missions, with the solitary exception of the Leipzig mission, were in agreement in holding that caste was a great evil and that it must be rooted out from the Church.[56] One case is of interest to show the attitude of the missionaries of the Wesleyan Missionary Society to the caste issue. In 1846 and 1847, two men sought recommendation for ordination. They were A.D. Ponniah and S. Devasagayam. They insisted that they held to caste on the ground that it was a recognition of civil and social privilege and they did not want to forfeit such privileges. The attitude of these two finally led to their withdrawal from the Methodist church. The missionaries then declared their

---

[54] FORRESTER, Duncan B. Caste and Christianity. Curzon Press, London & Dublin, 1980, p38.

[55] Madras Diocesan Record, July, 1894, Vol.VIII, No.3, p79.

[56] In the churches of the Leipzig Missionary Society, there were separate entrances for Sudras and for Panchamas, and different portions of the church were alloted to two classes, while in the observance of the Lord's Supper, Sudras took precedence of Panchamas. FINDLAY G.G. and HOLDSWORTH, W.W. History of the Wesleyan Methodist Missionary Society. Epworth, London, 1924, p136.

object that 'No person holding caste in any respect shall be employed as a paid agent in the church, or shall be admitted as a member of the society, and no candidate for admission into church shall be baptized until he has given satisfactory proof of having entirely renounced caste'.[57]

In view of the lack of success of mission among high castes, the strategy of the mission was bound to turn to the outcastes. The great increase in numbers came about only subsequently to 1858 when most Christian missions were confronted with this development. The churches which had for the most part been almost static for decades began to grow through group conversions from untouchable castes. In the mass movement, the decision to adopt the new faith was usually taken by the caste leaders.

Group conversion was not completely new. In the sixteenth century, Francis Xavier baptized the fishermen of the south western part of India in large numbers.[58] The whole caste of the Paravas had been baptized to get the protection of the king of Portugal. It was the first mass movement in India into the church. There were group conversions like the Paravas in the

---

[57] FINDLAY, G.G. and HOLDSWORTH, W.W. History of the Wesleyan Methodist Missionary Society. Vol.V. Epworth, London, 1924, p136f.

[58] Francis Xavier (1505-52), belonged to the Society of Jesus. He arrived on 6th May 1542 at Goa being commissioned by the king of Portugal. He had been appointed also by the Pope as legate to all the countries east of the Cape of Good Hope. Goa was the focus and central point of the entire Portuguese enterprise in the east. Xavier felt himself called to a different work than to be a parish priest of Goa. In 1536 the whole caste of the Paravas, the fisher folk of the coast of Coromandel, had been baptized to get the protection of the king of Portugal from the Muslim raiders from the north. But they were left for six years without pastoral care.

sixteenth century, Karta Bhajas at Krishna Nagar in Bengal and the Nadars in the south of Tamilnadu in the nineteenth century. But these were not on such a large scale as those in the second half of the nineteenth century.

> The Kasias of the Assam, the Kolls of Chota Nagpur, the Santals of Bengal, the low caste Hindus of the United Provinces, the Mhangs and Mhars of the Bombay Presidency, the Mhangs of the Western districts of the Hyderabad state, the Malas and Madigas of the Telugu country, the Arrians, Chogans, Palayans of the Travancore and Cochin states and Karens of Burmah have been pressing into the Kingdom of God and taking it by storm.[59]

The years between 1870 and 1930 were the real period of mass movements. During this period attention was drawn to the tribal people in West Bengal, Central India, in the Nilgiri Hills and in North East India; and to the depressed classes in south Travancore, Tamil Nadu, Andhra Pradesh, United province and North Western India. In 1930 it was estimated that 80% of the Protestant Christian community was made up of converts from these groups.[60]

The mass movement had a great impact on Indian society as well as within the church. In view of the circumstances under which mass movements developed, it constituted for many the most natural way of approach to Christ. It seemed to preserve the integration of the individual in his group, whereas individual conversion led to a complete break of the

---

[59] WHITEHEAD, Henry. Our Mission Policy in India. SPCK, Madras, 1907, p6.

[60] In 1851 it was estimated that there were only 91,092 Protestant Christians in India. In 1871 there were 324,258 Protestant Christians in India; by 1900 the figure was 854,867. RICHTER, Julius. A History of Missions in India. Oliphant Anderson & Ferrier, Edinburgh and London, 1908, p408.

convert with his group. Pickett, looking at the positive aspect of mass movements, says that in this respect they offered resistance to the identification of Christianity with westernization.

> Mass movements have offered effective resistance to the identification of Christianity with westernization. Western social patterns that the Indian public regards with disfavour have not left all mass movement converts untouched, but neither have they penetrated deeply into any such community. The church of the villages, which is predominantly the church of the mass movement, is highly Indian in social pattern and customs. [61]

Pickett also draws attention to the other side of the mass movement. Mass movement converts may import into the church the caste barriers to which they have been accustomed. They tend to show caste exclusiveness and hold to undesirable caste customs. This may help to allow the prejudices and customs that are inimical to the life in Christ to remain intact.

d. The Raj

Missionary attitude to the 'Raj' is one episode of immense practical and ideological complexity. Missionaries placed evangelization and social reform in the forefront in preference to political freedom. It was quite natural in an era of unhindered expansion and consolidation of British power. It was also natural for the missionaries to assume that they were part of the phenomenon of the British permanence in India.

In the Christian mission one thing which the Indians noticed was the missionaries. It is interesting to note the opinion of the educated non-

---

[61] PICKETT, J.W. Christian Mass Movements in India. Abingdon Press, Cincinnati, 1933, p332.

Christian Indians towards the West which the missionary was assumed to represent. Ram Mohan Roy (1772-1833), the pioneer social reformer in 19th century Bengal, saw acceptance of Christianity as an act of surrender to colonialism. He commented:

> It seems almost natural that when one nation succeeds in conquering another, the former, though their religion may be quite ridiculous, laugh at and despise the religion and manners of those that are fallen into their power.... It is therefore not uncommon if the English missionaries, who are conquerors of this country, revile and mock at the religion of its natives.

He went on to say, however,

> But as the English are celebrated for the manifestation of humanity and for administering justice, and as a great many gentlemen among them are noticed to have had an aversion to violate equality, it would tend to destroy their acknowledged character.[62]

This was generally true among the missionaries, whose general consensus was that the British rule in India was providential and the British thought of themselves as guardians or trustees for the people of India. Within this broad consensus, attitudes to political reform and involvement varied. There were some who preferred to be silent.

> As regards the attitude of missionary towards political movement in India, the position I would take is not heedlessness, but

---

[62] GHOSE, J.G. ed. English Works of Rammohan Roy. Calcutta, 1885, p170-71.

generally speaking in his capacity as a missionary, non-interference and silence.[63]

The silence did not arise from any lack of concern about their political interests, or from any want of sympathy, but from the conviction that their special work was to teach those fundamental truths with reference to men's relation to God and to one another. In his editorial note, H. Gulliford declared that his sympathies were with the hard pressed civil service rather than their Indian educated critics in the Congress. He dreaded the prospect of power being placed in the hands of such opponents of Christianity as Annie Besant and other extremists.[64]

The silence was broken at times when it seemed to be contrary to the truth. Following Jallianwalla Bagh and Martial Law in 1919, the action of the Punjab government was condemned as unchristian in the editorial of the Church Missionary Review of the CMS. Before this the CMS had been silent on political matters and had viewed Punjab's relative stability and progress as God's reward.[65]

The missionaries functioned within the prevailing ideological consensus concerning India and the British rôle, perhaps with exception of a few like C.F. Andrews, who were totally committed to the nationalist cause.

The final victory of the Christian faith in India depends upon the spiritual power manifested in bringing about the unification of races

---

[63] GREAVES, Edwin. The Attitude of Missionaries towards political and social movements in India. Harvest Field. Vol. XXXVIII/9, September, 1918, p333.

[64] Harvest Field. Editorial. Vol.XXXVIII. No 9. September, 1918, p326.

[65] Church Missionary Review, LXXI, 1920, p194-5.

within one body, the Church. The great principle of racial equality has to be fought out once more within the church, as it was fought out in St Paul's time. Christian love and devotion must be strong enough not only to break down all dividing barriers but also to build up a new order (spiritual and social), greater and nobler than any which India has hitherto expressed.[66]

The rise of extremism posed a challenge to the ideal of empire and this caused more serious thinking. Before 1919 the nationalist movement did not pose any real threat either to British rule or to the missions. The movement under the leadership of Mohandas Karamchand Gandhi from 1919 shook both the government and the missions. His contribution to the achievement of India's freedom is well known. He was an ardent advocate of the application of the principle of non-violence in political life. In the face of rising nationalism the missionaries experienced the challenge not only in the political context of the empire but also within the Church in India.

The missionaries had supported moderate loyalist nationalism but derided radical militants among them. Missionary enterprise had expected to win the intelligentsia through western education as one means of evangelizing India, but when that strategy failed, the focus concentrated on the evangelization of the masses and the outcastes. But nationalism was the natural outcome of western education introduced for the enlightenment of the Indians. Education helped many Indians, mostly from the upper classes. In fact the exposure to western political thought had a contrary effect in

---

[66] ANDREWS, C.F. India in Transition. CUP, Occasional Paper, 1910, p13. Charles Freer Andrews (1871-1940) came to India as an Anglican Missionary in 1904 and taught at St Stephen's College, Delhi. He worked in close association with Rabindranath Tagore at Santiniketan. He also worked with Mahatma Gandhi both in South Africa and in India.

that it enabled Indian intellectuals to think of their country in terms of a national unity. Instead of becoming allies of the status quo, they became its critics.

The missionary attitude needs to be seen within the context of the Raj. On the one side there was the India of the ecclesiastical establishment - the churches of the cantonments and civil stations. The chaplains were there to serve the needs of the entire expatriate community. They were serving the church and community but in an inescapable way serving the imperial system. On the other side were the missionaries at the grass root level serving the masses who were poor, outcastes and illiterate. In between the two general categories there were missionaries in educational institutions. Perhaps it will be interesting to note the opinion of some in the Indian civil service and in the mission during the transition period from the Raj to independence.

The opinion in general was that the British Raj was the way best suited to India of maintaining good government. The need was for a good government with impartial men to provide the greatest good for the greatest number of Indians. Within this general view, opinion differed:

> In spite of the ridicule to which it is subjected at various times,
> I think the British Raj did a very good job of work. It is possible
> that it was paternal, but this suited the staff generally and was
> known locally as 'Ma Bap' or in other words as 'my mother and
> my father'.[67]

---

[67] Memories of the British in India - Plain Tales from the Raj: A Catalogue of BBC recordings and Transcripts of Interviews, India Office Library, Oral Archives. ARMITAGE, E.C. 1920-50. District Traffic Superintendent and Railway Board Representative, Catalogue No. MSS EUR,T-76/1. India Office Library, London. See also ROYLE, Trevor. The Last Days of the

The British Raj, in years to come, is going to be viewed as one of the wonders of the world. But it was essentially a partnership, it was a government by Indians and British working together, in close partnership and its success was partly from what I could call the intelligence of the Indians, their sense to accept what happened to their country, that it had been overrun or conquered by foreigners, and to get the best out of it that they could, and they did.[68]

Standards of living for civil servants, missionaries and Indians varied. Recollecting from memory, one missionary of SPG says that 'As compared with the Indian Civil Service or Indian Medical service or with the Mercantile community that were expatriates, life was very different. I mean they were living in larger houses, and it was only right, they had very much larger salaries, very much larger, simply because they had greater responsibilities, they had greater social responsibilities'[69]. But in comparison to the Indians, the former missionary Lesslie Newbigin describes his first experience on arrival in India in 1936 as shocking. He expresses his astonishment on finding what looked to him like a spacious palace. 'We had not reckoned that the word "bungalow" meant anything so palatial.'

As Newbigin worked among the Indians, he observed that the fundamental problem was the unwillingness of missionaries to entrust full responsibility to the Indian leaders whom they had trained. The relation

---

Raj. Coronet, London, 1990.

[68] Sir Penderel Moon, 1929-44, Secretary to Governor of Bombay, ICS, India Office Library, Catalogue No.MSS.EUR T-48, p42.

[69] CASHMORE, Thomas Herbert. 1917-33 missionary of SPG. Interviewed on 16.10.1973. See Catalogue No.EUR T 13-14, India Office Library, London.

between missionaries and their Indian colleagues was shocking.

> I must say I could not help being horrified by the sort of relation that seems to exist between the missionaries and the people. It seems so utterly remote from the New Testament. There seems to be no question of getting alongside them and sharing their troubles and helping them spiritually. There never seems to be a word of encouragement. We drive up like lords in a car, soaking everybody else with mud on the way, and then carry on a sort of inspection, finding all the faults we can, putting everyone through their paces.[70]

The question is whether it was the equality of all or the equality of the missionaries and exceptional Indian Christian leaders![71] Khushwant Singh, the Indian novelist and journalist, puts the attitude of the Indians in general to the British in terms of admiration for their sense of justice and incorruptible officers but dislike of their arrogance and racial consciousness.

> British India was never close to the Indians. If they ever made friends it was in a benign attitude towards their servants. It was very rare to see a close friendship between an Englishman and an Indian at higher levels. There was a certain amount of entertaining and banter but there was no relaxed sentimental affection between the two.[72]

Khushwant Singh is talking about British imperial government and his criticism is to be understood in the context of his personal life in which he

---

[70] NEWBIGIN, Lesslie. Unfinished Agenda, An Autobiography. WCC, Geneva, 1985, p41.

[71] WEBSTER, J.C.B. British Missions in India. In CHRISTENSON, T. and HUTCHINSON, W.R. ed. Missionary Ideologies in the Imperialistic Era: 1880-1920. Denmark, 1982, p38f.

[72] SINGH, Khushwant. India Office Library, Catalogue No.EUR MSS R 193/12. ROYLE, Trevor. The Last Days of the Raj, p334.

enjoyed many close friendships with the British. What Singh refused to accept was that there was ever a feeling of brotherhood between the people of India and their rulers. In comparison to the civil servants, the life style and racial harmony advocated by the missionaries during the 'Raj' was admirable. The life style of missionaries was very simple in comparison with the British civil servants.[73] But the image of a missionary is different in the country from which he comes and in the country in which he works. In the home country he is an example of self-sacrifice and self-dedication for the sake of Christ, but in the Colonial context the identity of a missionary was generally seen in terms of a comfortable life style, association with the Raj, and being on reasonably good terms with the government.

Conclusion

One crucial issue for the missionaries in terms of method was whether to continue to expend energy on the people who showed no inclination to accept the Gospel in the hope of a response in future, or to build up the Christian church from the lower strata of Hindu society. The apparent poor success in India among the higher castes and the educated was a matter of

---

[73] The salary of T.B. Macaulay, a Law member of the Council in Calcutta, was £10,000 a year; the salary of a chaplain in the establishment £1200 per year; that of Alexander Duff was £300 a year, of some Indians in the CMS Rs 170 a month, a teacher in a mission school Rs30 a month, and an ordinary Indian Labourer Rs7 a month (then £1=10 rupees). See NEILL, Stephen. A History of Christianity in India: 1707-1858. CUP, Cambridge, 1985, p390.

great concern but the turning of the strategy to the outcastes was also not that easy in view of the prevalent attitude to the castes. The positive outcome of this strategy was the affirmation of the dignity of man that became characteristic of most of the Protestant denominations from the middle of the nineteenth century.

Attention was drawn to the concept of an Indian church, self-governing, self-propagating, self-supporting and free to develop its own form and pattern. This issue brought division among the missionaries. For example in the early 1920's the majority of the Danish missionaries with the backing of the Home Board advocated a more distancing attitude to the Indian aspiration for freedom. A minority saw no alternative but to leave the Danish Missionary Society, ashamed at its half-heartedness towards the Indianisation of the church.[74] Some missionaries identified themselves with the educated Indian Christians for revitalizing India with a concern for independence, but others distanced themselves.

The Indian Christian community was brought into being and supported by the labours of missionaries. Therefore it was natural on the part of the community to look upon the missionaries as friends, protectors and guides. But while the Hindus and Muslims feared the loss of identity due to British social reform, and the threat arising from the evangelistic activities of the missionaries, the issue for Christians was different. The community was concerned to maintain an identity in relation to other religious communities in India while at the same time having an identity

---

[74] CHRISTENSON, T. Danish Mission in India. In Missionary Ideology in the Imperialistic Era: 1820-1920. CHRISTENSON, T and HUTCHINSON, W.R. ed. Denmark, 1982, p128.

in relation to Christians in other parts of the world. While the other religious communities were trying to defend their faith, the Indian Christians were trying to gain an identity through questioning their own faith, practice and ecclesiastical control of the church. In this context apologetic became the means to defend against the charge of lack of nationalism.[75]

One important feature that distinguished the Christian community was its complex nature in contrast to the homogeneity of the others. The Christian community was the Indian nation in miniature, as it was drawn from all grades of Hindus, Muslims, Parsees and Sikhs. Religiously it shared the spiritual outlook derived from these sources and added to it an equal variety of denominational attitudes adopted from the continents of Europe and America. The consolidation of the diverse elements into a unit involved a considerable sociological problem.

In Hindu society, the traditional possibility of mobility within the caste system was closed to the untouchable. Conversion was a kind of group identity crisis in which the group passed through a negative rejection of their lowly place in Hindu society to a positive affirmation of a new social and religious identity by one affirmation of the equality of the dignity

---

[75] Christian Indians as well as non-Indians played a very conspicuous part in pioneering the national movement in its early stages and fostering national consciousness among the Indian people. Some of the Christian leaders were in a very large measure responsible for bringing into being the Indian National Congress in 1885. The names of K.M. Banerjee, Lalbehari Day, Hume, William Wedderburn are well known and their memory is cherished with deep gratitude and reverence. BHATTY, E.C. Indian Christian Community and National Movement, National Christian Council Review, November, 1942, p446.

of man. Group conversion resulted in the revival of castes within the churches as the converts from particular castes began to develop a sense of solidarity among themselves. Therefore the issue on the one hand was how to express and maintain unity in the midst of divisions which were based on caste, and on the other hand, the uncompromising opposition to caste by implication which raised the question of an alternative possibility of operating as a community in the Indian sense - a group the composition of which is defined by religion and which operates in competition with other communities.

The issue of caste is a complex one. The debate is as alive now as it was in the beginning of mission. In his study <u>Caste and Christianity</u>, Duncan Forrester states that the two poles round which the present discussion revolves are well presented by Professor F.G. Bailey and Professor Louis Dumont. Bailey defines caste as a peculiarly rigid and extreme form of social stratification. Dumont on the other hand defines caste as integrally connected with Hinduism and quite inconceivable apart from the Hindu context which provides the ideology without a grasp of which no adequate understanding of caste is possible.[76] Each represents one extreme in a spectrum of interpretation.

Forrester argues that Dumont's view has difficulty in interpreting non-Hindu groups within India like the Syrian Christians. Such groups operate each as a caste within the caste system while rejecting the Hindu beliefs which Dumont believes to be fundamental. Bailey abstracts caste from its

---

[76] FORRESTER, Duncan B. <u>Caste and Christianity</u>. Curzon Press, London, 1980, p2-3.

cultural and religious setting and finds it on the whole rather similar to other patterns of social structure which have developed in quite different situations.

One implication of the missionary attitude to caste, which Forrester draws out, is that the people like Krishna Mohan Banerjee and Lalbehari Day who accepted the missionary critique of caste quite logically discerned that the principle which justified the rejection of caste had clear implications for the relations of missionaries and Indian Christians and for the competitive denominational barriers between Christians! The missionaries did not like the reformation they themselves had in large measure initiated, and did their best to snuff it out as soon as it challenged their own social and ecclesiastical prejudices![77] This point will be discussed in the next chapter.

The work of the missionaries among the outcastes and tribals of Indian society is a glorious chapter in the history of Christianity in India. The people that were exploited systematically and kept down by caste for centuries could find hope for human dignity and made striking progress in their social and cultural life. Similarly the work of the missionaries among the tribals has brought a tremendous response and challenge to the Indian society.[78] The tribals do not come under the caste structure of Indian society but for generations they were in bondage to their fear of malevolent spirits. Christianity has given the tribals a unique social position in relation to their neighbours and they have experienced a spiritual and social

---

[77] FORRESTER, Duncan B. Caste and Christianity. Curzon Press, London, 1980, p130.

[78] THOMAS, M.M. & TAYLOR, R. eds. Tribal Awakening. CISRS, Bangalore, 1965.

64

liberation effected by Christianity. The very fact that the outcastes and tribal people are considered as human beings with dignity and brought into the fellowship in the Church is a source of both challenge and tension within the Christian community and Indian society.

CHAPTER TWO

NATIONALISM AND CHRISTIAN IDENTITY

The history of Christianity in India is often viewed as an eastward extension of western ecclesiastical history. The nineteenth century histories of Christianity in India, despite certain shifts of emphasis, shared certain common characteristics. The most obvious was that they were written by Western authors, published in the west for a western readership, and comprised the history of Western missions and missionaries, their work, methods, successes and failures in India.[1] They were not histories of the Indian Church and even when individual Indians were accorded considerable space, they were generally assigned to 'mission result' rôles.

The change in the aims and methods of the writing of this history during the twentieth century has been to show that the history of Christianity in India is a part of, not separate from, the general history there.[2] The university academic communities in India have largely ignored ecclesiastical history, regarding it as being peripheral to the main stream of Indian history. The credit for making the history of Christianity in India a

---

[1] See KAYE, John William. Christianity in India: An Historical Narrative. Smith Elder, London, 1859. SHERRING, M.A. History of Protestant Missions in India from their Commencement in 1706 to 1871. London, 1875. RICHTER, Julius. A History of Missions in India. Edinburgh & London, Oliphant Anderson & Ferrier, 1908.

[2] THOMAS, P. Christians and Christianity in India and Pakistan: A General Survey of the Progress of Christianity in India from Apostolic Times to Present Day. London, 1954. FIRTH, C.B. An Introduction to Indian Church History. CLS, Madras, 1961. PHILIP, T.V. Protestant Christianity in India since 1858. In Christianity in India. PERUMALIL, H.C. and HAMBYE, E.R. eds. Prakasam Publications, S.India, 1972.

respectable undertaking goes to a group of historians including Kaj Baago, Geoffrey Oddie, Duncan Forrester, John Webster and Daniel Potts. They took seriously scholarly developments in secular academic circles and drew attention to the need to look for the relationship between the Indian Christian communities and Indian society, philosophy and religion.[3]

The breakthrough came when the history of Christianity was seen not just as an extension of Christianity from the West but as set in the context of the social, religious, political and cultural history of India. The figures included in this process were the Indian Christian leaders, or rebels who were cast in the rôle of heroes. The history that was seen in this perspective provided at least a corrective to the general understanding.

> It is well known that the movement for political independence in India can be traced back to the work of Surendranath Banerjee, who in 1876 founded the Indian Association of Calcutta. What is less known is that he may have been inspired so by a group of Christians in Calcutta who in 1868 had formed the Bengal Christian Association with a view to create a national independent Indian Church...... The first independence movement among Indian Christians in Calcutta is

---

[3] BAAGO, Kaj. The First Independence Movement among Indian Christians. Indian Church History Review. Vol.1, No.1, June, 1967, p65-78. The Pioneers of Indigenous Christianity. CLS, Madras, 1969. ODDIE, Geoffrey A. Social Protest in India: British Protestant Missionaries and Social Reforms: 1850-1900. Manohar, New Delhi, 1979. Indian Christians and the National Congress:1885-1910, Indian Church History Review. Vol.II, No.I, June, 1968, p45-54. WEBSTER, John C.B. The Christian Community and Change in Nineteenth Century North India. Macmillan, Delhi, 1976. History of Christianity in India: Aims and Methods. Indian Church History Review. Vol.XIII, No2. Dec 1979, p87-122. FORRESTER, Duncan B. Caste and Christianity: Attitudes and Policies of Anglo-Saxon Protestant Mission in India. Curzon Press, London & Dublin, 1980. POTTS, Daniel E. Baptist Missionaries in India: 1793-1837, CUP, Cambridge, 1967.

of interest therefore, not only for the history of Christianity in India, but for Indian history in general.[4]

In the attempt to make the history of Christianity in India as representative as possible, attention must be given to the question of the identity of the Church. One of the main reasons why the Indian Church did not develop its own identity was due to the lack of understanding of its own history. Any search for the identity of the Church could not ignore the question of national identity. All historical writings inevitably involve an element of interpretation even when they are claimed to be scientific and objective. But it is important to inquire whether the history of the Church in India is comprehensible in isolation from secular history. The Church as a community may be the symbol of God's identification with mankind in history, but this identification is not because it has an entirely separate history of its own or a monopoly of God's presence! 'The Church does have a history but that history has meaning and relevance only in relation to the history of mankind in its fullness and variety' as Ian Clark wrote.[5]

The change in the perspective of the history of Christianity in India during the twentieth century was partly inevitable because of the nationalistic reaction to British rule and missionary paternalism. Inevitably, many Christian nationals became impatient with imported divisions. Therefore a general overview of Indian nationalism at this juncture would be appropriate in order to understand the intricate nature of the rise of nationalism in

---

[4] BAAGO, Kaj. First Independence Movement Among Indian Christians. Indian Church History Review. Vol 1, No1, 1967, p65.

[5] CLARK, Ian D.L. Church History or History of the Church? Indian Church History Review. Vol VIII, No 2, 1974, p110.

India. The object in this section then, is to emphasize that the growth of the national movement gave Indian Christians a certain amount of self-confidence in voicing their demand for independence. What is attempted in this chapter is to give an interpretation of Indian nationalism, and then to focus on the course of events in north and south India involving the move towards independence from missionary paternalism and denominationalism.

Indian Nationalism

The awakening of the Indian people to nationalism is of great historical importance. The encounter between the East and the West took place with the establishing of British rule. The cultural renaissance and Hindu reformation together with the emergence of religious and political nationalism all played their part in this encounter. While the encounter itself cannot be explained in simple terms of Western influence and Indian response, the interpretation of nationalism depends in part at least on the understanding of the impact of the West on India.

British rule, the evolution of national political institutions and ideas, the influence of economic thought and practice, the introduction of western education, the emergence of a national intelligentsia, the spread of western Christianity and its effect on indigenous life and thought, all these were the channels of the western impact. The elite, being oriented to western education, became the leaders of this national awakening which found expression in the organization of the National Congress in 1885 and in the aspiration for political freedom and national community. In this context the churches in India were faced with a new reality with implications for their own identity.

There were outstanding Indian Christians who responded positively to the national awakening. Among them were Susil Kumar Rudra (1861-1925) the Principal of St. Stephen College Delhi, Surendra Kumar Dutta (1878-1942) the Principal of Foreman Christian College Lahore, K.T. Paul (1876-1931) Secretary of the YMCA, one of the founders of the National Missionary Society and President of SIUC, and Vedanayakam Samuel Azariah (1874-1945) one of the founding fathers of NMS, Chairman of the National Christian Council, the first Indian Anglican Bishop and a pioneer of ecumenism. They were not narrow in their view. In the words of K.T. Paul,

> I fully realize the dangers of nationalism. With that warning clearly in our minds, I invite you to contemplate the infinite significance of all that is connoted by that most sacred entity, 'India'. Let it not stir us to any narrowness or exclusiveness: India herself ever kept an open door, with proverbial hospitality and tolerance.[6]

Their concern was to discern the identity of the Church in the context of India's thought, aspiration and action. In analysing the situation they emphasized the structure of the Christian community in relation to the emerging national community. The impact of the national struggle for freedom developed a new sense of selfhood in the churches and they began to see the Church transcending western culture and western Christian denominations. In the words of M.M. Thomas:

---

[6] PAUL, K.T. Responsibility of Christian Citizenship in India. Presidential Address to All Indian Christian Conference, Bangalore, December 27-29, 1923.

Thus God spoke to the churches through Indian nationalism about the uniqueness of the gospel and the oneness of the body of Christ; and the new understanding has helped the churches without giving up their positive attitude to the Western heritage and partnership with Western churches, on the one hand to relate themselves to the nation in its struggle for selfhood and on the other to work for the unity of the churches in Southern and Northern India.[7]

Nationalism, as the story is generally told, begins as Sleeping Beauty and ends as Frankenstein's monster.[8] It has been defined in various ways.[9]

---

[7] THOMAS, M.M. Indian Nationalism. Religion and Society, June, 1959, pp 4-26.

[8] MINOGUE, K.R. Nationalism. B.T. Batsford, London, 1967, p1.

[9] KOHN, Hans. Nationalism is a state of mind, permeating the large majority of a people and claiming to permeate all its members, it recognizes the nation-state as the ideal form of political organization and the nationality as the source of all creative cultural life and economic well-being. The supreme loyalty of man is therefore due to his nationality, as his own life is supposedly rooted in and made possible by its welfare. The Idea of Nationalism: A Study in its Origin and Background. Macmillan, New York, 1945, p16.
SMITH, Anthony tries to demonstrate the distinction that exists between nationalism and ethnocentrism. He conceives nationalism as an ideological movement, for the attainment and maintenance of self-government and independence on behalf of a group. Nationalism fuses three ideals: collective self-determination of the people, the expression of national character and individuality, vertical division of the world into unique nations. Theories of Nationalism. Duckworth, London, 1971, p23, p171. For Definitions of Nationalism, see pp153-191.

CHATTERJEE, Partha, using the case of India, shows how Indian nationalism did effect significant displacements in the framework of modernist thinking imbibed from the West. Yet despite constituting itself as a different discourse, it remained dominated by the very structure of power it sought

There are as many definitions as there are scholars. It can remind people of various things: fascism, nazism, wars, massacres and also liberation of nations from colonial rule. One way to look at nationalism is from both western and eastern perspectives.[10] Nationalism in the west, according to Plamenatz, is defined predominantly as a cultural phenomenon though it has taken political form. The main thrust is the desire to preserve and enhance a people's natural and cultural identity when that identity is threatened, or the desire to transform and even create it, where it is felt to be inadequate or lacking. England and France were the first to lead other European countries on the path of nationalism. Later when nationalism emerged in other European countries, it was the demand for nation-states rather than any cultural issues which acted as the principal motivating force. On the other hand eastern nationalism in which he also includes Slavs, is said to surface among people recently drawn into a culture hitherto alien to them. People in these backward countries were not culturally well-equipped to form nations. Hence there were two paths open to them: either

---

to repudiate. So the historical outcome has been transformation of third world nationalism by ruling classes into a state ideology legitimising their own rule. Nationalist Thought and the Colonial World: A Derivative Discourse. Zed Books, Delhi, 1986.

GELLNER, Ernest. Nationalism is primarily a political principle, which holds that the political and the national unit should be congruent. Nations and Nationalism. Basil Blackwell, Oxford, 1983, p1.

[10] PLAMENATZ, John. Two Types of Nationalism. In. KAMENKA, Eugene ed. Nationalism: The Nature and Evolution of an Idea. Edward Arnold, London, 1976. p23-36.

to regenerate their own culture or to imitate the model of the west. According to Plamenatz, the first path has invariably led to failure, and the second to mere ambivalence. Eastern nationalism is both imitative and hostile to the models it imitates.

The assumption of Plamenatz is that nationalism is fundamentally a European ideology which surfaced out of the modern historical conjuncture. The non-European societies gained access to this ideology through their contact with and imitations of the European counterpart. The European brought order and scientific administration for the colonial people. This led the educated colonial peoples to adopt the principle of nationalism to get rid of an acute sense of inferiority. The rise of nationalism in this context is considered one of the spread of ideas which have marked the growth of the modern world.

The modern world is the product of an industrial age. Society is understood to have moved through three distinct phases, pre-agrarian, agrarian and industrial. In the transitional phase individuals are displaced from their traditional position and nationalism becomes the means by which the disadvantaged people try to alter the situation in their favour. Therefore it is the social and economic needs in the industrial setting that force people to adopt the ideology of nationalism. So nationalism is a contingent phenomenon and can best be understood by placing it in its proper historical context.

There are difficulties in accepting the view of nationalism as applying equally in both West and East. One is that the factors which in other countries are regarded as essential to the growth of national sentiment either do not exist at all in India or tend to produce separation rather than cohesion. 'The concrete reality of Afro-Asian politics is the caste, the religious community or the traditional leadership, and the nationalist elite is partly a question of what sort of conflict one prefers.'[11] The other is how much the understanding of nationalist thought, provided by the nationalist thinkers or leaders, would help us to comprehend nationalism. There is a nationalist way of understanding nationalism. That means to accept the analysis of the nationalists that nationalism is a natural principle adopted by people sharing a certain common language, culture and history. On this view all the people in the colonial societies were naturally against alien domination though it was only the charismatic leaders who brought them into the mainstream nationalist movement. Therefore the best way to approach nationalism is through the ideas and actions of these leaders. This is to accept a nationalist way of understanding nationalism.

To overcome the above limitations, some scholars have gone to the other extreme. Nationalist ideologies are hardly worth analysing because they suffer from pervasive false consciousness.[12] To treat nationalism as a mere form of false consciousness is to wish away the problem completely. This extreme view at least compels us to look at the network of interests which lie behind the monolithic conception of the nationalist ideology.

It is necessary to recognize the variations and the uneven penetration of colonialism. The impact in India of colonialism is normally regarded as a change from semi-feudalism to capitalism. Such change is seen within the

---

[11] MINOGUE, K.R. Nationalism. B.T. Batsford, London, 1967, p88.

[12] See GELLNER, E. Nations and Nationalism. Basil Blackwell, Oxford, 1983, p124-125.

great account of the modes of production. It is seen as the inauguration of politicization for the colonized. The colonial subject is seen as emerging from the indigenous elite which came to be described as bourgeois nationalist.

This definition has been challenged by the subaltern studies group, a group of scholars exploring 'subaltern themes' in South Asian History.[13] They deal with a wide range of themes covering a vast section of Indian society. What unites these scholars is not only the commonality of the theme but also a way of looking at history as a complex interplay of domination and subordination. Their contention is that history in general and the history of nationalism in particular was studied from above, from the point of view of the elites, colonial as well as indigenous. According to these historians, history ought to be studied from below, from the point of view of the people. The most significant outcome is that the instrument of change is pinpointed in the 'subaltern'. The moments of change are

---

[13] a. See the volumes of Subaltern Studies: Writings on South Asian History and Society edited by GUHA, Ranjit. In the five volumes, there are at least a dozen scholars dealing with a wide range of themes, covering a vast section of Indian society.

b. The Subaltern approach to religion is inspired by the Italian Marxist Antonio Gramsci. Gramsci varied the classical Marxist approach to religion and proposed that religion of the proletarian (subaltern class, as he termed it) could not be always understood as having been imposed by the ruling class. Sometimes subaltern religion will mirror the religion of the ruling class but sometimes it will develop its own form of religion in opposition to the wishes of the ruling class as a way of maintaining cultural identity. See SCHREITER, Robert J. Constructing Local Theologies. SCM, London, 1985, p136.

pluralized and plotted as confrontation rather than transition.

One has to discern two kinds of political language. One is the language of nation building and involves the rituals of the state, political representation, citizenship, citizen's rights. This is the Indian colonial heritage and it is what Indian nationalism owes to the colonial experience. The other language derives its grammar from relationships of power, authority, hierarchy which predate the coming of colonialism but which have been modified by having been made to interact with the ideas and institutions imported by British rule. The Indian elite classes equivocate and use both the languages, and Indian history has moved in a direction of greater interlacing of the two languages in Indian institutions and practices. But the first language has been a privilege of the Indian elite classes while the lives and aspirations of subaltern classes have been enmeshed on the whole in relationships articulated in the second. The historiography of Indian nationalism has been dominated by colonial elitism and bourgeois-nationalist elitism. Both originated as the ideological product of British rule in India and have survived the transfer of power. Both share the prejudice that the making of the Indian nation and the development of consciousness of nationalism were exclusively or predominantly elite achievements.

In colonial or neo-colonialist historiography these achievements are credited to British colonial rulers and in the nationalist or neo-nationalist writings they are credited to Indian elite personalities. The central modality common to the first is to describe Indian nationalism as a sort of learning process through which the native elite become involved in politics because of the expectation of rewards in the form of a share in the wealth. The central modality of the other kind of elitist historiography is to present

Indian nationalism as primarily an idealist venture in which the indigenous elite led the people from subjugation to freedom. The central motif is to uphold Indian nationalism as an outstanding expression of the goodness of the native elite. Thus national
ism is written as a sort of spiritual biography of the Indian elite.

The contention of the subaltern group is that both help to know about the structure of the colonial state, but fail to acknowledge, far less interpret, the contribution made by the people on their own independently of the elite. It is their aim to understand the consciousness of the subaltern on their own independent of any elite initiatives. The weakness of the subaltern approach is the tendency to break the world into two opposing totalities, the elite and the subaltern. A study either from the points of view of the elite or the masses, must necessarily be partial and inadequate. History does not offer a clear choice to historians in terms of either-or. In reality one finds that the elite as well as the masses exist in a process of interaction. To assume that the life of the masses is always determined by the elites or they are always engaged in acts of resistance, is to make such complex processes of interaction simple. The other difficulty is that common people have left few written documents for the historians to work upon. Therefore any works on popular history have to depend, in a great measure, upon the documents of the elite.

The historians studying Indian nationalism trace the locus of political activities under the Raj to the localities and local interests. Anil Seal contends that unevenness in India's development produced the same disparities among Muslims as among Hindus.[14] Consequently it is unreal to talk about a common Hindu or Muslim interest. His contention is against the view that describes the Islamic community in India as a block of people whose conditions were generally equal, whose interests were generally the same, and whose solidarity was generally firm. Neither Hindus nor Muslims were monolithic communities. Likewise, Paul Brass, in his study of Muslim separatism in the United Provinces, comes to a similar conclusion. He rejects the view that sees Muslim separatist politics as stemming from a combination of backwardness and minority position.[15] According to Brass, Muslims in the United Provinces were not significantly behind the Hindus and in many respects were more advantaged than Hindus in urbanization, literacy and social communication. The different religious communities in India were all involved in the Indian national awakening. While the involvement could be addressed from the point of view of self-interest of a community, it is important in the context to identify the processes by which people come to identify their interests. The central question in sociologically orientated theories of nationalism concerns how and why ethnic group cohesion grows and develops at particular times among some people. In south India as in Europe and in Africa, it has been more common for language to provide a basis for nationalism in religiously diverse societies, whereas in north India, religion has united linguistically distinct peoples, particularly the Muslims. But it would not be correct to

---

[14] SEAL, Anil. The Emergence of Indian Nationalism. CUP, Cambridge, 1971.

[15] BRASS, Paul, R. Language, Religion and Politics in North India.CUP, Cambridge, 1974.

conclude from these cases that religion is inherently a more powerful motive force in identity formation than language, because it is not inconceivable that the language differences may yet become more significant in north India as well.[16]

The attachment of values to symbols of group identity does not happen spontaneously. There is always a particular segment of the group which takes this task upon itself. Again Brass comments that ethnicity and nationalism are not given but are social and political constructions.[17] They are the creations of elites, who draw upon, distort and sometimes fabricate materials from the cultures of the groups they wish to represent in order either to protect their well being and existence, or to gain political and economic advantage for their groups as well as for themselves. Brass's argument differs from those who consider ethnicity and nationalism to be reflections of primordial identities and who have searched the past to find evidence of the existence of ethnic identities and nationalism throughout recorded history.[18]

It is a well-known story that the western educated elite developed

---

[16] BRASS, Paul R. Language, Religion and Politics in North India. Cambridge University Press, 1974, p404. There is also recent evidence from the south Asian subcontinent, in the case of Bangladesh, that language which at one time plays a secondary role to religion, may at another time become primary. The unity created in the state of Pakistan by the bond of Islam was in turn broken by movement of Bengal linguistic-cultural group toward regional autonomy and ultimately towards sovereignty.

[17] BRASS, Paul R. Ethnicity and Nationalism. Sage Publication. Delhi, 1991.

[18] See SMITH, A.D. Ethnic Origin of Nations. Oxford, 1986.

asense of common identity and destiny due to relative lack of opportunities. This group mobilized their people to remove western power. The important aspect is the character and influence of this elite group. But in India it is not that simple, because there were layers of leading groups. The multi-layered struggle began at different times in major provinces beginning from the late nineteenth century. The existence of an elite group provides the necessary but not the sufficient condition for the transformation into a self-conscious community. The elites who started simply to reform Indian society found themselves overtaken by growing nationalism. This led to the emergence of two groups: the moderate who gave precedence to social reform and the extremists who wanted independence first and reform afterwards.

The nineteenth century Indian elites were in a dilemma regarding social reforms and freedom from foreign rule. M.N. Srinivas says that the urge to reform traditional Indian society preceded the urge for freedom. However the British failure to admit Indians to higher administrative service and evidence of racial discrimination led to the founding of the Sarvajanik Sabha in 1870, the Indian Association in Bengal in 1876 and the Indian National Congress in 1885. Thus the elite who had started out simply to reform Indian society found itself overtaken by growing nationalism.[19]

Every group which seeks to build a sense of consciousness, however, at some point creates a myth concerning its origin and destiny which is designed to instil pride among its members in its past and to create

---

[19] SRINIVAS, M.N. Social Change in Modern India. University of California Press, 1966, p84-88.

confidence in its ability to mould its own future. An oppressed group whose contemporary condition compares poorly with its golden past and its hope for the future may also add a myth to explain the causes of its decline, attributing it to the intervention of one alien group or another.

In the context of British social reform, the Hindus, and later the Muslims, feared loss of identity so they tried to defend their traditional interests, faith and practices. The Indian Christians were in a dilemma. They were concerned to establish an identity in relation to other religious communities while at the same time to retain an identity in relation to Christianity in other parts of the world. Most of the members of the Christian community consisted of people drawn from many different castes and religious communities, and from economically weaker classes. They had embraced a faith which had not yet become a part of the Indian cultural milieu. The Indian Christian community which the missions helped to build up initially shared political conservatism, but also the impact of the national struggle for freedom caused a sense of selfhood in the church in India. They began to see the Church transcending western culture and denominations. They began to think of unity and indigenization as a witness to the universal gospel. The Christian community began to relate itself more than before to the national stream of life and became involved in the nation's struggle, in order to define a new goal for the church in India.

Mission and Independence

The awareness of weakness, division and dependence naturally came first to those Indian Christians who were educated and had independent means of sustenance. They began to express their protest against missionary control and denominational identity in the country. One important consideration is to look at these protests for the development of ecclesiastical union in twentieth century India. Its place in the context of rising nationalism adds another dimension to the interpretation from the vantage point of the dissenting elite.[20] In the following section their protest is described which made the missionary church awaken to the fact of nationalist feelings. It will shed light on the context in which such aspirations emerged and flourished. Alongside the question of the possible influence from the missionary movement on the emergence of the ecumenical movement, Indian nationalism encouraged a less than rigorous concern for denominational exclusivity.

a. North

The birthplace of the national consciousness that began to develop in the second half of the nineteenth century was Bengal. The revolt of 1857 is called in Indian history the First War of Independence. It was not aimed at the creation of a united free India. The spontaneity was the outburst of hatred against the conquerors. Therefore it was perhaps not just a coincidence that the protest in the fifties against the exclusive missionary control of the church was also made first in Bengal.

The dream was to construct a United Church of Bengal on the broadest possible basis so as to include in its communion a great variety of

---

[20] T.V.Philip claims that the real impetus for Christian unity came from Indian Christians. It was the protest of the Indian Christians against western denominationalism that led to the discussion of church unity at some of the missionary conferences. PHILIP, T.V. Protestant Christianity in India since 1858. In. PERUMALIL H.C. and HAMBYE E.R. Ed. Christianity in India. Prakasham Publication, S.India, 1972, p294.

opinions. The broader basis was the Apostles' Creed because this creed embodied within its brief compass the essential teaching of the holy Scriptures. It comprised also a survey of those articles and belief which are necessary to salvation; it was the symbol of the primitive church, and in the first two centuries or so after the apostles it was put into the hands of catechumens who recited it at their baptism as their confession of faith. Therefore Lalbehari Day wanted to make the Apostles' Creed, with the exception of one article, the creed of the United Church of Bengal.[21] The exception was the article on the descent of Christ into Hades. He wanted to expunge it from the creed partly because it might give rise to unnecessary controversy, and partly because it is not to be found in its most ancient forms as preserved in the writings of the fathers.

> By founding the United Church of Bengal on so broad and catholic a basis, we should be in communion with every church in Christendom, the Greek and Latin churches not excepted. I for one would rejoice if our brethren of the Native Roman Catholic Church of Bengal would unite with us in the formation of a National Church, which they can do by abjuring the dogmas of the infallibility of the Pope and the insufficiency of the holy Scriptures as a rule of faith; for I look upon R.C.C.,

---

[21] Lalbehari Day (18th December 1824-28th October 1894). He was born at Talpur, Burdwan, Calcutta. His father belonged to Vaisya caste. He decided to become Christian at the age of nineteen. It is possible to identify the external influences that operated to induce him to change his religion through the Christian character of the teaching in the General Assembly's Institution and the piety and learning of his missionary teachers. He was baptized in 1843, ordained in 1855 as minister of Free Church of Calcutta, and then entered the secular service as headmaster of Berhampur College in 1867, fellow of the University of Calcutta form 1877.

though disfigured with corruption, as a branch of the true visible Church of Christ.[22]

The Indian and Bengali pastor and author Lalbehari Day had a spirit of earnestness, perhaps implanted in his childhood, which he carried into his Christian life.[23] He was very clear in his perception. He set forth his ideas in a letter dated 7th June 1846 to G.M. Tagore who at that time was an enquirer after Christ.

> It is not only desirable but it is our bounden duty to stand connected with a church which is after the model of the scriptural church, which manifests purity of doctrine, which has an evangelical ministry in it and which by its constitution and institutions, tends to the alarming of the ungodly, the awakening of the careless and the edification of the saints. One form is more scriptural in its constitution than another, and to know which is most scriptural is an important point, but you must grant, dear sir, that important as it is in some respects, it loses its significance when compared with the saving doctrine of Christianity.[24]

---

[22] DAY,L. Desirablness and Practicability of Organising a National Church in Bengal.1870, p10-11.

[23] 'A Hindu is the most religious fellow being in existence. He gets up from his bed religiously, anoints his body religiously, washes religiously, dresses religiously, sits religiously, stands religiously, eats religiously, drinks religiously, sleeps religiously, learns religiously, remains ignorant religiously and becomes irreligious religiously. It is this religiousness forming so prominent part of Hindu character, and called into activity by combined influence of English education and Christian missions which has created that spirit of religious inquiry over which I am now rejoicing'. MACPHERSON, G. Life of Lal Behari Day. Edinburgh, T. & T. Clark, 1900, p42.

[24] MACPHERSON, G. Life of Lal Behari Day. T. & T. Clark, Edinburgh, 1900, p48.

It was G.M. Tagore, the Barrister-at-Law, who had first breathed among Bengali Christians the idea of a United National Church. Day continued the same vision in his addresses and writings, calling all native Christians of Bengal to repudiate all denominational distinctions and to form themselves into a United National Church. His arguments were that union in love is the essential element of the Christian religion and division is alien to its spirit. His vision was to form a united church in Bengal as a sign of healthy development of native Christianity. Commenting about different denominations, he said:

> When I look upon Bengal as a field of missions and of Christianity, I am reminded of what in horticulture is called forcing gardens, where, in an ungenial soil, productions of milder climates are reared in hot-houses and other similar structures by producing an artificial temperature and humidity of the atmosphere.... Our mission stations and our native churches are so many forcing gardens. We have an episcopalian pinery, a presbyterian orangery, and a congregational melonry. But these magnificent pineapples, exquisite oranges and excellent melons, do not add to the resources of the country.[25]

The concern was for a true partnership in the mission field. In his address delivered at the United Monthly Missionary Prayer Meeting on 6 December 1858, held in the Union Chapel, Calcutta, he advocated that the goal of every true hearted missionary ought to be to gain the affection and to win the confidence of the people to whom he has been sent. Particularly referring to the European Christian laymen, he said:

> Can you not do more? I do not say with regard to your pecuniary

---

[25] DAY, L. Desirableness and Practicability of Organising a National Church: A Lecture Delivered at the Bengal Christian Association on Monday, 13 December 1869. Calcutta, 1870, p3-4.

contributions...... Can you not do more in other higher and better respects? Can you not love the people of this land more than you have hitherto done? Can you not cherish toward them a more kindly feeling than you have hitherto done? Can you not look upon every native as your brother? What I mean is that a better acquaintance with the people, and the cherishing of a more brotherly feeling towards them, are highly desirable.[26]

He used to deplore the evils and hindrances to the spread of Christianity caused by the variety of beliefs with regard to doctrines when it was not difficult to remove them. It does not mean that he did not take seriously the differences between the different confessions but his contention was that in essentials, in the fundamental doctrine of Christianity all agreed. It was better to unite on the basis of that which is common to the creed of us all. Therefore he said that the religious history of Britain justified the reasonableness of framing both the Thirty Nine Articles and the Westminster Confession of Faith. But Bengal Christians have nothing to do with the storms of past European religious controversy!

Lalbehari Day was very unyielding in his character. He advocated that Indian ordained ministers should be put on an equal footing with the missionaries and have membership in the Scottish Church Council. He was ordained along with two other native ministers. They had expected in accordance with the principle of presbyterian parity to be treated on a footing of equality with the European missionaries, at least in so far as their ecclesiastical status in mission was concerned.[27]

---

[26] DAY, L. Searching of Heart. Serampore, 1858, p15.

[27] A similar case was of Gopi Nath Nundy, the first Indian to be ordained by the American Presbyterian Mission in 1844. In 1848, he claimed both the status of a full missionary and full membership in the mission. See

The mission council was composed of all the missionaries but none of the three newly ordained native missionaries were made members. Alexander Duff, who had pioneered reform through education as mentioned in the last chapter, proved to be strongly opposed to their being admitted as members. The two other members, being frightened, yielded to Duff but Day did not; rather, he threatened to leave the mission. Eventually a compromise was reached and it was arranged that Day should be placed in independent charge of the Culna mission.

With regard to church government Day never aspired to become the constitution-maker but he hoped for a united church, the constitution of which would be a compromise between the distinctive principles of each of those three forms of ecclesiastical polity:

> This union will be possible only on one condition, the condition viz, that we hold that no unchangeable form of church government is prescribed in the New Testament for the adoption of Christians in all ages and under all circumstances.[28]

The vision of Day found expression in the formation of the Bengal Christian Association in 1868 under the presidentship of Krishna Mohan Banerjee.[29] 'Obviously it was a great relief to missionaries that Krishna

---

WEBSTER, J.C.B. The Christian Community and Change in 19th Century North India. Macmillan, Delhi, 1976, p212.

[28] Day, L. Desirableness of Organizing a National Church. Calcutta, 1870, p12.

[29] Krishna Mohan Banerjee (24th May 1813 - 11th May 1881). He belonged to an orthodox Kulin Brahmin family. He was born in Shampukur, Bengal. He gained admission to Hindu College where he was open to the knowledge of both the worlds but not to Christianity. He became an enquirer only after the encounter with Alexander Duff. He was baptized

Mohun Banerjee was elected President, since this would guarantee that the more radical elements did not get the upper hand - a development that could be dangerous for the missionary control.'[30] Banerjee was an active participant in the Young Bengal Movement which originated in the Hindu College and was formed under the inspiration and leadership of Henry Louis Vivian Derozio, a young Eurasian teacher of the College. Banerjee edited the Bengal Spectator, one of the periodicals published by the Young Bengal Group, and was in the forefront of the movement.

Banerjee was a Christian apologist. In the beginning he carried on his criticism of Hinduism in the form of theological and philosophical treatise arguing for the superior claims of Christianity.

> All that can be said to this is that awful and mysterious as it is, yet so it is. Not the revelation alone which Christians deem it their privilege to possess, but the light of nature shows that thus it is with us. Revelation and Philosophy alike witness to man's helpless misery in this respect, but it is only the Bible that furnishes an account of the cause hereof, and reveals the remedy for it.[31]

His conviction was that Christianity stood for the system which the disciples held and taught. When the disciples were called Christians, first

---

according to presbyterian rites in October 1832. In 1836 he resigned from the school due to a difference of opinion with the authorities and took theological studies at Bishop's College, Calcutta under the Principal Mill. He was ordained as priest by Bishop Wilson in 1839. He was the first Indian to be entrusted with an episcopal church, Christ Church, Cornwallis Square, Calcutta. In 1868 he joined Bishop's College as a lecturer.

[30] BAAGO, Kaj. Pioneers of Indigenous Christianity. CLS, Madras, 1969, p2.

[31] BANERJEE, K.M. Truth Defended and Error Exposed. Calcutta, 1841, pxiii.

at Antioch, sects and divisions were unknown. It signified the system professed by all Christians.

> Of all the new things which India has derived from her connection with England, the greatest and most important is the presentation of Christian knowledge which proclaims deliverance from sin and offers to regenerate society. While eagerly accepting minor advantages, are we to refuse that very benefit which concerns the soul and promises to prove in India which it has already proved in Europe, the power of godliness in human nature both as regards individuals and communities?[32]

However, by 1865 Banerjee's position on the relationship between Christianity and Hinduism began to change. He tried to establish a positive relationship between Hinduism and Christianity. The publication of 'Arian Witness' even surprised the older missionaries.[33] Its purpose was to show the striking parallels between the Old Testament (particularly Genesis) and the Vedas, whereby he wanted to prove that Christianity was, if not identical with, then certainly the logical conclusion of original Hinduism.

> This essay aspires likewise to the patriotic honour of proving that while all Hindoos who have been instructed in western literature, science and history have departed from the faith derived from their immediate forefathers, Hindoo Christians can

---

[32] BANERJEE, K.M. Claims of Christianity in British India.Calcutta, 1864, p18.

[33] BANERJEE, K.M. Arian Witness to Christ: Jesus Christ the True Prajapati (Testimony of Arian Scriptures in Corroboration of Biblical History and the Rudiments of Christian Doctrine, including dissertations on the original Home and early Adventures of Indo-Arians), Calcutta, 1875. Banerjee tried to show in this book the common background of the Arians (Aryans of India) and the Hebrews as the original home of the Arians had been Media, from where also came Abraham. BANERJEE, K.M. The Relation between Christianity and Hinduism. Calcutta,1881.

alone have the satisfaction of knowing that the fundamental principles of the Gospel were recognized, and acknowledged, both in theory and practice, by their primitive ancestors, Brahminical Arians of India, and that if the authors of the Veda could by any possibility now return to the world, they would at once recognize the Indian Christians, far more complacently as their own descendants, than any other body of educated natives.[34]

The significance of all this was that Christianity far from being a foreign religion was the fulfilment of the Veda. In the relation between Christianity and Hinduism, he further explained the similarity between the book of Genesis and Veda with respect to the sacrificial system.

Christ is the true Prajāpati - the true Purusa begotten in the beginning before all worlds, and Himself both God and Man. The doctrines of saving sacrifice, the 'primary religious rites' of the Rig-Veda - of the double character priest and victim, variously called Prajapati, Purusha, and Viswakarma - of the ark by which we escape the waves of this sinful world - these doctrines, I say, which had appeared in our Vedas amid much rubbish, and things worse than rubbish, may be viewed as fragments of diamonds sparkling amid dust and mud, testifying to some invisible fabric of which they were component parts, and bearing witness like planets over a dark horizon to the absent sun of whom their refulgence was but a feeble reflection.[35]

The vedic idea of the Purusa sacrifice was fulfilled in Christianity, Christ being the prototype of Prajāpati (the Lord of the creation). Banerjee knew such ideas would startle the Christians in India but he reminded them that the first Christians similarly had blamed Peter for mingling with

---

[34] BANERJEE, K.M. The Arian Witness. In BAAGO, Kaj. Pioneers of Indigenous Christianity. CLS, Madras, 1969, p95.

[35] PHILIP, T.V. Krishna Mohan Banerjea. CLS, Madras, 1982, p196.

the uncircumcised. There might have been several factors in his change of outlook in his later writings but one of them was his definite and active spirit of nationalism and pride in his own heritage. It was no longer Christ and Hinduism contrasted but Christianity as a fulfilment of Vedic religion.

There was growing uneasiness among the Indian Christians in Calcutta with respect to missionary control. James Vaughan, the CMS missionary at Calcutta, gave a lecture at the
Allahabad Missionary Conference in 1872. He said that most of the educated native Christians were showing feelings of bitterness, suspicion or even dislike towards European missionaries.

> It cannot be denied that bitterness, suspicion and even dislike largely enter into that feeling. An impression has somehow or other taken hold of those brethren that they have been wronged, misunderstood and misrepresented by the missionaries, that the missionaries do not really love them, nor seek their advancement, that they assume more the tone of Lords over God's heritage than that of gentle and loving shepherds.[36]

One of the leaders of the radical group in Bengal was Kali Charan Banerjee.[37] He intended to read for the ministry and had expressed the same in his letter to the chairman of the Bengal Free Church Mission Council.[38] A misunderstanding arose with Duff and some of other miss-

---

[36] VAUGHAN,J.Native Church in Bengal.In: Report of Allahabad Missionary Conference.1872,p270.

[37] Kali Charan Banerjee (1847-1907). He was the son of a Bengali Kulin Brahmin. He entered Alexander Duff's College in 1858. He became a Christian in 1864 and after passing the Bachelor of Law examination in 1870, became a practising lawyer.

[38] BARBER, B.R. Kali Charan Banurji. CLS, Madras, 1912, p24-25.

ionaries on the issue of what his status was to be and the care of his family in case of his death. Another deciding factor was Lal Behari Day, pastor of the Manicktollah Free Church. Day had been compelled to resign because he felt that the pay was insufficient to support him and that Indians were not given sufficient rights as ministers and missionaries. So Kali Charan gave up his scholarship and theological studies and read law. He started a newspaper called, The Bengal Christian Herald, later called The Indian Christian Herald, with as coeditor, Joy Govind Shome. The object of this paper was stated in the first issue:

> To the native Christian of India in general and to those of Bengal in particular, we propose to give a voice; The Bengal Herald is to be their public carrier. In having become Christians, we have not ceased to be Hindus. We are Hindu Christians as thoroughly Hindu as Christians. We have embraced Christianity but we have not discarded our nationality.[39]

Kali Charan and J.G. Shome were opposed to the transfer of the theological and ecclesiastical differences of the West to India. Being impatient with the discussion of the question whether the time had come for independence and self-governing, they left their churches in 1887 and formed the Calcutta Christo Samāj. It was a Christian Samāj parallel to the Brahmo Samāj[40] and organized in a similar way. The Samāj was accepted

---

[39] Church Missionary Intelligencer. Vol.VII, London, 1871, p261.

[40] This movement was founded by Raja Rammohun Roy. Its forerunner was the Atmiya Sabhā (Spiritual Society), founded in 1815 for the purpose of religious discussion. This ceased to exist after few years. In 1830 Rammohun Roy, together with Dwarkanath Tagore and others formed the Brahma Sabhā, which later was called 'Brahmo Samāj' for worship, prayer and religious discussion. Worship included recitation from the Upanishads, a sermon and hymns. The society continued under the leadership of

as something not altogether desirable yet inevitable. In his address at the first anniversary of the Samāj in 1888, he set forth the object of the Samāj as the propagation of Christian truth, the promotion of Christian union, and the welfare of Indian Christians.[41]

The Samāj required its members to subscribe to the Apostles' Creed, to believe in lay baptism, in lay ministry and in the ministry of women. The members met weekly in private homes for common worship led by the members in turn both men and women, as Kali Charan was an ardent supporter of the right of women to preach and to minister in the churches. No pastor was elected and there was no distinction between clergy and laity. They believed that truly indigenous theology would develop if the Indian church were left alone to work it out.

During the Decennial Conference of 1891 at Bombay at the gathering of missionary workers from all parts of India, Kali Charan presented a paper in which he contended that the conception of self-support had unfortunately been reduced to a question of rupees. A self-supporting congregation was understood to mean a congregation which finds the money required for the benefit of its pastors. It would have been better to include in the conception the capability of finding within itself the pastor. Before a congregation was declared to be self-supporting, it must be possible for it to find within itself, both men qualified to sustain and propagate church life and money sufficient to provide for their support.

Debendranath Tagore, Keshub Chandra Sen and P.C. Mozoomdar. It played an important part in the reform of Hinduism.

[41] BARBER, B.R. Kali Charan Banurji. CLS, Madras, 1927, p32.

It is desirable that the conception of the Native Church in India should be realized in the near future. In order to effect this consummation, the foreign churches should not burden Indian Christians with the demands of their own matured organizations, but leave them free to start from simple beginnings and to educate themselves into complex developments, such as might come naturally to them under the leading of the Divine Spirit. The attempt to make them begin at the end is responsible for their ill success hitherto in reaching the end.[42]

The work of Christo Samāj met with strong resistance and it never became what its founders had hoped. It is typical that the Samāj consisted mostly of educated lay people who were financially independent of the missions and could afford to disagree. Christo Samāj was dissolved in 1894. Perhaps it would be right here to add a reference to a similar protest against western denominationalism in Western India.[43] A group of three ministers formed an alliance in 1871 which is generally referred to as the Bombay Native Christian Church or The Western India Native Christian Alliance. The ministers were, Narayan Sheshadri of the American Mission of Bombay, Dhanji Bhai Nauroji of the Scottish Free Church Mission and Appaji Bapuji of the Church Missionary Society. It was a short lived alliance as it went out of existence by 1895 but what is important is that their voice was raised at a time of national awakening. They announced their objective in a letter, dated 29th November 1870.

---

[42] LOVETT, Richard. History of the LMS: 1795-1895. Vol.II, London, p279.

[43] See SINGH, D.V. Nationalism and the Search for Identity in 19th Century Protestant Christianity in India. Indian Church History Review. Vol.XIV, No2, December 1980, p105-116.

To all our native brethren in western India, beloved of God, called to be saints, grace to you and peace from God, our Father and the Lord Jesus Christ. Beloved by the grace of God, we are made members of the body of Christ. By one Spirit, we are all baptized into one body, whether we be Jews or Gentiles; whether we be bond or free; and have been all made to drink into one Spirit. So we being many are one body in Christ, and every one member of one another. It follows from this, dear brethren, that as all members of the body are united to one another, the body to the head, so we also are united to one another, and to the Lord Jesus as our great-Head.[44]

Their conviction was based on a two-fold union - union with each other, and with the Saviour. It is the Christian duty to manifest this double union in the world. The object is to convince the non-Christian population that there is one body, one Spirit, one Lord, one Faith, one Baptism, one God and Father of all, who is above all and through all and in all. The great importance of taking such a step was inferred from the Saviour's intercessory prayer that His people may be one, that the world may believe.

Their object was to promote the spirit of union and concord. Such union would develop the capabilities and the resources of the native churches to make a united effort in evangelistic labours. One important point was their affirmation of the spirit of union among Indian Christians. It was vital to cultivate and promote that spirit as well as to manifest it to the people. In one of his speeches Dhanji Bhai Nauroji in 1881 said:

They belong, it is true, to various denominations, but seldom if ever, do they make anything of denominational differences. The fact is, they do not know and are not eager to know, what these

---

[44] <u>Church Missionary Intelligencer</u>. Vol.VII, London, 1871, p262.

differences exactly are. They are Christians, and they glory in that name. Consequently, their Episcopalianism or Presbyterianism or Congregationalism, or any other ism that may exist among them, does not prevent them from regarding each other as members of the same body.[45]

The protest of these dissenters in western India was very short-lived but it expressed an affirmation of the essential unity of Indian Christians. Their protest was an independent initiative for unity in witness and evangelism. One of the reasons for it being so short-lived was their dependence on the mission. Perhaps in their enthusiasm they over-rated the strength and under-rated the difficulties of their position.

They tried to do a little too much and failed. The experience of the past two years has taught them their mistake. The members of the Alliance have been somewhat embarrassed by reason of their connection with foreign missionary societies. Any one who desires to work in connection with the Alliance, must in order to do so effectively, dissolve his connection with his mission.[46]

b. South

The movement in Bengal had its impact in Madras in south India under the leadership of S. Pulney Andy.[47] He was a medical doctor but

---

[45] Bombay Guardian. Vol 26, New Series, April 9, 1881, p83.

[46] Indian Evangelical Review. Madras, 1873, p122.

[47] S. Pulney Andy was born at Trichinopoly in 1831. He came from a respectable high caste Hindu family. He was trained at Madras Christian College and went to England as the first Indian student ever to register for British Medical Degree. After returning from U.K., he worked as a government doctor in Travancore and was baptized without joining a church. He settled in Madras in 1861 and began to work for the realization of his favourite idea of a National Church in India.

worked for realization of a National Church in India. He was influenced by the ideas of Lalbehari Day of Bengal. 'I came across a lecture delivered at the Bengal Christian Association on Monday, 13 December 1869 by Lalbehari Day, entitled, The desirability and practicability of organizing a National Church in Bengal. I will ask every one of you to procure a copy and pursue it for yourselves.'[48]

The National Church was inaugurated on 12 September 1886. It wanted to prove that a church can exist in south India without the aid of European funds and European supervision. The services conducted under Pulney Andy's leadership were of the nature of united worship, on the model of the united prayer meetings introduced by the missionary conference. But they were also concerned not to give the National Church the form of an additional sect. They felt it to be necessary to aim at uniting the various denominations.

> The sectarian prejudices of the West have not taken deep root among Indian Christians, except their dependence on their respective mission societies which stands as the principal draw back for them to avail themselves of the advantages derivable from an independent church of their own. A little countenance, sympathy and cooperation on the part of missionary bodies out here would facilitate the formation of the much needed indigenous church in this land and the funds of the mission thus made available could be more beneficially utilised for evangelical, educational and other useful purposes, by their respective societies.[49]

---

[48] See Address Delivered by S. Pulney Andy at the opening of the National Church of India on the afternoon of Sunday, 12 September 1886, p24.

[49] Annual Report of the National Church: 1894-95, Madras, 1895, p292.

The united church was named as the National Church of India during the first annual meeting in 1886-87. The reasons were to keep it in uniformity with the one started by the Christian brethren in Bengal, to denote that the idea originated with the natives of India and to confess that if there was any chance of the different races inhabiting this land becoming a nation by any power, it would be through the vivifying influence of Christianity alone. The object of a united Church was to be a witness against the institution of caste which had been a cause of disunion among Indian people. The implanting of a sectarian Christianity would be another element of discord. It was through the movement for unity among Christians that they expected to break down the barriers.

Andy was less scholarly in his attitude to Hinduism but in his lecture, 'Are not Hindus Christians?', 1894, he wanted to prove that Adam and Eve were identical with Parameswar and Pārvati, and their sons Subramanya and Ganapati, none other than Cain and Abel. The prophecies about Christ were to be found in the Vedas, particularly in connection with the Prajāpati.

> Let me entreat my Hindu brethren... In the old original form of Hinduism, one can still find the true religion from the days of creation and if Hindus will turn to that, they will discover that Christianity, far from being a foreign religion, is Hinduism as it was in the beginning.[50]

It was during his stay in England that he conceived the idea of a National Church for India. It was at the time when Essays and Reviews

---

[50] ANDY, Pulney S. Are not Hindus Christians? Madras, 1894, p14-15.

was published and was creating a great sensation in England. He felt that if Christianity was to take root in India, it would be necessary to get rid of the sectarian shackles that had interfered with spiritual growth. He expected that by the religious union, it would be possible to break down the pride and the rank of the caste system and then all could meet on a common platform to worship.[51]

The friends of the National Church had forwarded a petition to the Board of Directors of the several missionary societies. It was to request them to authorize the local missionaries to permit their converts to unite in order to raise up their own independent church. It was signed by 146 Indian Christian leaders who asked for assistance in their endeavour to gain an independent church. However this request received very little attention.

The movements in north and south India did not have the success that their founders had hoped. Most of the Christian community was not in favour of these movements for independence. But seen in the perspectives of nineteenth century India, their vision of a united independent church however inadequate it may be, was rooted in the nationalist movement which found expression in the formation of the Indian National Congress in 1885.

---

[51] One root of these ideas could be found in the national religion of Freemasonry. He thought that if Masonry could succeed in bringing all religions to one common platform to own and serve the true living God, Most High, then what was there to prevent the different sections of Christ's church from coming together to worship Him in a similar manner. He was fully aware that native Christians were from necessity, obliged to belong to the sectarian churches from mere accident of their baptism. ANDY, Pulney, Memo, p 17.

c. National Missionary Society

Although the dream of Christian elites was not successful, at least an institutional expression of an indigenous platform for missionary activity was achieved in the formation of the National Missionary Society in 1905. Reform movements within Hinduism created an opinion that Christianity was a religion of the rulers. But in fact the progressive individuals of the Christian community were actively involved in the nationalist movement. Against this background the Indian Christian leaders maintained that a self-supporting, self-directing united Church was the goal.

The story of the origin of the National Missionary Society (NMS) goes back to the Student Voluntary Movement (SVM) for India organized in 1896. A group of Euro-American missionaries had inspired nationals for SVM and it was organized with much enthusiasm.[52] In the period of heightened nationalism, the SVM appeared to be a recruiting agency to become a missionary through a foreign missionary organization. The movement ceased to exist by 1905 but its end coincided with the birth of the NMS. The NMS promised to offer missionary opportunity under an Indian society and assumed the function of a missionary recruiting agency. The NMS officers were the officers of SVM. The transfer of power and

---

[52] G.S. Eddy was one of the great youth workers of the volunteer movement. He had come to India to help the national leaders for the Christianization of the great land. He met V.S. Azariah at the 4th National Convention of the YMCA in Calcutta, December 1896. They jointly laboured in 1905 to set up the NMS. V.S. Azariah was the first secretary of the NMS till 1909. Azariah was succeeded by K.T. Paul.

outlook was facilitated by these intimate relationships. The NMS was constituted on 25th December 1905 and it was in fact a child of Indian national
aspiration.

The NMS incorporated a new policy in its revised constitution of 1920
to adopt as far as possible indigenous methods of missionary work. In this
revised constitution it was spelled out that the object of the Society should
be to undertake missionary work in India and adjacent countries and to lay
on Indian Christians the burden of responsibility for their own country's
evangelization. The policy of the Society was to foster missionary spirit and
promote cooperation and unity among Christians.

The officers of NMS till 1920 were sincere nationalists who were also
active in other stimulating agencies. The vision of the founding members
of the society was that if India were to be evangelized then the work must
be done through the participation of Christian nationals. The object was to
awaken among people a national consciousness, create a sense of patriotism
and to unite them in the cause of the evangelization of India.

Christians in all parts of India were united in this common endeavour
of evangelism through the NMS. Ebright comments that the response of the
politically aroused students and young people of India was a contributing
factor to the rapid development of the NMS. 'They responded as they did
because it was a natural reaction to the spirit of the time. The NMS offered
an outlet for Christian service under indigenous leadership working
through a society that belonged to the Christians themselves. It was Indian
Christian nationalism in action.'[53] Some thought that NMS was afraid of

---

[53] EBRIGHT, D.F. <u>The NMS of India: 1905-1942</u>, Chicago, 1944, p103.

setting itself against denominational prejudices as it was committed to perpetuate in its different centres the denominational cleavages of the supporting congregations. It did succeed in drawing together in a common enterprise all sections of Indian Christians, but the need was to go further than this.

Conclusion

There is a wide measure of agreement among scholars concerning the passive role played by the Indian Christian community as a whole in the Independence struggle, but there is also recognition of the fact that quite a number of individual Christians, particularly the educated, were actively involved in the struggle. The influence of nationalism was manifested within the mission context by a growing dissatisfaction with the comprehensiveness of foreign control.

The coincidence of colonialism and the modern missionary movement provided a problematical starting point for the process of defining the identity of the Christian community in India. It was obvious that the elites pioneered the search for an identity of the community in order to form an indigenous united church. In general there was resistance to transmitting western church traditions to India and a growing impatience with all confessionalism. Such traditions were viewed as fostering divisions which seemed to be meaningless in the Indian context.

The Indians who were interested in the formation of an Indian Church and who protested against missionary control, were not similarly interested in drafting the union schemes or envisaging central organizational structures. This resulted in the formation of the Christo Samaj and the National Church in Madras. While both failed for want of support, their very appearance at that time was indicative of a certain unease among the intellectuals concerning the place of Christians in Indian society. A more successful expression of the new self-consciousness was in the form of the National Missionary Society. It sought to utilize indigenous personnel and funds for its evangelistic work. To forget this chapter in the history of Christianity in India would be to ignore a valuable phase in the context of national awakening.

The indigenous dissenters and their endeavour for an Indian church was fragmentary. It did not have the charisma of a great movement. But in their piecemeal venture they were convinced of their goal. Historically speaking it began in the second half of the nineteenth century. The real intention of the indigenous movement for unity through dissent was to have an indigenous church free from denominations. The protest was an elite phenomenon parallel to the growth of the social reformation movement and the political agitation for self-government. In this venture the common determinant was the new spirit in the nation.

The protest of the Indian Christians against denominationalism was part of the national stirring and it is no surprise that it first came from Bengal. They were the educated Christians who were also economically independent of missions and consequently could afford to disagree. Though they could not accomplish any instantaneous results nevertheless these efforts infused a spirit which underlined for many Indian Christians the comparative unimportance of western imposed denominational structures. It must be given credit in the context of the church union movement, but their vision of the evolution of an ecumenical Christian Community from grass root perspective is still a dream of the future.

It is against this background that one has to understand the much-acclaimed twentieth century movement in India for a united Church transcending the denominational identity. The search for an Indian Church by overcoming the denominational divisions found expression in long discussions, drafting and redrafting of union schemes, joining and withdrawing from negotiating committees. It established a pattern where the identity was primarily based on the question of church order and polity and resulted in the formation of the Church of South India and the Church of North India. The next section will contain an outline of the history of the negotiation in north India and the theology of union, in order to identify the basic issues involved in this long search.

PART TWO
CHAPTER THREE
THE STORY OF THE NEGOTIATIONS

The story of negotiation is the story of the Round Table Conferences (hereafter RTC) and the Negotiating Committees (hereafter NC) stretching over the period from 1929-70. The story of negotiation was first published by James Kellock.[1] It was an account of the negotiation in north India through the eyes of a participant and related to the formation of the Presbyterian alliance, the United Church of North India (hereafter UCNI), and RTC and Joint Council up till the time of the third revised edition of the plan in 1957. He tried to show how patient negotiations over a long period had borne fruit in producing a real 'breakthrough' towards reaching a measure of agreement, and this was embodied in the third revised plan.

Kellock's work is to be set alongside the book of Bishop Stephen F. Bayne; Bayne's book was a reprint of the Ceylon and the North India and Pakistan schemes with certain documents emanating from the 1958 Lambeth Conference, the General Council of the Church of India, Pakistan, Burma and Ceylon (hereafter CIPBC), and a summary prepared by Archdeacon Donald Sully to give a brief account of the negotiations and an Anglican understanding of them.[2] Bayne prepared the book for the information of the various provinces of the Anglican communion which were asked by the CIPBC to give their verdict on the third edition of the Plan. Many who were

---

[1] KELLOCK, J.Break Through for Church Union in North India and Pakistan. CLS, Madras, 1965.

[2] BAYNE, S.F. Ceylon, North India and Pakistan. SPCK, London, 1960.

connected with the subject found his work helpful. Kellock's book can rightly be called a history of the church union movement in north India. The first six chapters relate to the history of the movement and chs. vii-xvi deal with the major issues which confronted the negotiators. Following this an outline of the history of the CNI handling the period after 1956 was published in the Indian Church History Review by D.M. Kennedy. It was in two parts, having three sections. The first section covered from Pachmarhi to Calcutta 1956-60, the second section from Calcutta to Pachmarhi 1960-65 and the third section from Pachmarhi to Nagpur 1965-70.[3]

I will attempt in this chapter to give an outline chronological survey of the RTC and NC from 1929. The primary sources for the events during the period are derived from the minutes of the meetings.[4] I will highlight

---

[3] KENNEDY, D.M. The History of the Church of North India. Indian Church History Review, Vol.VI, No 2, 1972, p102, pp101-45. Vol.VII, No.1, 1973, pp1-27. The Pre-history of the negotiations (1929-56) was not included in his presentation. He presented an outline, dealing only with the period after 1956. In the words of the author 'The pre-history of the negotiations (1929-56) has its own importance but the question has already been raised whether the inclusion of this material will make the history both too voluminous and too belated.'

[4] Minutes of the Round Table Conferences 1929-1948. Minutes of the All India Conference on Church Union, 1931. Minutes of the Continuation Committees of the RTC 1935-48. Minutes of the Negotiation Committees 1955-1970. Minutes of the Continuation Committees of the NC 1955-64. Minutes of the Working Committees 1967-70. Minutes of the Special Committee July 1970. Minutes of the Negotiation Committee 1951-54 are missing. Minutes of the Inaugural Committee 1970. The name of the churches are taken from the minutes. Ref. Microfilm No.1179. Bodleian

the major decisions taken and include the names of the churches which were represented at the meetings. An analysis of the participants in these events indicates fluctuations until 1941 amongst those attending the meetings. However from the fifth RTC 1941, they were CIBC, Methodist (British and Australian), MCSA and UCNI. They were joined by the Baptists again in 1951, and by the Brethren and Disciples of Christ in 1957. In reading the minutes of these committees, one gets a first impression of a long-drawn-out debate whereby one paragraph was eventually written and then changed over and over again. The impression is that it produced a great multitude of plans and counterplans but led to nothing of any great significance.

The story of negotiation for union is complex and the debate was not only carried on in the committees. Referring to the CSI, Bengt Sundkler comments that the real debate was carried on through people in their studies in Oxford and in Cheltenham, rather than in India! [5] For example, one impression of a missionary attending the Negotiating Committee in North India was that with regard to Anglican opinion, the negotiation appeared to be not with the Anglicans of the Church in India but with Lambeth. 'If Lambeth were tough on an issue the Anglican delegates would be of similar texture: and when certain leading prelates in the U.K. gave a green light, only then were the Anglican negotiators prepared to withdraw

---

Library, Oxford.

[5] SUNDKLER, Bengt. Church of South India. Lutterworth Press, London, 1965, p179.

their suggested amendments.'[6] What was needed was an equilibrium 2between the various church traditions if there was to be any church union at all. The group of Indians and Westerners in the committees represented their local churches as well as the pressure to be faithful to the inherited traditions.

FIRST PHASE: 1929-51

First Round Table Conference 10-11 April 1929 Lucknow.
Churches Represented:
Australian Churches of Christ Mission
Australian Methodist Church
Baptist Church
Church of the Brethren Mission
India Mission Disciples of Christ
Methodist Episcopal Church
United Church of Northern India
Wesleyan Methodist Missionary Society
Visitor: S.P.G. and Evangelical Synod of North America.

The UCNI was formed in 1924 through the union of Presbyterian and Congregational churches. It had sent out official invitations to several churches and missions for a wider union with other churches in north India. The Wesleyan Methodist Church was the first to respond to this invitation. After the first preliminary meeting of representatives in October 1927, a RTC was felt to be desirable for those willing to discuss the possibility of union. The invitation was sent out and the response to it resulted in the first RTC. The Metropolitan of the Anglican Church in India was entirely in sympathy with the proposal but he did not think it wise for the Church of the provinces of India, Burma and Ceylon to enter into official negotiation until

---

[6] HENRY, Bruce. An Impression of the Negotiation Committee on Church Union. Church Union News and Views, February, 1960, p7.

after the Lambeth Conference had expressed its opinion upon the proposed scheme for union in South India.[7]

Church polity was first on the agenda. In the general discussion it was revealed that a pure congregationalism, recognizing the absolute autonomy of each separate congregation, was not acceptable in India and was rarely found in operation. Government by presbyters or some form of central authority as in the case of the Methodist Episcopal and the Wesleyan Methodist churches had been proved to be effective in India and in practice had been to a greater or lesser extent adopted even by churches founded on a congregational basis. However all the elements of real value in congregationalism were to be preserved in a united church as had been done to some extent in the UCNI. Provision had to be made to avoid the insecurity of pastoral appointments revealed in the churches with a congregational basis, so that the ministers might be assured of another appointment on the termination of their pastorate in a particular sphere. Congregational liberty was to be secured so far as it was consistent with the larger good of the Church. There was to be a policy of supervision by superintendents or bishops under constitutional control.[8]

The union was contemplated with full recognition of the convictions of each church. Each had its gift to bring to a united church whereby the whole church might be enriched. It was agreed to recognize the place of the child in the church and the necessity of a definite profession of faith on the part of every member. There was agreement on the necessity of order in the

---

[7] Minutes of the Ist RTC, p2.

[8] Minutes of the 1st RTC, p3.

observance of the Sacrament of the Lord's Supper. One considerable problem was the administration of the Lord's Supper by laity but this was thought to be a possibility if care was taken to safeguard the interests of good order. The possibility of including such groups as the Friends, who did not have any outward ritual for the observance of either baptism or the Lord's Supper, was not excluded.

The value of recognizing the existing organic relationships with churches in other parts of the world was a vital element during the discussion. The object was to secure a union with a broader outlook than that which might be achieved by a purely national church. At the same time it was realized that a united church must have complete autonomy in the administration of its own affairs. A statement of faith was desirable as the basis of Christian unity but it was to be a statement in the simplest and broadest terms.

Second Round Table Conference 18-20 November 1930 Delhi.

Churches represented:
Australian Methodist church
Baptist church
Church of the Brethren
Church of India, Burma and Ceylon
Methodist Episcopal church
Society of Friends
United Church of Northern India
Wesleyan Methodist Church
Visitor: United Presbyterian Mission of the Punjab and the delegates of the Joint Committee from South India.

The debate centred on the congregational liberty to be secured both in the sphere of the life and activity of the local church and in respect of its representation on the governing bodies of the United Church. The authority and responsibility for the government of the United Church was expected to be vested in the Council, constituted by lay and ministerial members, and the Church would have superintendents and bishops to discharge spiritual and administrative functions as constitutionally determined. Some delegates wished to put on record that in the event of the title 'bishop' being adopted, the term 'historic episcopate' should not be introduced into the constitution nor should it be implied that episcopal rank constituted a distinct order in the ministry of the United Church.

The statement by the members of the Society of Friends indicating the possibility of union with those observing the sacraments of Baptism and Supper of the Lord was received with a warm welcome but the Conference hoped that further negotiations would lead to the Society of Friends actually entering the united church. The difficulty of incorporating two practices, infant and believer's baptism, was left to be overcome by congregational autonomy. A broad doctrinal statement was adopted as a guide for the discussion among the uniting churches:

1. The acknowledgement of the Father, the Son and the Holy Spirit, one God blessed for evermore.

2. The acceptance of the Holy Scripture of the Old and New Testaments as containing all teaching necessary for salvation and as the ultimate standards of our faith.

3. The commendation of the historic creeds known as the Apostles' and the Nicene as containing valuable statements of Christian doctrine.[9]

---

[9] Minutes of the 2nd RTC, p10.

The delegates of the Joint Committee on Union in South India, J.J. Banninga and W.F. Tomlinson, were present as visitors. They explained the proposed Scheme of Union for South India. The Conference requested the South India Joint Committee to arrange a conference for both south and north with a view to a united Church for India.

All India Conference on Church Union 7-9 November 1931 Nagpur.

Churches Represented:
The Society of Friends
The Churches with B.M.S.
The Wesleyan Methodist Church
The United Church of North India
The Church of India, Burma and Ceylon
The Methodist Episcopal Church
The South India United Church

It was affirmed that in Christ individual Christians were joined together in faith and experience. The barriers of separation were identified as due to the conflicting types of church polity that had grown up in the West. It was imperative that these differences should not be perpetuated in India. The need was to associate members of the various churches for united evangelistic effort and other forms of Christian service and to make every endeavour to promote common acts of worship including the partaking of the sacrament of Holy Communion.

The restrictions on Christian fellowship were largely due to different conceptions of the ministry. Therefore the solution to this problem was essential for both the North and South India members. There seemed to be general agreement on the adoption of a constitutional episcopate responsible to representative assemblies and synods. The constitutional episcopate was not used as a synonym for the historic episcopate. The Joint Committee of South India found it possible to adopt the phrase on the distinct understanding that no doctrinal implications of apostolic succession, sacerdotalism or the three orders of the ministry were implied by this. A united church was expected to look at the inclusion of all possibilities. The Conference in general followed the South India pattern closely but the inclusion of a second episcopal tradition in the north (Methodist Church in Southern Asia, hereafter MCSA), as well as the Baptists, introduced a special consideration in the North.

Third Round Table Conference 6-8 April 1937 Lucknow.

Churches Represented:
The Church of India Burma and Ceylon.
The Methodist Church (U.K.)
The Methodist Church (Australia)
The Methodist Episcopal Church
The Society of Friends
The United Church of North India.

After the first meeting at Lucknow, there were eight years of exploration of common ground and the first draft of the basis of negotiation was produced at this third conference. This was an enlarged basis of negotiation, covering a much wider spectrum than that adopted during the second RTC.[10] The intention of the proposed basis was to pursue the negotiation

---

[10] 1. Doctrine: 'The uniting churches in Northern India hold the faith which the Church has ever held in Jesus Christ, the Redeemer of the world, in whom men are saved by grace through faith, in accordance with the revelation of God, which He made, being himself God Incarnate, they worship one God, Father, Son and Holy Spirit. They accept the Holy Scriptures of the Old Testament and New Testament as containing all things

and to secure definite suggestions for modification. The Baptist representatives were absent due to the inability of the Baptist churches to send delegates to this conference.

THE JOINT COUNCIL 1931-1945

Stanley Jones and Chitamber had attended the General Assembly of the UCNI in December 1929 as visitors and first made the suggestion of a Joint Council for union between the United Church of North India and the Methodist Church in Southern Asia. The UCNI issued an invitation for

---

necessary to salvation and as the ultimate standard of faith.They acknowledge the witness of the Apostles' Creed and the Creed commonly called the Nicene Creed to that faith which is continuously confirmed in the spiritual experience of the church of Christ.'

2. The Sacraments: 'The uniting churches believe that the sacraments of Baptism and the Holy Communion are means of grace through which God works in us. The Sacrament of Baptism shall be administered with water in the name of the Father, Son and Holy Spirit. The full privilege and obligation of membership shall belong to those who having attained to years of discretion and having gained some measure of experience in Christian life, and having received due instruction in Christian truth and in the duties of their Christian calling, make public profession of their faith and of their purpose with God's help to serve and to follow Christ as members of His Church. They shall make this profession at a public service.'

3. The Ministry: 'The Church is a royal priesthood, all have direct access to God. The Ministry is a representative ministry. They accepted constitutional episcopate together with the presbyterial and congregational elements in church order as necessary parts of the basis of union, without committing to acceptance of any particular interpretation of episcopacy. It expected to maintain full communion and fellowship with each of the various communions in which they belonged.' Minutes of the 3rd RTC, p7-8.

negotiation immediately after the RTC in November 1930, to which the Baptists and later on the Bengal LMS churches also responded. The Joint Council became a separate platform for negotiations which continued from 1931-45. Its first meeting was held at Allahabad in December 2-4 1931. The first plan of union in 1940 was issued after its 5th Meeting in February 1940 with a revised edition after the sixth meeting in March 1942.[11] The plan tried to avoid any commitment to the historic episcopate and followed a polity more Presbyterian in character. It was proposed that the united Church should have Bishops or General Superintendents without involving any question of Orders or of Apostolic succession. In the Preamble it was stated that

> ... being convinced that the situation in India calls for practical unity in their Christian witness to the non-Christian world, and being inspired by the belief that the will of God for his Church is set forth in Christ's prayer, 'That they all may be one...that the world may believe that thou hast sent me' [they] have entered into negotiations through a Joint Council with a view to concerting a plan of corporate union.[12]

The Council had expected a consummation of union by the end of 1945. The Plan made no mention of the historic episcopate, accepted existing ministers without unification of ministry or laying on of hands, and a polity of presbyterian character in which General Superintendents were to be appointed for five years but could be called bishops, if so desired. The parallel meetings of the Joint Council delayed definite decision in the RTC

---

[11] The second, third and fourth meetings of the Joint Council were held in 1935, 1936 and 1939 respectively.

[12] Plan of Union. Joint Council, 1940, New Indian Press, Calcutta, p1.

though there was close liaison between the two bodies. During the fifth meeting of the Joint Council, at the request of the RTC the representatives of those churches associated with the RTC but not involved in the negotiation undertaken by the Joint Council were present.

In fact it seemed at that time likely to achieve a quicker consummation than the RTC. The Baptists, being in favour of the Joint Council plan, had left the RTC mainly on the issue of congregational independence. The UCNI accepted the plan of 1942 at its General Assembly of 1944 but the MCSA in their Central All India Conference in January 1945 rejected the plan of the Joint Council, and resolved to proceed at once to explore afresh the possibilities of union on a wider basis than that of the Round Table Conference and the South India Scheme. The churches which had produced the plan looked in another direction. The Joint Council faded out and the RTC again came to the forefront. Commenting on the Joint Council, James Kellock says,

> We must turn back to look at a vigorous union movement which originated out of the Round Table Conference, eclipsed it for over a decade, and then faded out. This is the movement that had its focus in what is called the Joint Council. It took the ball from the RTC, played about with it for a time, carrying it a good deal nearer the goal, and then passed it back to the Round Table Conference.[13]

---

[13] KELLOCK, James. Break Through for Church Union. CLS, Madras, 1965, p4.

Fourth Round Table Conference 22-23 November Lucknow 1939.

Churches Represented
The Church of India, Burma and Ceylon.
The Churches connected with B.M.S.
The Churches connected with L.M.S.
The Methodist Church (U.K.)
The Methodist Church in Southern Asia.
The Methodist Church (Australia)
The United Church of North India.
Observer:The Disciples of Christ
       The Society of Friends

This was the conference that requested the Joint Council to invite to its meetings as observers representatives of those churches associated with the RTC but not involved in the negotiations undertaken by the Joint Council. The previous RTC had appointed a sub-committee to consider whether in their judgement the Joint Council Plan contained any proposals likely to hinder a wider scheme of union, and Canon T.D. Sully presented its findings to the RTC. It noted that the Joint Council had omitted all reference to the Apostles' and Nicene Creeds, a divergence both from the outline and from the basis of the RTC which might cause difficulty for wider union in the future. It also asked for a statement as to the exact difference between a call to an Office, and an Order, in reference to the ministry.[14]

Fifth Round Table Conference 31 July-1 August 1941 Allahabad.

The Church of India, Burma and Ceylon.
The Methodist Church.
The Methodist Church in Southern Asia.
The United Church of North India.

---

[14] Minutes of the 4th RTC, p3-4.

Due to the optimism about the Joint Council Plan and the uncertainty regarding the negotiations in south India, there was some hesitation for a while in proceeding with the work of the RTC. Indeed the Baptist churches had discontinued their cooperation with the RTC from 1940. However it continued to negotiate and the basis of union was further developed at a meeting of the continuation committee in March 1941 and during the fifth RTC.

The breakthrough during this conference was initiated by a proposal about ordination and consecration by the mutual laying on of hands with prayer, using a formula leaving no room for any scruple or doubtfulness regarding the unification of the episcopates of the Anglican and the Methodist Episcopal churches. The uniting churches believed that those who were called to exercise episcopal powers, within the limitations of a divided church, should be authorized to perform a wider ministry in the united church. It was the aim of the uniting churches that this wider and more effective exercise of episcopal powers was to be initiated by the mutual laying-on of hands with prayer. The bishops of CIBC with the presbyters of the uniting churches were to lay their hands upon the heads of the bishops of MCSA and the bishops of the MCSA and presbyters of other uniting churches were to lay their hands upon the heads of the bishops of CIBC.[15]

Sixth Round Table Conference 23-24 July 1947 Allahabad.

The Church of India, Burma and Ceylon.
The Methodist Church (British and Australian)

---

[15] Minutes of the 5th RTC, p3.

The Methodist Church in Southern Asia.
The United Church of North India.

This conference approved the 1941 proposed basis of negotiation with certain revisions. With regard to membership it was resolved that

> At the time of union, all full communicant members, members on probation or under institution, members under discipline, catechumens and other persons in connection with the uniting churches shall be accepted by the uniting churches with the corresponding status. The full privileges and obligations of membership in the united church shall belong to those persons who, having attained years of discretion shall make the confession at a public service. Those only shall be members of the united church who have by baptism been admitted to Christ's Church visible on earth. Baptism may be administered in infancy or upon profession of faith.[16]

The conference accepted the principle of the unification of the ministry by the mutual laying on of hands as an act of "supplemental ordination" to the ministry of the united church.[17] This act involved the acknowledgement of the limitations of a divided church since they were restricted in their authority and did not have the seal of the whole Church. The existing presbyters and bishops of each of the uniting churches were expected to accept the additional authority and grace that they lacked in separation through the laying-on of hands of the duly authorized persons of the other

---

[16] Minutes of the 6th RTC, p2.

[17] The term 'supplemental ordination' originated among American Anglicans. Those who proposed it for south India explained that supplemental ordination implies that those who receive it are real ministers of Christ's Church and that they receive through it 'further grace of orders and authority'. See Marshall, William J. The Unification of Ministry in the Church of North India. Indian Journal of Theology. Vol.19, No.1, January-March, 1970, p23.

churches uniting with them. The episcopate was to be both constitutional and historic without being committed to any particular interpretation.[18]

Seventh Round Table Conference 20-22 February 1948 Allahabad.

The Church of India, Pakistan, Burma and Ceylon.
The Methodist Church (British and Australian)
The Methodist Church in Southern Asia.
The United Church of North India.

The 1941 proposed basis for negotiation was approved with minor adjustments. The revised document contained the basis for negotiation and suggested elements for the constitution of the Church. The Conference authorized the continuation committee to draw up the details of the proposed constitution. One important aspect of the basis was a clear affirmation that:

> ...the will of God for His church is set forth in Christ's prayer 'that they may all be one... that the world may believe that thou hast sent me,' and...the situation in north India and Pakistan calls for practical unity in...Christian witness to the non-Christian world. [19]

The Conference accepted the principle of the unification of the ministry by the mutual laying on of hands in a solemn act of humility and rededication with prayer. This involved the acknowledgement of a common lack in all ministries due to divisions, in that they were limited in authority and did not have the seal of the whole church. In this act the grace of God

---

[18] Minutes of the 6th RTC, p4.

[19] Minutes of the 7th RTC, p2.

for the wider and more effectual fulfilment of ministry was sought.[20] It is anoteworthy that the wording 'supplemental ordination' with reference to unification of ministry as used in the sixth RTC was omitted.

SECOND PHASE 1951-65

The consummation of the union in south India in 1947 brought a feeling that the RTC basis provided the best foundation for definite negotiations for union. The Lambeth Conference of 1948 gave a measure of approval to the schemes worked out by the RTC and the Churches in Ceylon. It showed particular interest in the suggestion for the complete unification of ministry at the inauguration of the union. The acceptance of the basis of negotiation by the four participating churches made it possible to hold the first Negotiating Committee at Calcutta in 1951. This was when the Baptists rejoined the process. The Plan of Church Union in North India and Pakistan was published in 1951 with acknowledgement to the CSI and Ceylon schemes.[21] The Plan was the result of a series of meetings of the RTC, which was replaced by the Negotiating Committee. It was partly founded on the work already done by the Joint Committee on Church Union in South India, by the Negotiating Committee on Church Union in Ceylon, and by similar negotiating bodies in other parts of the world.[22]

---

[20] Minutes of the 7th RTC, p6.

[21] Plan of Church Union in North India and Pakistan. CLS, Madras, 1951.

[22] The first step towards union in Ceylon was taken by a Conference of church leaders. It met at Trinity College, Kandy in August 1934. The Ceylon Provincial Synod of the Methodist Church had sent an invitation in

The negotiating churches continued to be inspired by the belief that the will of God for His church is set forth in Christ's prayer 'That they may all be one...that the world may believe that thou hast sent me', and were convinced that the situation in North India and Pakistan called for a practical unity in their Christian witness to the non-Christian world.[23]

The Plan consisted of the basis of union, the constitution of the church, and the inauguration of union. The section 'basis' represented the general principles on which it was agreed that the churches would be able to enter union. The section 'constitution' represented only a preliminary

February 1940 to the other constituent churches of the National Christian Council of Ceylon to enter into negotiation. The churches that took part in the negotiation were, the Church of India, Burma, Pakistan and Ceylon, the Methodist Church in Ceylon, the Baptist Churches in Ceylon, the Presbyterian Churches in Ceylon, the Jaffna Diocese of the Church of South India.

The Joint Committee was set up in November 1940 and the report of that committee was accepted as a basis for negotiation. Therefore an official Negotiating Committee was constituted in November 1941. The section of the Scheme of Church Union in Ceylon dealing with Faith and Order was issued in November 1947. The Scheme of Church Union in Ceylon was then published in July, 1949. It was the third edition of the Scheme which was adopted by the Negotiating Committee in June 1955.

During 1971-73 all the churches officially voted in favour of the union but the decision was challenged in the courts of Sri Lanka with regard to the legality of the voting procedures. It is most unfortunate that the union continued to be impeded by interminable delays resulting from unresolved legal issues. Proposed Scheme of Church Union in Ceylon. United Society for Christian Literature, Madras, Colombo, 1949.

[23] Plan of Church Union in North India & Pakistan. CLS, Madras, 1951, p1.

sketch of certain important elements of the constitution. The basis at this stage did not include the reference to confessional statements of the uniting churches. Prior to 1951 it was not necessary to include the alternative of believer's baptism leading to full membership as the Baptists had been unrepresented since 1939. But it was agreed in the first NC to include the recognition of the alternatives of infant and believer's baptism to be incorporated in the section on the sacraments. Part II incorporated the elements of the constitution and Part III contained the first draft for the inauguration of union. But the details of the services and division of dioceses were left to be worked out by the NC.

The Plan affirmed the Church as the body of Christ and its members as members of His body. 'Those are members according to the will and purpose of God who have been baptized into the name of the Father, the Son and the Holy Spirit. They receive the call and grace of God with faith, continue steadfast therein, being maintained by the same faith through the various means of grace which He has provided in His church. Their vital union is with the Head of the body, and through Him their fellowship one with another.'[24]

The Plan acknowledged that owing to divisions, all ministries were limited in scope and authority, not having the seal of the whole church. They therefore accepted the principle of the unification of the ministry by the mutual laying on of hands in a solemn act of humility and rededication with prayer. In this act they sought the grace of God for the wider and

---

[24] Plan of Church Union in North India and Pakistan 1951. CLS, Madras, p1.

more effectual fulfilment of their ministry. The basis also contained an important statement regarding the intention of the unification of the ministry. By mutual laying on of hands to signify unification, the aim was not to declare invalid ordination previously received, nor to replace it by a new ordination, nor to grant for a second time any grace, gifts, character or authority previously bestowed.[25]

The first Plan of union as prepared by the NC in 1951 was not accepted by the uniting churches because of the intention regarding the unification of the ministry, and because the matter of unification of the episcopate of the Anglican and Methodist episcopal churches was not clear. The constitution in part II of the Plan needed more clarification on the polity of the church. Therefore the plan was revised in 1954. It included (a) the insertion of the words 'as the inspired word of God' in respect of OT and NT; (b) the assertion that while some men who have been deacons may later be ordained presbyters, the diaconate properly represents a distinctive calling in the church; (c) agreement on the distinctive functions of the deacon being a specific share in the public worship, sharing responsibility in church administration and a pastoral function under the direction of the presbyter.

The initial unification of the ministry was to be by mutual laying on of hands in a solemn act of humility and rededication. The unification of ministry focused upon the belief in God's answer to prayer which meant that any difference between ministers hitherto episcopally ordained and

---

[25] Plan of Church Union in North India and Pakistan 1951. CLS, Madras, p9-10.

those not so ordained would be transcended. The intention of the union of episcopate was on the one hand to supply the former bishops of the Methodist Church in southern Asia with the special link with the episcopate of the Primitive Church which the Anglican Communion claimed to have preserved, and on the other hand to enable the former bishops of the CIPBC to enter into the spiritual heritage of the episcopal branch of the Methodist Communion.[26] But the 1954 Plan was not accepted by all churches as further clarifications were needed on the subjects of membership and baptism.

Negotiating Committee 10-12 August 1955.

The Baptists
The Church of India, Pakistan, Burma and Ceylon
The Methodist Church in Southern Asia
The Methodist Church (British and Australian)
The United Church of North India
Observer:The Brethren
    The Council of Baptist Churches in Assam

The Committee discussed the distinctive functions of the deacons as set out in the Plan. While the united church was expected to be free to develop the form of diaconate most appropriate to the life of the church, it was hoped that it would be possible so to use this office as to set other ministers free for the functions which properly belonged to another distinctive calling. The ministry of the diaconate could be undertaken for life by those who had been accepted for this ministry by diocesan authorities and had received due training. The values of the lay diaconate as

---

[26] Plan of Church Union in North India and Pakistan 1954. CLS, Madras, p2, p9, p10, p14.

known in the Baptist churches was to be maintained and developed together with the value found in other forms of the lay ministry such as the Presbyterian eldership. The proposal of a special commissioning was introduced by James Kellock.

Step 1: Service of inauguration of union forming a united church.

Step 2: The bringing together of two episcopates.

Step 3: The representative act of unification of the ministry.

Step 4: Declaration and confirmation of appointment of existing bishops and consecration of new bishops.

Step 5: Diocesan service of unification.[27]

The suggestion of bringing together two episcopates before the unification of the ministry aroused sharp criticism. This appeared to be an act between only two of the uniting churches while the others functioned merely as spectators.

Negotiating Committee 3-6 April Pachmarhi M.P.1957.

The Church of India, Pakistan, Burma and Ceylon
The Methodist Church (British and Australian)
The Methodist Church in Southern Asia
The United Church of North India
The Baptists
The Church of Brethren
The Disciples of Christ
Observer: American Baptist Bengal Orissa Mission

The five negotiating churches were joined by the Church of Brethren and the Disciples of Christ. While the Disciples of Christ joined the negotiation for the first time, the Church of Brethren had in fact joined the

---

[27] Minutes of the NC, p12.

continuation committee of the NC since October 1956. The seven churches that participated in the meeting of the NC in 1957 happened to be associated with the missions from English speaking countries with the exception of a small part of the UCNI.

In June 1956 a proposal had been made by the leaders of five delegations to rearrange the Plan. The rearrangement was inevitable because the RTC prepared a basis for negotiation first and then the draft of the constitution. Inevitably it led to repetitions. It was proposed to make a conflation of the basis and constitution in a unitary document. The work was entrusted to Leslie Wenger. The conflated version borrowed a great deal from the Ceylon scheme. The plan was rearranged with the permanent elements of the constitution of the church in part I and the procedure and principles of the inauguration of union in part II. The main outcome of the NC was the publication of the revised edition of the 1957 Plan.

It was decided that the negotiation in North India and Pakistan would bring into being two autonomous churches in full communion, one in each country, with two separate ceremonies of inauguration. The bringing together of the two episcopates was to take place at the Indian service of inauguration of union, at which all the existing bishops of the churches involved, from both India and Pakistan, would be present. The plan received the approval of some churches but not the required two thirds majority. The death of Augustine Ralla Ram, secretary of the NC since 1929, resulted in a change in its leadership. Ralla Ram was succeeded by Donald Sully.

The Negotiating Churches

The churches connected with the Council of the Baptist Churches in Northern India (CBCNI) arose out of mission work under the auspices of the Baptist Missionary Society which goes back to the mission beginning with William Carey in 1793. The Baptists were divided into Particular or Calvinistic and General Baptist. The General Baptist Missionary Society was formed by G.K. Pike and others in 1818 and they had established a mission in Orissa. This remained the principal field of the society until its amalgamation with the Baptist Missionary Society in 1891. The Baptists established links with each other through the provincial unions: The Bengal Baptist Union, The Baptist Union of North India, The Utkal Christian Church Central Council, The Baptist Church of Mizo District. The Council of Baptist Churches in North India was constituted in 1958 with the representatives from the four provincial unions. The Baptist Church of Mizo District subsequently withdrew in order to seek unity in North-East India, leaving three provincial unions to take part in the negotiation.

The mission of the Church of the Brethren in India dates from 1894 within the states of Maharashtra and Gujarat. Since 1946 the Brethren churches had been independent in their administration. Their basic unit was the local church and congregations were grouped into districts. There were two districts, one in Gujarat and the other in Maharashtra.

The mission of the Disciples of Christ started in 1882 with stress on local autonomy. One group of disciples of Christ, known as the convention of the churches of Disciples of Christ, took part in negotiations. This convention was formed in 1935. The group had about 30 local churches mainly in Madhya Pradesh.

The Church of India, Burma and Ceylon started as part of the Anglican ecclesiastical establishment. The bishopric of Calcutta was established in 1813, with separate dioceses for Madras in 1835 and for Bombay in 1837. It became autonomous in 1930. The CIPBC had fourteen fully organized dioceses in India and five missionary dioceses.

The Methodist Church (British and Australian Conference) missionary work began in Bengal in North India in 1860, and then spread to Banaras and Lucknow, thus forming the Bengal, and Lucknow and Banaras districts. The Australian Methodists began to work in the second district in 1909. The Church was subject to the Annual Conference in Britain and Australia.

The United Church of North India (UCNI) is a merger of Presbyterian, Congregational and Moravian churches. Its origin goes back to the Presbyterian and Congregational missions of the early 19th century. The Presbyterian mission came from Scotland, U.S.A., Ireland, England, Canada, Australia and New Zealand. They organized one Presbyterian Church in India in 1904 and the southern section joined with the Congregationalists in 1908 to form the South India United Church. In 1924 the Presbyterian Church in India joined with the Congregationalists, the fruit of the evangelism of missionaries by the American Board of Commissioners for Foreign Missions, to form the UCNI. Due to the evangelistic work among the hill tribes in the North-East, a very numerous group had joined the Presbyterian Church in India in 1921 and became part of the UCNI. But the UCNI joined the final negotiation without these churches of the North-East.

The Methodist Church in Southern Asia owes its origin to the work of the American Methodist missionaries. The work had begun in India in 1856. The Church was organized as part of the American Methodist Church. The Annual Conference was formed in 1864 and the Central Conference in 1884. The membership of MCSA in India was about 560,000, the largest among the negotiating churches.

The Negotiating Committee 2-4 December 1959 Jabalpur.

In 1958, the Lambeth conference had made certain suggestions for change to facilitate relations of communion between a united church and the Anglican churches. These were taken up by the episcopal synod of CIPBC who then forwarded a suggested modification of the procedure for the unification of ministry to the NC for their consideration. The committee accepted certain verbal and procedural changes in the inauguration service which were incorporated in a revised issue of the proposed service, but decided against considering any amendment of the Plan.

The proposed changes for unification of ministry in fact became a concern among the other uniting churches. Therefore the UCNI made a statement on the unification of the ministry and requested that this be printed in the minutes of the NC. The object of the statement was to note that within one of the churches with which it sought union, there were those who found a conscientious barrier to full acceptance of other ministers. Therefore some act of commission was needed through the episcopal laying on of hands with prayer. The UCNI did not itself find any necessity for this particular type of commissioning in the union. In the act of union UCNI was ready to acknowledge the ministry of episcopally ordained ministers, without needing to signify that acknowledgement in this particular way. In addition the UCNI did not regard such a procedure as a necessary condition for bringing about the unity of the church, since they believed that unity is created by Christ alone in His atoning and reconciling death and risen life.[28]

Nevertheless the UCNI expressed its willingness to share in such an act, if that would enable the brethren who had such conscientious scruples to recognize more heartily the unity of the church and its ministry. The willingness was based on the acknowledgement that the laying on of hands is not only used in ordination but is also a spiritual and traditional symbol of the bestowal of spiritual gifts by God, not only on the ordained ministers of the Church but on the whole church itself.

Following the NC, concerns were expressed in several of the negotiating churches at the statement made in the Preamble to the decision of the General Council of the CIPBC in Jan 1960.

> In leaving it to the wisdom of God to determine what is to be bestowed on each participant, which we may expect to be different in each case, it is on the human level, legitimate to place different interpretations upon what God does in this act. Thus it is our conviction that in the rite, episcopal ordination is bestowed upon those not previously so ordained, though it does not repeat any ordination previously received.[29]

In 1961 the continuation committee of the NC decided to remind the negotiating churches to make their decision for union on the basis of the intention of the representative act of the unification of the ministry which

---

[28] See Appendix E of the minutes of the NC, 1959, p18.

[29] Quoted in the Minutes of the Continuation Committee of the Negotiating Committee, 11-12th April 1961, p7.

was given in the Plan itself.[30] In their General Council Meeting from 13-17 January 1963 the CIPBC passed an important resolution clarifying the famous Preamble of three years before. While it did not withdraw the statement, it expounded it in a conciliatory way and affirmed explicitly its acceptance of the intention of the churches in coming together as contained in the Plan. The willingness on the part of the negotiating churches to go on wrestling with the issues made it possible to look forward to further negotiation.

THIRD PHASE 1965-70

The Negotiating Committee 16-19 March 1965 Pachmarhi M.P.

It was recognized that there was need to revise the Plan for resubmission to the Churches with a positive statement on the approach to unity. The fourth and last edition of the Plan in 1965 included a statement of faith of the uniting churches as a supplement to the Plan of church union which acknowledges the witness to the catholic faith. The five steps for unification as suggested in the third edition of the Plan of 1957 were reduced to four in the fourth Plan. The bringing together of the two episcopates as suggested in Step 2 during the inaugural service was dropped. Instead, the total ministry, including the bishops and the presbyters, was to be united as step 2 in the Representative Act of the Unification of the Ministry.

The fourth plan also deleted the appendix which in the previous plan

---

[30] Plan of Church Union in North India and Pakistan 1957. CLS, Madras, p55-58.

attempted to deal with the issue of the unrepeatability of baptism and with the possible desire on the part of some on grounds of conscience to undergo a second baptismal act. During the meeting the recommendations of the sub-committee were presented on the issue of baptism.[31] In the light of the recommendations, the following statement was inserted in section iv of the plan as a new paragraph and the old paragraph iv was numbered as v.

> The Church of North India and Pakistan is keenly aware of the fact that divergence of conviction on certain matters of faith and practice is something which can only be borne within one fellowship by the exercise of much mutual forbearance and charity. Nevertheless it believes that it is called to make this act of faith in the conviction that it is not the will of the Lord of the Church that they who are one in their faith in him should be divided even for such causes as these. It further believes itself to be called to this venture in the confidence that in brotherly converse within one church, those of diverse convictions will be led together in the unity of Spirit to learn what is His will in these matters of difference.[32]

The admission of godly women to the office of deacons as practised in the early church was regarded as one of the proper forms of the ministry of trained women. It was hoped that in the course of time, the CNIP under the guidance of the Holy Spirit would constitute such a diaconate and specify its conditions and functions. The question of admission of women

---

[31] 'In as much as the CNI\Pakistan will have within its membership both persons who practice infant baptism in the sincere belief that this is in harmony with the mind of the Lord, and those whose conviction it is that the sacraments can only properly be administered to a believer, both infant baptism and believer's baptism shall be accepted as alternative practices in the CNI\Pakistan' Minutes of NC, 1965, p5.

[32] Minutes of NC, 1965, p5.

to the ordained ministry was left for the consideration of the Synod of the Church.

The uniting churches maintained that God would certainly answer their prayer so that any difference between bishops from the alternative traditions, or between ministers episcopally or otherwise ordained, would be transcended. By transcending these and other differences, as they were known to God Himself, the CNIP believed it would receive from Him at the outset a ministry fully accredited in the eyes of all its members, and as far as may be, of the Church throughout the world.[33]

Three of the seven churches, the Baptists, the Brethren and the Disciples, baptized only those who consciously professed faith and repentance. The other four, the Anglicans, the Methodist churches and the UCNI, baptized infants as well. The statements of the CIPBC, UCNI, MCSA, Methodist (British Conference) and CBCNI were declared to be consistent with the doctrinal standard of the proposed united church. This consistency was seen to be in the teaching of the doctrine of trinity, the person and work of Christ, the Holy Spirit, the fall of man and his redemption, the unique authority of the canonical scriptures, and the Apostles' and the Nicene Creeds.

In authorizing the fourth and final edition of the 1965 Plan it was expected that the churches should take their decision to unite or not with the least possible delay. While realizing that the time required for constitutional procedure varied in different churches, it was expected that the decisions would be communicated by March 1969.

---

[33] Minutes of NC, 1965, p12-13.

Negotiating Committee 14-17 January 1970

Council of Baptist Churches of Northern India
The Church of Brethren
The Disciples of Christ
The Church of India, Pakistan, Burma and Ceylon
The Methodist Church in Southern Asia
The Methodist Church (British and Australian)
The United Church of North India
Observers: Bishop J.W. Pickett and Mrs Pickett, Bishop Sundaram
Overseas Representatives from USA, UK, Australia

A special committee of 21, representing the seven negotiating churches, was constituted by the NC to act on its behalf until the Inaugural Committee should take over as per the Plan of Union. During the NC Bishop Sadiq presented the need for non-stipendiary ministry in order to relate to the needs of India. The NC requested the united church to give early and serious consideration to this study, and to the encouragement and the use of non-stipendiary ministry at all levels.

The Committee was informed about the details of the voting of the negotiating churches.[34] The Utkal Christian Church Central Council decided to enter the union whereas in other areas of CBCNI the vote was 'divided. In view of the required 2/3 majority, the CBCNI recommended that the Provincial/Council/District unions and the individual churches which had decided in favour of the union were free to join the proposed United Church.

The Convention of the Churches of the Disciples of Christ in its meeting in November 1969 unanimously accepted the Plan of union to join the CNI. The Annual Conference of the Church of Brethren in 1969 decided

---

[34] Minutes of NC, 1970, p6-8.

to join as the two districts had voted in favour of the union. The Methodist Church (British and Australian Conference) had voted in favour of union on the basis of the 1957 plan and re-affirmed this in 1969.

The General Council of CIPBC in January 1966 had voted unanimously in favour of the fourth edition of the plan. Having received the required majority, the CIPBC decided to join the CNI. The two dioceses in West Pakistan in 1965 decided to proceed along with the North India group. The Church of Pakistan was inaugurated on 1st November 1970 with the union of the dioceses of the CIPBC, MCSA and the United Church of Pakistan.

The UCNI in its Assembly of 1962, along with subsequent ratifying votes by the church councils, voted in favour of the union on the basis of the 1957 plan. The UCNI General Assembly held in 1968 formally decided to enter the union.

On behalf of MCSA, R.B. Desai gave the total results of the voting on the fourth edition of the plan of union in MCSA. This was 662 for, and 298 against; thus the MCSA had accepted the plan by a 2/3 majority. On behalf of the executive board of the MCSA, J. Satyavrata gave a report on the steps being taken in the MCSA for an orderly transition to union.[35]

However this orderly transition did not take place on account of some unhappy incidents which occurred. The Executive Board of the MCSA transmitted a request of their Agra Conference to the NC meeting on 17th

---

[35] Among the MCSA the plan of 1957 did not get the two thirds majority vote as only 6 out of 11 Annual Conferences were in favour. The focus of objection was on the 'Laying on of hands'. The General Conference at Dallas, Texas, in April 1968 passed the Enabling Act, permitting the MCSA to enter into union if the MCSA in India was in favour.

January 1970 for a postponement of the date of the inauguration of the union. Bishop Lance requested permission for Mrs Agnes Loyall to make a statement on women's work which was not granted by the Secretary of NC as Mrs Loyall's name was not on the list of those invited to Nagpur for the Sub-Committee.[36] At the same time Townsley of MCSA presented a resolution to include a statement regarding the Endowments of the MCSA in the minutes. It was the feeling of some of the members of MCSA that these matters were not given proper consideration and patient hearing. Bishop Lance wanted to record his dissenting vote as he felt that this lack of due consideration to Townsley's motion by the NC was an indication of the prejudiced attitude of the group.[37]

The misunderstanding arising from the NC seemed to the members 2of the NC only to be a procedural matter, without any intention to thwart, oppose or offend the Bishops or the members of the MCSA.[38] However the Central Conference of the MCSA in India on 6th August 1970 at Delhi rejected the Plan to join the CNI by 106 to 48. This unfortunate incident led to the inauguration of the Church of North India on 29th November 1970 in the city of Nagpur without the MCSA.

The Inauguration of the Church of North India

Under the presidency of Rt. Rev. Gurbachan Singh, retiring moderator of the General Assembly of UCNI, the inauguration of the CNI took place

---

[36] C.C. Pande was the Secretary of the NC since 1967 on retirement of T.D. Sully.

[37] Minutes of NC 1970, p23.

[38] Minutes of the Working Committee, 3 (a), March 1970.

in the All Saint's Cathedral Compound in a great shamiāna (tent) at Nagpur on the morning of Sunday 29th November 1970, this being the first Sunday in Advent. The Most Rev. Lakdasa De Mel, metropolitan of the CIPBC, the Rev. Dr Benjamin Pradhan, chairman of the NC and a Baptist, and the Rev. C.C. Pande, secretary of NC and a Methodist, became the nucleus of the ordained ministry of the CNI. This was done by prayer and laying-on of hands by the accredited representatives of the six uniting churches, assisted by four ministers from outside the area of union, the Most Rev. P. Solomon, Moderator of CSI, the Rt. Rev. Mar Theophilus, representing the Metropolitan of the Mar Thoma Syrian Church of Malabar, the Rev. W. Manners of the Presbyterian Church of Assam and the Rev. E.L. Wenger of the Baptist Missionary Society.[39]

The three then admitted to the ministry of the CNI six Bishops designate, nine Bishops elect and four retiring bishops together with representatives and accredited ministers of all six uniting churches, chosen in such a way that, as far as possible, each diocese of the CNI would be represented by at least one presbyter, who later would assist the diocesan bishops at diocesan unification ceremonies.

Thus six uniting churches came together in one visible fellowship to form the CNI on 29th November 1970. The CIPBC had 340,000 members, UCNI 188,000, CBCNI 110,000, the Church of the Brethren 18,000, Methodist Church (British and Australian) 10,000, the Disciples of Christ 7,500. The total of 673,500 members of the CNI represented various heritages in north

---

[39] Minutes of the Inaugural Committee, December, 1970, p2.

India.[40] This union did not deny the gracious gifts of God manifested in various ways in different traditions. They recognized each other to be part of the one Church of Jesus Christ. They anticipated the day when the special insights granted to several churches would be brought together for mutual enrichment of all in the living fellowship of one church, being guided by the Holy Spirit. They expected to be used as an effective instrument proclaiming by word and deed the gospel of Christ.

Post-Union Phase
Negotiation with the Methodist Church in India

The Juridical Council of the Methodist Church in 1972 had declared that the decision of MCSA in 1970, which reversed an earlier decision to join the union, was beyond its legal authority. This had kept the door open for the Methodists (MCSA) to join at a future date. The General Conference of the United Methodists on 15th-25th April 1980 at Indianapolis, Indiana, USA, granted the necessary Enabling Act authorizing the Central Conference of the Methodist Church in Southern Asia to reorganize and become the Methodist Church in India; this was inaugurated on 7th January 1981 at Madras.[41]

The Church of North India then invited the Methodist Church in India

---

[40] Methodist Recorder. Thursday, November 26 1970, p11.

[41] The Book of Discipline. Methodist Church In India, Bombay, 1982, p20.

(MCI) to enter into union negotiations.[42] The first meeting of the Union Negotiations Committee, on which each group had seven members, was held in August 1985. The terms of reference for the Committee were to inform the churches of the progress of negotiations and empower it after careful study and prayerful deliberations to draw up a concrete plan for union between CNI and MCI. The basis for starting negotiation was the 1965 Plan for church union in North India and Pakistan.[43]

The second meeting of the NC was held in April 1986. There was no fundamental differences between the two churches in the concept and function of the episcopate. Therefore the demand was for immediate steps towards mutual recognition and unification of the ministries, as an interim goal to union. During the third meeting of the NC in January 1987 it was decided to undertake on a priority basis a deeper study of issues involved in achieving intercommunion between the CNI and MCI at an early date, and to draw up a concrete proposal along with the procedure to be followed to achieve this as an interim goal towards the larger goal of union. The proposal also was related to the issue of ordained ministry including the episcopate.

---

[42] Invitation was sent to MCI as per the decision of the 31st meeting of CNI Synod Executive Committee, 28-30 September 1984. The MCI in their Second General Assembly, Jabalpur, 31st December 1984 - 7th January 1985 accepted the invitation of the CNI.

[43] Bishop Lance on behalf of MCI, proposed that the following three main areas out of thirteen be accepted by the CNI as the first step to growing together in unity: 1. Unification of the episcopate of the MCI within the new church; 2. Recognition of the ordained ministry of the MCI; 3. Intercommunion between the MCI and CNI.

During the fourth meeting in August 1987, it was proposed by the CNI that the Faith and Order statement in the 1965 Plan of Union, should this be affirmed by the MCI, could provide a basis for moving towards the interim goal of intercommunion and mutual recognition of ministries. It was hoped that this would be possible as the erstwhile MCSA had participated in formulating these statements and had subscribed to them. The NC asked the CNI and MCI to affirm and adopt the following statement as an expression of their commitment to the goal of union:

a. The goal of union (the nature and form of which is to be mutually decided) between the Church of North India and the Methodist Church in India is to be pursued with a sense of commitment.

b. Negotiations for establishing intercommunion between the CNI and MCI in India must be undertaken on a priority basis to foster mutual fellowship and cooperation on the way to union of these two churches.

The fifth NC in September 1988 recommended that the interim goal of intercommunion should be pursued by unifying the three-fold ministries of the two churches as a step towards the ultimate goal of the union of these two churches. The CNI executive committee of March 1989 was not in a position to approve the recommendation of the fifth NC as it was made without first receiving the MCI's firm commitment to the goal of church union.

The CNI in its executive committee of September 1987 had affirmed its commitment to the goal of union as recommended by the fourth NC, whereas the MCI was interested to discover the possibility of a unification of the ministry and intercommunion outside the structural union. So the basic issue was whether mutual recognition and uniting of the ministries of the two churches could only take place as part of, and within, the structural union of the two churches, appealing to the 1965 Plan of Union. After having journeyed on the way of negotiation for organic union for nearly forty years, the CNI would need to know the reason if it were to opt for early intercommunion with the MCI.[44]

The Joint Council of the CNI, CSI, and Mar Thoma Church

The Joint Council was formed on 4th July 1978. The invitation was sent by the CNI to form three commissions of representatives of the three churches to explore the ways and means of further cooperation and witness in India. This move was welcomed during the meeting of the CSI and Mar Thoma Negotiations Commission, held on 17th May 1974. Therefore the three churches appointed their representatives to the Theological Commissions of their respective churches and these commissions began to function as a Joint Theological Commission.[45]

---

[44] Report of the General Secretary of the CNI 1986-89, the Seventh Ordinary Synod, October 1989.

[45] The first meeting of the Joint Theological Commission was held in January 1975 at Madras. The object of the Commission was to explore the possibilities of close cooperation between the CSI, the CNI, and the Mar Thoma Church and to discuss the question of faith and order and other relevant issues. The aim of this was that there might be Union between these churches, keeping in mind the ultimate goal of all Christ's people in India i.e. the fulfilment of the Mission of the Church. During their third meeting in September 1976, the JTC passed the proposal for a new model of union for these three churches which was accepted and the Joint Council was inaugurated in July 1978, at Nagpur. This Joint Council is not a traditional church union negotiation aimed at organic union but it is an attempt to manifest organic oneness through a common structure, while retaining the autonomy of the three churches. According to the Preamble of thle constitution, the object of the Joint Council is:- 1.To serve as the

One of the important issues with which the Joint Council has been grappling since its inception is organic oneness. One major task was to find a common name fulfilling all the aspirations of the three uniting churches for the future united church in India. The difficulty was expressed by some, that to adopt a common name would be a question of losing the identity of the three churches. The failure to adopt a common name by the three churches has raised the question of the very existence of the Joint Council if the only purpose was to have closer fellowship and to be an instrument of common action. At the same time it is claimed that the Joint Council is a unique relationship of communion of three autonomous churches. The search still continues to explore a visible manifestation of unity.

common organ of the three churches and of the whole church of Jesus Christ in India. 2.To help the churches to fulfil the mission of evangelization of the people of India, and to witness to the righteousness of God revealed in the gospel of Jesus Christ by striving for a just society. See Minutes of the Joint Theological Commission of the CNI, CSI and Mar Thoma Syrian Church. Chandran, Russell J. ed. The Joint Council of the CNI, CSI and Malankar Mar Thoma Syrian Church: A Brief History and Interpretation. ISPCK, Delhi, 1984. The Constitution of the Joint Council of the CNI, CSI and MTC. ISPCK, Delhi, 1981.

CHAPTER FOUR

THE THEOLOGY OF THE UNION

Each church union has a particular basis and a rationale which even when they are not clearly spelt out might be implicit in the procedure followed and formulas chosen. For example, J.W. Winterhager gives a comparison of unions in Canada and South India. He sees the two movements as representing two radically different approaches to union. He regards the Canada project as the purest embodiment of the principle of Nathan Soderblom that union should come about through the fulfilment and enrichment of the various traditions. Then he characterizes the South India pattern as also based on dialogue and sacrifice of traditional ways. John Webster Grant however says that one can object that both Canadian and South Indian history have been distorted to provide pure types for easy identification. Instead a fairer way of stating the contrast might be to note that the Canadian union was largely inspired by considerations of life and work, while those who carried on the conversation in South India had to grapple with more difficult problems of faith and order.[1]

While it is difficult to categorize a scheme with a particular type, it is important to note the rationale of formulating a scheme and its own way of dealing with denominational differences.[2] The general challenge in any

---

[1] GRANT, J. Webster. The Canadian Experience of Church Union. Lutterworth, London, 1967, p34.

[2] GRANT comments that the size, comprehensiveness and Canadianism were emphasized repeatedly in the discussion leading to the formation of the United Church of Canada on 10th June 1925 despite the refusal of a

scheme of union is to continue efforts to evolve an indigenous and ecumenical church. I will deal with this subject in chapters five and six. The danger in the success of any scheme lies in the co-existence of denominational Churches alongside the United Church in the same place which leads to ongoing tension. The two schemes of union in South and North India were almost parallel but the consummation in South India took place earlier than in the North.[3] In the Tranquebar Conference on Church Union, held on 1-2 May 1919, the thirty three ministers of the South India United Church (SIUC) and the Anglican churches had issued a manifesto which was a significant milestone in the history of church union.[4]

> We believe that the challenge of the present hour in the period
> of reconstruction after the war, in the gathering together of the
> nations and the present critical situation in India itself, calls us

---

substantial part of the Presbyterian church to enter it. It was the result of the interaction of a particular view of the mission of the Church with a particular national situation. The Canadian ideal was not to be a melting pot but a mosaic to which all would contribute their distinctive gifts. The Canadian Experience of Church Union. Lutterworth, London, 1967, p23-24, p36.

[3] The Presbyterians were in the vanguard in the South India Union Movement. They had formed an All India Presbyterian Union in 1900. In 1908, its south Indian section joined with the Congregational union to form the South India United Church. With this Church, the Lutherans of the Basel Mission in Malabar joined in 1919.

[4] It was a conference of Indian ministers but the presence and influence of the two missionaries, G.S. Eddy and H.A. Popley, who had helped in the drafting of the manifesto, cannot be overlooked. H.A. Popley was the secretary of the Forward Evangelistic Movement of the SIUC and G. Sherwood Eddy was the YMCA secretary, who was visiting India for evangelistic purposes.

to mourn our past divisions and turn to our Lord Jesus Christ to seek in him the unity of the body expressed in one visible church. We face together the titanic task of the winning of India for Christ - one fifth of the human race. Yet confronted by such an overwhelming responsibility, we find ourselves rendered weak and relatively impotent by our unhappy divisions - divisions for which we were not responsible, and which have been, as it were, imposed upon us from without; divisions which we did not create, and which we do not desire to perpetuate.[5]

Those who gathered at Tranquebar had stated in their resolution their desire to combine the Congregational, Presbyterian and Episcopal elements in the forming of a united Church.[6] During the negotiation, the three churches were agreed on matters of Faith and the difficulty was mainly in the sphere of Order. The Anglican churches in South India, who were to

---

[5].BELL, G.K.A. The Document on Christian Unity. OUP, London, 1929, p278-79.

[6] Three fundamental principles were noted to have guided the Committee all through its deliberations:1.The Church after union should be a real spiritual home for all its ministers and members in which each can worship and serve God according to the dictates of his own conscience-.2.The Church after union must be such that no one entering it should feel that by so doing he had cut himself off from his former Christian fellowship. That fellowship must continue in the resultant Church.3.The church will be an autonomous body over which no State, Church or Society has any authority, though this Church will try to keep in fellowship with other parts of the Church universal. Church Union News and Views, Vol.I, No.I, July, 1930, p13. One important event needs to be noted for reference, that during this period of negotiation, the World Conference on Faith and Order was held in Lausanne in 1927 and the spirit of that conference must have had an effect on the south India movement through the nine delegates. After the meeting of the Joint Committee in February 1929, the report of this committee was issued under the title 'Proposed Scheme of Union.'

withdraw from the Anglican Communion in order to become part of the CSI, were under pressure to postpone any final decision and action until after the Lambeth Conference had met in 1948, but the inauguration went ahead even so. The Church of South India was constituted on 27th September 1947, by the South India United Church, the South India Province of the Methodist Church and the four dioceses of the Church of India, Pakistan, Burma and Ceylon.

The inauguration of the CSI and the achievement of the independence of India in 1947 provided added incentive for the negotiators in the north to move forward. It is difficult today to imagine ourselves in the position of those negotiators who drafted the Plan of union. The issues with which they had to deal were both complex and important. My object, after the chronological survey of the negotiation in north India, is to interpret the theology of union that led to the formation of the Church of North India.

Basis of Union

The attempt to reconcile the divergent western traditions was the first task for the negotiators. It was not an easy one as the very process challenged the concept of denomination and advocated a return to the doctrine of the Church as the whole body of Christians, worshipping and witnessing to one Lord in a particular locality. The 1965 Plan of church union in north India and Pakistan was the basis of the formation of the CNI. The object was defined in the statement of intention given in the preface of the Plan:

> We are agreed in seeking a united church which will be an integral part of the universal church and yet develop the special

and distinctive gifts which God has given to the people of India and Pakistan in the expression of their worship, their faith and their common life.[7]

An assessment of the fourth plan has been done by W.J. Marshall in his doctoral dissertation. He gives a commentary on the Plan and examines it not as 'an abstract statement of doctrine but as a programme which has been put into action, an example of obedience to God's will for unity.' His study brings the theological insights of the plan of union into focus as a result of his experience of ministry in the Church of Ireland, the CIPBC and subsequently in the CNI. In his summary he notes that:

> One dominant insight which informs the Plan as a whole is the Church's dependence on God. It is remarkable that such a simple, obvious truth should have such profound and far-reaching consequences. Surely everyone knows that the Church depends completely on God and only exists through His continuous action? But it is precisely this truth which divisions in the Church tend to obscure.[8]

According to Marshall, the Church's dependence on God may seem a very obvious truth but it is too often obscured by division between denominations. This insight draws attention to the point that Christians of different denominations are not there merely to justify their own positions and stress the rightness of their own beliefs, but together to seek from God the full expression of truth. Such a view of truth has far reaching implica-

---

[7] The Plan of Church Union in North India and Pakistan. 1965. CLS, Madras, pIX.

[8] MARSHALL, W.J. The Church of North India/Pakistan: A theological Assessment of the Plan of Union. Ph.D Thesis, Dublin University. 1975; and Faith and Order in the North India/Pakistan Unity Plan. ISPCK, Delhi, 1987, p119. The book is part of his Ph.D Thesis of 1975.

tions for unity. In this perspective the statement of intention of the Plan is not an end in itself but a foretaste of unity that is to be a sign and instrument of God's purpose in the world. The movement for unity is not to have a united church with a mere fusion of denominations but to highlight what is common to the uniting churches and to seek for truth that corrects and reconciles the partial insights.

The negotiators in north India affirmed from the beginning the value of diversity and there was a conscious structural need to respect continuing diversity and avoid homogeneity.

> We do not desire that any one Church shall absorb other churches, nor that one tradition shall be imposed upon all; but rather that each Church shall bring the true riches of its inheritance into the united Church to which we look forward. We intend that it shall be a Church which, while holding to the fundamental Faith and Order of the Universal Church, shall assure to its members freedom of opinion in all other matters, and also freedom of action in such varieties of practice as are consistent with the life of the Church as one organic body.[9]

The search for consensus implies a search for an ecumenical perspective on ecclesiology. It would have been impossible for the negotiating churches ever to have contemplated union with one another unless they had been satisfied that each party to the union held the essentials of the catholic faith. It was possible to continue the debate, to hold together the different presuppositions and divergences regarding the nature of union only with open recognition of each other in Christ. The historical reasons which lie behind the schisms in the West had comparatively little interest

---

[9] The Plan of Church Union, Fourth Revised Edition. 1965. CLS, Madras, pX.

for many Indians. They were convinced that the Church should be one, but to say that all were concerned to promote any scheme of union would be hardly true. Bishop Waller wrote that they wanted a national expression of Christianity.

> They are convinced that the Church should be one; they are duly resentful at the cleavages introduced by the foreigners. They want a national expression of Christianity - an Indian church. If any leader could show them a way of securing that they would follow him, regardless of history in the west. If the way to union must be through long discussions and a particular scheme on which foreigners must unite, they will listen with attention to the debate and they will join in it for or against particular points but their real feeling, perhaps is rather that the sooner it is all over and they get union the better everyone will be pleased.[10]

In this respect the remark of an Indian, G.V. Job, one of the Rethinking group, which will be discussed in the next chapter, is pertinent. He emphasized that in the New Testament one will find a triangle but not a quadrilateral: one faith, one Lord, and one baptism.[11] In the west the reason for ecclesiastical skirmishes was the fourth side of the quadrilateral, namely the historic episcopate and related ministries. It so happened that the negotiations lingered for a long time due to the reaction against an exaggerated principle or due to the fear of omitting certain matters of importance on the part of negotiating churches, but there was a conscious attempt to build up extensive theological consensus as a prerequisite for any

---

[10] WALLER, E.H.M. Church Union in South India. SPCK, London, 1929, p30-3I.

[11] JOB, G.V. and Others. Rethinking Christianity in India. A.N. Sudarisanam, Madras, 1938, p21.

real consideration of structured commitment between the churches. The commitment was not to be at the cost of principles or through compromises but in obedience to the will of the Lord of the Church.[12]

It was acknowledged by the negotiators that the division in the Church was a testimony to departing from faith in Jesus. That is a decisive issue for the question of Church unity. If it is accepted, then unity is an overcoming of the fragmentation of the history of the Church, through faith in one Lord. One obvious problem in such an affirmation is to maintain unity in the context of great differences among the confessions and creeds of the various epochs of the history of the Church, which contain statements opposed to each other even though they talk about the same Jesus Christ. The content which has been preserved chiefly in the specific forms in different denominations needs to be seen in the light of the common affirmation of faith in one Lord. Therefore it is wrong to contend that one of the denominations has the exclusive expression of the Christian faith.

It might be helpful to note the view of Bishop Newbigin, a senior statesman of the ecumenical movement and one of the strong supporters of the church union movement in India. He took a major part in the negotiations which led to the establishment of the CSI. He is known as an able apologist for the Church of South India. In his defence of the South India scheme of union he examines the theological issues involved in the various grounds on which the unity was opposed. He tries to raise consciousness of the fact of division in the Church. His contention is that the New

---

[12] Plan of Church Union: Compromise or Comprehension? (ii), <u>Church Union News and Views.</u> Editorial, May 1969, p17f.

Testament leaves no room for the commonly held view that the unity of the Church, being spiritual, does not require organic union. His thesis is that the New Testament rejects the Greek antithesis between the spiritual and the material and treats the spirit and body as correlates. The divisions arise when people put human constrictions alongside the Gospel as part of the foundation of the Church. Therefore he stresses the sinful character of the divided Church.[13] The plea for restoration of the broken unity through the reunion of the churches could be understood from Newbigin's interpretation of the Church as 'the congregation of the faithful'.[14] The faithfulness is defined in relationship to Christ as the ground of faith. At the heart of this faith is incorporation in Christ by faith.

> There is one mediator, given once for all, at the centre of the world history, by whom we are reconciled to God...He is present in the word and sacraments of the Gospel. In the word of the Gospel truly read and preached, and in the Sacraments which He gave, duly administered, Christ himself is present in His saving power, to evoke faith, to reconcile sinful man with holy God, to build up the Church, which is His body, by drawing all men to himself.[15]

The incorporation is by baptism into a visible fellowship which is the body of Christ yet the body of Christ is divided. Both the Catholics and the

---

[13] NEWBIGIN, Lesslie J.E. The Reunion of the Church. SCM, London, 1948.

[14] The Kerr Lectures were published as The Household of God. SCM, London, 1953.

[15] NEWBIGIN, Lesslie J.E. The Household of God. SCM, London, 1953, p49.

Protestants as visible institutionally in the course of history are guilty of schism. The distortion of Protestantism is to define the Church as that which bears apostolic witness - the message, and the distortion of Catholicism is to define the Church as a continuation of the apostolate - the structure. Then Newbigin gives a third interpretation which he calls the 'Pentecostal' - the community of the Holy Spirit. It is the living Spirit which can and does give its own life to bodies which lack in some measure the fullness of the Church's true teaching and order. It is grace that defines and determines the relation.

> It will be clear from what I have said that I believe that the Catholic-Protestant debate which has characterized the ecumenical movement needs to be criticized and supplemented from what I have called the Pentecostal angle, that in fact the debate has to become three-cornered. I think it is clear that the Protestant-Catholic dilemma is seen from this angle to be a false one....In our Lord himself there is no such separation. He is himself the message. He is the word made flesh. In him word and deed, message and being are one.[16]

Newbigin is very clear about the absolute nature of the call to unity. According to him the word ekklesia in the New Testament is an exclusive word, describing the body of Christ in the world, something of which it is unthinkable to predicate plurality except in the sense of the plurality of local churches.[17] Newbigin spotlights the double aspect of the unity of the church. One is the spiritual unity and the other is visible unity. His argument is that organic unity is the other side of the spiritual unity,

---

[16] NEWBIGIN, Lesslie J.E. The Household of God. SCM, London, p94.

[17] NEWBIGIN, Lesslie. The Reunion of the Church. SCM, London, 1948, p23.

springing necessarily from it. Newbigin's view has been questioned. Van Dusen questions such an implication because he questions whether Paul ever envisioned a visible corporate unity of the kind that is in the mind of those who look toward a single institutional Church of Christ as the ideal for the corporate life of His followers on earth. He thinks that Paul's thought moves between the 'Congregation' and the Church universal as 'the Body of Christ'.[18]

The negotiating churches assumed the organic unity of the Church as expressing the spiritual unity of the body of Christ. The theological basis of union was John 17. It was used as a proof text. The central point of argument was that the unity of believers is to lead the unbelieving world to faith in Jesus as the one sent by God. The idea of mission was based on the prayer of Jesus that all believers may be brought to the unity of the divine that the world may see the love of the Lord embodied in them and may behold the glory. This as the basis was categorically affirmed in the Plans of Union, starting from the seventh Round Table Conference in 1948.[19]

One of the persons involved in the negotiation process in north India was Leslie Wenger. He agrees with T. Evan Pollard's exposition of John

---

[18] VAN DUSEN, H.P. One Great Ground of Hope. Lutterworth, London, 1961, p125. NEWBIGIN, Lesslie. The Reunion of the Church. SCM, London, 1948, p50-54 argues that the conception of the nature of Christian unity grounds itself upon unequivocal New Testament teaching. See also JONES, Stanley. The Proposed Church Union in north India. The Guardian. Vol.XXXIII, No.31, Thursday, 4th August, 1955, p1,4-6, where Stanley Jones argues for a Federal Union and against episcopacy.

[19] Minutes of 7th RTC 1948, p2. Plan of Union 1951, p1.

17:21 by a parallelism with the doctrine of the Trinity - that the unity of the disciples of Christ is to be a unity with distinctions. But Pollard's contention is that John 17:21 is frequently quoted in discussion concerning church union and church unity but never interpreted in the light of its immediate context nor in the light of the whole Gospel. 'The ardent protagonists of union quote it as if it were the final sanction or even the absolute command of our Lord that the churches, as we know them in this twentieth century, should unite.'[20] Wenger contends that Pollard uses the context only to show the pattern of this unity and almost ignores the twofold purpose of the unity. 'If the full context is taken and the unity is to be, as Pollard finally says, that of perichoresis or mutual interpenetration, it is hard to see how it can be achieved merely by intercommunion and mutual recognition and inter-change of ministries between denominations.'[21] Wenger argued that the connection of John 17:21 with church union schemes may not be obvious at first sight, but its full exegesis will give a profound basis for organic church union.

The scholars have differed about the interpretation of this chapter.[22] But John 17 is a farewell speech. It is not unusual for a speaker to close a farewell address with prayer like Moses in Deuteronomy 32 where he turns

---

[20] POLLARD, Evan T. That They All May be One (John 17:21) and the Unity of the Church. Expository Times. Vol.LXX, No5, February 1959, p149-50.

[21] WENGER, E.L. That They All may be One. Expository Times. LXX, No.II, August 1959, p333.

[22] See for a list of different interpretations In: BROWN, R.E. The Gospel According to John. Geoffrey Chapman, 1971, p775.

from the people to address the heavens and then in chapter 33 he blesses the tribes for the future. The prayer of Jesus is a prayer of communion between the Son and the Father and then a prayer of petition. The expectation is that the disciples may share this union by sharing God's glory among themselves. It is in the mission of the disciples that the name of God will be glorified on earth. The belief in Jesus entails an appreciation of the relationship of the Son to the Father. Those who come to believe in Jesus through the words of Jesus do so through the work of the Paraclete. The unity of believers, for which prayer is made, is more radical and fundamental. It is rooted in the being of God, revealed in Christ, and in the redemptive action of God in Christ.[23]

Discussion of the theological basis of union occupied an important place during the negotiation and it is hardly surprising, given the fact that it indicates an intention to identify what is important and constitutive for any area of concern. The basis operated as a strategy for finding and ordering the life of the uniting churches. Having agreed on the principles of a basis for union, the negotiators then had to wrestle with defining the faith and order of the proposed united church. The faith and order section of the scheme provided a medium through which the bond of unity in Christ was expressed. It was used as a foundation for building the unity of the churches. In the following section an attempt is made to look at the statement of faith as contained in the Faith and Order section of the scheme which found acceptance by the uniting churches and a place in the faith

---

[23] BEASLEY-MURRAY, George R. John. Word Biblical Commentary. Vol.36, Texas, 1987, p291-307.

and order section of the Constitution of the Church of North India.

The Statement of Faith.

The Statement of Faith has been classified in section III of the Constitution of the CNI as 'The doctrines of the Church'. It can be summed up as the Lordship of Christ, primacy of Scripture, acknowledgement of the Creeds, by conversing in brotherly love to hold together the divergent convictions on certain matters of faith and practice, and acknowledging the statements of faith of the uniting churches as consistent with the doctrinal standards of the CNI.[24]

The Statement of Faith is precise and no attempt was made during the negotiations to write an elaborate statement of faith though it was stated that the CNI might later do so. In fact the CNI adopted an affirmation of Faith and Commitment in October 1986. It is not a substitute to the classical Creeds but a faith-response to the contemporary Indian context.[25] This affirmation of faith acknowledges the richness of the uniting traditions, the doctrine of the Trinity, the rich heritage of the country and a call for justice and freedom for the powerless.

The suggestion that the churches can and should agree on common faith to restore the unity of the Church on the surface appears to be self-evident and highly desirable. It appears to be a reasonable and practical appeal but in fact it is neither as simple or unchallengeable as it might first seem. Christianity itself is still an essentially contested concept, and that is

---

[24] See Appendix I.

[25] See Appendix II.

reflected in the numerous church divisions.[26] A common Christian faith goes back to the general conviction that Christianity was in fact one thing. It was generated from the early Church's experience that God was in Christ reconciling the world to himself (2 Cor.5:19).

One faith is a confession of trust in the consistency of God's grace. An agreement that finds expression of oneness in language is helpful for maintaining the identity of the community of Christians. They are tellers of a tale in which they confess themselves to be participants and of which doctrine is an abbreviated statement. As long as the abbreviated statement contains the essential elements of faith then it can claim to be catholic. The faith that finds expression in language is integrally related to the life and activity of a particular community.

A consequence of this was the affirmation of one Lord, one faith and one baptism (Eph.4:5). This one faith was encapsulated in the early Church's confession of the Lordship of Christ (Acts 2:36, Rom.10:9). Such a confession required a fresh appropriation of an inherited Jewish monotheism. Oneness of faith came to form in various semi-credal statements of faith. The multiplicity of confessional form was not a threat to the oneness of faith prior to the beginning of the fourth century. All creeds and summaries of faith were local in character. It was taken for granted that they enshrined the universally accepted catholic faith, handed down from the Apostles. Beginning with the Council of Nicaea, the custom was established to frame formularies of agreement on matters of faith which

---

[26] SYKES, Stephen. The Identity of Christianity. SPCK, London, 1984, p11-34.

were intended to have a far more than local authority. The desire for a common statement of faith is a process of communication. One of the main concerns of the negotiators for union was the desire to restore unity by affirming one faith. It is very difficult for any one Christian communion to produce within its own denominational history and life, a comprehensive account of the story of the Church and the need to hold together the relation between the different traditions. The negotiators knew that after the union of churches in India, there would still remain different denominations in the world, yet they were also convinced that it would be a united church to the extent that it was bringing into one organic life the heritage of the uniting churches. That conviction was based on the faith that the movement for unity was a movement towards Christ. In other words it was a challenge to return to be closer to Christ.

> The Church of North India holds the faith which the Church has ever held in Jesus Christ, the Redeemer of the World, in whom men are saved by grace through faith, and in accordance with the revelation of God which He made, being Himself God Incarnate, it worships one God, Father, Son and Holy Spirit.[27]

The language of the CNI's above statement of faith is largely drawn from the declaration of the constitution of the Church of India, Burma, Pakistan and Ceylon. It is different from the Church of South India in that the CSI scheme begins with the acceptance of the Holy Scriptures of the Old and New Testaments as containing all things necessary to salvation and as the supreme and decisive standard of faith, followed by Creeds and the statement of Trinitarian faith. In the context of a scheme of union for

---

[27] The Constitution of the CNI. ISPCK, Delhi, 1987, p4.

divided churches, the north India scheme held to the faith only by a renewed hold upon God's revelation of Himself in Christ.

In the statement of faith, the Holy Scripture is accepted as containing all things necessary to salvation and as the standard of faith, and the Apostles' Creed and Nicene Creed as witnessing to and safeguarding the faith which is continuously confirmed in the spiritual experience of the Church of Christ. Scripture is no doubt the source of the Christian faith which is clearly accepted in clause two of the doctrines of the Church of North India, but Christology forms the starting point. Scripture is common to all, but each denomination finds its own particular emphasis in Scripture which enables its members to justify their own existence rather than promote the unity of the Church. Scripture as a witness to the common origin of all Christians points to the person of Jesus. He is the historical starting point for the historical form of the Christian faith.

Confession of Jesus as Lord involves the question of the Father and the Spirit. This was set in the debates with heretical beliefs which seemed to threaten the clarity of the confession of Jesus as Lord. It is witnessed in the framing of the credal statement of the ancient Catholic Church at Nicaea in 325, at Constantinople in 381 and at Chalcedon in 451. The concern was to ensure unity in the statements about Jesus, the Father, and the Holy Spirit. Confession of faith in Jesus as Lord implied a confession of faith in the reality of God the Father and God the Holy Spirit in unity with Jesus. Therefore the statement of the CNI included that 'It worships one God, Father, Son and Holy Spirit.'[28]

---

[28] The Constitution of the CNI, ISPCK, Delhi, 1987, p4.

After affirming its faith in a triune God, the CNI was allowed to bear divergent convictions within one fellowship. Holding the fundamentals of the faith of the Church universal, the principle was to allow freedom of opinion in all other matters, and freedom of action in such differences of practice as were consistent with the general framework of the Church as one organic body. Therefore in the statement of faith the CNI acknowledged the witness to the Catholic faith as contained in the confessions of faith adopted both at the time of the Reformation and subsequently and formulated by the uniting churches or their parent churches. In particular the CNI accepted as consistent with its own doctrinal standards Declaration (I) of the Constitution of the Church of India, Pakistan, Burma and Ceylon, the Confession of the Faith of the UCNI, the Doctrinal Standards of the Methodist Church (British Conference), the Baptist Church Covenant of the Council of the Baptist Churches of Northern India and the Declaration of Principle of the Baptist churches.

It is obvious that various traditions went to make up the CNI. A genuine appreciation and admiration for traditions other than one's own and sharing each other's experience is the basis of the agreed statement of faith. The various traditions are not seen as opposed but complementary. A positive approach to the validity of the principle of plurality of doctrine within limits might be in order. What is involved in taking them seriously depends on the meaning of the doctrine. Plurality of doctrines within the CNI mirrors the pluralism of Christianity. To accept plurality of doctrine is not to allow latitude of belief but to hold together the plurality of doctrine through the unity of God. The different convictions in the CNI are not a sign of doctrinal relativism but plurality of interpretation of one story. The presupposition of such a view is that in a reconciled community one doctrine cannot be imposed on others. The unity of the Church is based on the presupposition that the Church is a historical community intended to be one in Christ and the divergence of conviction on certain other matters of faith and practice is something which can only be borne within one fellowship by the exercise of much mutual forbearance and charity.

The statement of faith included only the necessary minimum doctrines but the negotiators wrestled with different issues for a long time. The chronological survey of negotiations show how the issues were discussed and agreement reached. In the following section attention is drawn to some important issues which found place in the debate and on which agreement was finally reached.

a. Baptism

The question of baptism was an important issue because of the participation of the Baptists in the negotiation. Therefore it was decided to regard as equivalent alternatives for entry into the Church both a pattern where baptism in infancy is followed by later profession of faith and a pattern where believer's baptism follows upon a presentation and blessing in infancy. This involved a mutual recognition of convictions about baptism. The rite of initiation occupied a major point of debate during the period of negotiation. 'Those shall be the members of the united church who have been baptized with water in the name of the Father, and of the Son and of the Holy Spirit.' Declaration of this personal acceptance of God in Christ is made either at the time of baptism when it is believer's baptism or at the time of confirmation when it is infant baptism.

It was recognized that the baptism is incomplete as a rite of initiation unless that baptism is confirmed by a personal declaration of faith. The Christian parents are free to decide whether their children will be dedicated as infants and then receive believer's baptism or be baptized as infants and then declare their personal faith at the time of confirmation. The persons baptized with water in the name of the Father, of the Son and of the Holy Spirit, who had openly confessed their faith and been admitted by confirmation or other such services to participate in Holy Communion were accepted as members in full standing. But it was impossible to omit all reference to children or catechumens. Therefore they were specially recognized to be within the Church whose nurture in the Christian way is a special care.

Pastoral problems were inevitable in a united Church where differing practices of administration were allowed, because a person may be troubled by grave scruples about his own baptism. The issue would arise if a person baptized in infancy subsequently wished to receive baptism as a believer. The Plan of 1957 allowed the matter to be referred to the Bishop of the diocese for pastoral advice and direction. If the Church claims to hold the authority to baptize, it needs to be very sure that it is right if it refuses to baptize one who comes with genuine faith.

Baptism is the sign of having died, been buried with Christ and risen with him, which is an expression of faith union. 'Baptism is a sign of cleansing from sin, of engrafting into Christ, of entrance into the covenant of grace, of fellowship with Christ in His Death and Resurrection and of rising to newness of life.'[29] But the debate was on the unrepeatability of God's

---

[29] The Constitution of the CNI. ISPCK, Delhi, 1987, p16.

gracious act of accepting a child or an adult as a member of the family. The question is whether God's gracious act is so tied to a liturgical act that it could become the ground of unrepeatability of baptism. If so the unrepeatability raised the radical question of the meaning of baptism.

Baptism administered in water in the name of the Father, Son and Holy Spirit is interpreted as being a participation in Christ's death and resurrection, a washing away of sin, a new birth, an enlightenment by Christ, a reclothing in Christ, a renewal by the Spirit, a liberation into a new humanity, an act of justification, God's gift of anointing and the promise of the Holy Spirit, a sign and seal of common discipleship, a bond of Christian unity, the notion of a new covenant, an analogy to circumcision. It is a decisive beginning of an initiatory process but the importance of the community of faith is the context for the individual's act of faith and growth. These form the basis for holding together the two practices of baptism of believers and infants.

The issue of baptism was a test case of the reality of freedom of conscience during the negotiation. The difficulty was two-sided. When one is baptized, he is also baptized by someone else who is asked to act as if the earlier baptism had never taken place, in spite of the fact that infant baptism is solemnly recognized as one of the modes of administration of this sacrament. Similar difficulty could not be ruled out in other situations. For instance, someone who has received believer's baptism may later have a further spiritual experience and then wish to be baptized again. During the negotiations this was one of the most sensitive issues.

The third edition of the Plan of Union (1957) included an Appendix B giving guiding principles in regard to Baptism. It laid down that a member already baptized in infancy, who desires to take Believer's Baptism should be helped to seek the remedy for what he believed to be a grave lack in his own baptism, not by re-baptism, but by some other means which effectively re-affirms his baptism and symbolizes for him his engrafting into Christ. The Appendix contained the controversial note that 'the Church holds that there is but one Baptism which is therefore unrepeatable in the life of any person, no matter by which practice it was administered.' If a person should persistently maintain that only his baptism as a believer will satisfy his conscience although he was baptized in infancy, the minister concerned will refer the matter to the Bishop of the Diocese for pastoral advice and direction.

It appeared to some to suggest that the liberty of individual consciences would be overridden by church regulations. Therefore the fourth edition of the Plan in 1965 deleted the Appendix B of the 1957 Plan. Only section 4 of this Appendix B was added to the fourth and final edition of the 1965 Plan in the section on the Doctrine of the Church (Section IV:4 / Section III:Clause 5 of the Constitution of the CNI).[30] The purpose of the new paragraph was to recognize and accommodate both views and both practices even at the risk of anomaly. Such anomaly was allowed with the expectation that it would be swallowed up in the greater unity. It was expected that such problems could be met on the basis of mutual charity and accommodation within the new context, as the traditional arguments for or against one practice were used in a context not of unity but plurality. One aspect of baptism that was stressed was that baptism in itself is not a

---

[30] The Constitution of the CNI. ISPCK, Delhi, 1987, p4.

completed act but the beginning of a process which is God's saving and reconciling activity in the life of an individual who is within a fellowship.

b. Lord's Supper

The Plan laid down two essential conditions that the bread and wine be set apart with the unfailing use of Christ's words of institution; and the celebration of Holy Communion be entrusted only to those who by ordination received authority. It also recommended that every service of the Lord's Supper was to have as its basis six recommended elements, to which only one addition, clause (c) below, was made during the negotiation.

(a) Thanksgiving for God's glory and goodness, with the expression of penitence, and prayer that all may communicate worthily.

(b) Commemoration of Christ's life and work through the ministry of the Word and through the recitation of the Creed.

(c) Intercession for the Church and the world.

(d) Showing forth, and pleading before the Father, Christ's sacrifice once for all offered, invoking Christ's merits for the whole Church, remembering His resurrection and ascension and the outpouring of the Holy Spirit, who continuously indwells and inspires the Church, and looking for Christ's coming again in glory.

(e) Presenting ourselves, our souls and bodies, as a living sacrifice to God.

(f) Communion and fellowship with God, with one another, with the people of God on earth, and with all the company of heaven.

(g) Offering to God our sacrifice of praise and thanksgiving for the grace received in Holy Communion.[31]

---

[31] The Constitution of the CNI. ISPCK, Delhi, 1987, Section V, Clause 16, p19.

Criticism has been levelled against the clause (d) which was supposed by some to pave the way for a sacrificial theory of the eucharist and in invoking Christ's merit for the benefit of the whole church may mean to include the living and the dead.[32] Such a reading is difficult to rule out as this sacrament is seen as a means of grace by which the believer is united to God and through which God works in us.

The Liturgical Commission of the CNI prepared the order of the Lord's Supper in 1973. The structure of the Lord's Supper is set out in the two main divisions, the proclamation of the Word and the Prayers, and the Communion with four actions clearly indicated, the taking of the bread and wine, the thanksgiving, the breaking of the bread, and the sharing of the bread and wine.[33] The Synod's executive committee in 1985 while commenting on the WCC document on 'Baptism, Eucharist and Ministry', said of the eucharist that the CNI appreciates the focusing of attention on the central significance and experiential aspect of the eucharist in terms of the 'real presence' of Christ in this sacrament. They noted that the significant focus is on the missionary aspect of the eucharist in section 17 and 26, especially the comment in 26 'In so far as Christians cannot unite in full fellowship around the same table to eat the same loaf and drink from

---

[32] BOYD, Robin. The Theological Basis of the Teaching of the Lord's Supper in the North India Plan. Indian Journal of Theology. Vol.11, No2, 1962, p47.

[33] An Order for the Lord's Supper prepared by the Liturgical Commission of the CNI and approved by the Executive Committee of the Synod in April, 1973 and March 1974. ISPCK, Delhi. An Alternative Order for the Lord's Supper, ISPCK, Delhi, 1974, Revised 1976.

the same cup, their missionary witness is weakened at both individual and corporate levels.'[34]

The object of the sacrament is to use that occasion to rethink the meaning of the Lord's Supper for the fellowship. One is expected to see the fellowship at the Lord's table as not just the goal of union but the source of power for subsequent missionary activity of the Church. Marshall makes a good remark that the Plan of 1965 treats the sacrament of Holy Communion at the level of worship rather than doctrine. It does not attempt to define the nature of Christ's sacrifice. The bond of union lies in the fact that Christians celebrate the Eucharist together rather than that they have the same theories about it.[35]

c. Episcopacy

The episcopate was accepted in a constitutional form. The continuity with the historic episcopate was being affirmed but no particular interpretation of the fact of the historic episcopate was thereby implied or should be demanded from any minister or member of the United Church. They were aware of the fact that this was one of the main causes of dispute in the history of Christianity. Some regard episcopacy as being of divine appointment and episcopal ordination as being an essential guarantee of the sacraments of the church. Others regard episcopacy as a form of church government which has persisted in the church through the centuries and as such may be called historic.

---

[34] THURIAN, Max. ed. Churches respond to BEM. Vol.II. WCC, Geneva, 1986, p72.

[35] MARSHALL, W.J. A United Church. ISPCK, Delhi, 1987, p43.

(a)The episcopate shall be both constitutional and historic.

(b) By constitutional is meant that bishops shall be appointed and shall perform their functions in accordance with the constitution of the Church.

(c) By historic is meant the episcopate which is in historic continuity with that of the early Church. It is accepted as a means of expressing the continuity of the Church down the ages and its unity all over the earth.

(d) The Church is not committed to any one particular theological interpretation of episcopacy, nor does it demand the acceptance of such an interpretation from its ministers or members.[36]

It was often pointed out that in a mission field situation episcopacy was likely to be more suitable than local autonomy. For example the Baptist churches in India had their local autonomy much modified to the central authority. The united Church accepted the three-fold ministry of Bishop, Presbyter and Deacon but in practice it can be more accurately described as a two-fold ministry of Bishop and Presbyter. The acceptance of episcopacy in practice is not without criticism.

> Obviously episcopacy in the CNI was not supposed to be what it is in the Anglican Church and members of the free or non-episcopal churches joining the CNI had neither accepted nor are they supposed to accept everything that goes on with episcopacy or in the name of episcopacy. It is unfortunate, however, that in certain respects some dioceses of the CNI, have become more 'Anglican' than the 'Anglican churches' and in certain dioceses of the CNI, in view of their sheer numerical strength, certain groups are trying, in a subtle manner, to thrust upon others

---

[36] The Constitution of the CNI. ISPCK, Delhi, 1987, p24.

some of their former practices and ideas which are peculiar to Anglicanism.[37]

The question of the lay diaconate was not overlooked but the uniting churches having carefully discussed this found no uniformity of functions in various types of lay workers in different negotiating churches. They accepted the ordained diaconate as it existed in the Anglican church in India as a step to the ordained ministry, leaving the united church to organize this later as might seem best.

d. Unification of Ministry

In the case of the Church of South India, the episcopal and non-episcopal ministers were accepted side by side as the ministers of the united church. Care was taken to see that consciences were not over-ridden either by church authorities or by majorities. The fact remained that a congregation formerly Anglican could choose to be ministered to by one not episcopally ordained. After thirty years of inauguration, the united church was expected to determine for itself whether it would continue to make any exception to the rule that its ministry is an episcopally ordained ministry, and generally under what conditions it would receive ministers from other churches into its ministry. In fact the thirty year period was reviewed by the sixteenth Synod of the CSI in 1978 and it unanimously resolved that:

> On completion of the thirty-year period as stipulated in the constitution, chapter ii, section 21, the CSI solemnly proclaims that hereafter there shall be a fully unified ministry of episcopally ordained ministers in the CSI and that in as much as the united church is the basic reality which gives unification to the ministries episcopal and non-episcopal, the present practice of

---

[37] ADHIKARI, Prabhudan. Episcopacy in the CNI. The North India Churchman. June, 1979, p2.

receiving ministers from any church with which the CSI is in full communion shall continue and that the period of such reception shall be indefinite.[38]

During the thirty-year period it was expected that the ministry would become increasingly episcopal, but uncertainty whether it would at the end of it lead to a purely episcopal ministry was one of the chief grounds of concern in some Anglican circles. The presence in the church of ministries of diverse origin caused anxiety about the privileges of former Anglicans under the pledge in some parts of the Church.[39] The limit to intercommunion set by the Anglican communion was a disappointment to some. Such matters led the negotiators in north India to desire a unification of the ministry from the beginning. In fact the Lambeth Conference 1948 tended to encourage such an attitude.

> The unification of the ministry in a form satisfactory to all the bodies concerned either at the inauguration of the union or as soon as possible thereafter, is likely to be a prerequisite to success in all future proposals for the reunion of the churches.[40]

Since 1948, every plan in which Anglicans were involved envisaged as a vital part of the inauguration some form of unification of ministry by laying on of hands by ministers, at least one of whom is a bishop within the

---

[38] The Constitution of the Church of South India. CLS, Madras, 1982, piv.

[39] The uniting churches had pledged themselves that the united church will at all times be careful not to allow any overriding of conscience either by church authorities or by majorities, and that it will not in any of its administrative acts knowingly transgress the long-established traditions of any of the churches from which it has been formed etc. For a full text of the Pledge, see SUNDKLER, Bengt. Church of South India. Lutterworth, London, 1965, p259.

[40] The Lambeth Conference 1948. SPCK, London, 1948, Part 1, p40.

historic succession. In this way it was hoped that there would be inter-communion from the beginning between the united church and the churches of the Anglican communion.

Mutual acknowledgement and recognition was the basis whereby all persons who were communicant members of any of the uniting churches were accepted as communicant members of the united church, and the same mutual acknowledgement and recognition meant that all the ministers of the uniting churches at the time of the inauguration of the CNI were brought into the ministry by the use of a common service of unification.

At the heart of the service of unification was the prayer that God would pour out His Holy Spirit on all the ministers of uniting churches to endue each according to his need with grace and authority. Therefore they had to work out a formula of laying on of hands for the act of unification without the implication of re-ordination and also to bring together the two episcopates. The history of the negotiation is a clear witness to the strong desire between the churches for an agreed statement.

The object in accepting the episcopate was to witness to the riches of God's grace in this form of ministry, but the difficulty was to find a way whereby this positive witness can be given without being bound to it as a controlling negative judgement on others. The Lambeth Appeal in 1888 and 1920 was burdened by an implied negative judgement on others:

> To this end, we who send forth this appeal would say that if the authorities of other communions should so desire, we are per-suaded that, terms of union having been otherwise satisfactorily adjusted, Bishops and clergy of our Communion would willingly accept from these authorities a form of commission or recognition which would commend our ministry to their congregations, as having its place in the one family life.........It is

our hope that the same motive would lead ministers who have not received it to accept a commission through episcopal ordination, as obtaining for them a ministry throughout the whole fellowship.[41]

There was no explicit mention of mutual laying of hands but at the heart of the 1920 Lambeth Appeal the suggestion was for an act of mutual commissioning with the laying on of hands. The commission given to non-episcopal ministers was described as 'episcopal ordination' though it is made clear that their previous ordination was not called into question. In the 1941 Round Table Conference in north India the proposal was introduced for 'mutual laying on of hands'.[42] In 1947 the RTC's acceptance of the unification of ministry by mutual laying on of hands in an act of 'supplemental ordination' led to much debate. In fact the proposal was introduced originally in 1943 in the south India negotiation and was a difficult one for the negotiating churches in south India to accept. The supplemental ordination was interpreted as something one divided church was able to supply another. Each was supposed to receive from others what it lacked and to supply to others what they lacked. This became the intransigent problem and the term 'supplemental ordination' was dropped. The Lambeth Conference of 1958 was happy to say that 'the plan for reunion in north India and Pakistan may go forward, and that the intention of the plan may be secured, that the ministry of the united Church shall be

---

[41] BELL, G.K.A. ed. <u>Documents on Christian Unity</u>. 1920-4, OUP, London, 1924, p4.

[42] See Minutes of 5th RTC, 1941, p3.

fully accredited in the eyes of all its members and as far as may be of the church throughout the world.'[43]

The CSI laid down the principle that church union is effected by churches acknowledging one another as churches in the act of union with provision for the conscience clause. From the day of union the CSI in its own eyes was one church with a unified ministry. There was pressure to postpone any final decision and action until after Lambeth 1948 but the inauguration of the CSI took place on 27th September 1947. The Lambeth Conference 1948 drew up the recommendations to govern the relation between the Anglican churches and the CSI. It proceeded with the assumption that from the point of view of the Anglican church the ministry of the CSI was not a unified one.

The aim of the unification of the ministry in North India was to make it possible without abandonment of any previous conscientiously held belief. The hope was to have unification by a service of laying on of hands with prayer in which God is asked to give whatever He sees to be needed for the fullness of ministry in the united Church. That was central to the plan. The question was whether any one of the uniting churches can properly lay down the sense in which it understands the rite, either as bestowing episcopal ordination upon those not previously so ordained or as being in no sense ordination at all.

The real difference was that, unlike the CSI, the rite included the laying on of hands. It led to many interpretations. In the second edition of the book, The Reunion of the Church (1960), Bishop Newbigin added a new introduction in which his criticism of the North India Plan was made.

---

[43] Lambeth 1958, Resolution No24(a). SPCK, London, 1958.

He said that the procedure laid down for the unification of the ministry is substantially 'supplemental ordination'. He defined it as the attempt to combine a recognition of an existing ordination with the addition to it of something which also has the character of ordination.

> It is true that the phrase 'supplemental ordination' has been abandoned in the proposals now before us. But the substance of them is the same - the attempt to combine a recognition of an existing ordination with the addition to it of something which also has the character of ordination. The Lambeth Conference of 1948 was surely wise in saying that this proposal requires much more thorough theological scrutiny before it can be recommended as the medicine for the healing of the Church. I feel bound to submit that the Conference of 1958 was not wise in deciding, without scrutiny, to advise all concerned to take only that medicine.[44]

The rite of unification was based on the assumption that God will do what is necessary in the context of church divisions to vindicate that which cannot be justified theologically. The unification was not based on the unanimity of interpretations but unanimity of trust. The factor which made it possible in the meeting of minds was the thought that unification was not to be seen as the victory of either view of the ministry over the other.[45]

---

[44] NEWBIGIN, Lesslie J.E. The Reunion of the Church. SCM, London, 1960, pxxv.

[45] 'The UCNI recognises that, within one of the Churches with which it seeks union, there are those who find a conscientious barrier to full acceptance of other ministers, unless in some act a commission is given to them by prayer, with episcopal laying on of hands....the UCNI does not regard such a procedure as a necessary condition for bringing about the unity of the Church, since that unity has already been created by Christ alone in His atoning and reconciling death and risen life. Nevertheless the UCNI has stated its willingness to share in such an act, if it will enable the brethren

The main change in the act in the fourth edition of the plan was the omission of the separate unification of the episcopates of the CIPBC and the MCSA. The positive element of this fourth edition included the formula regarding the intention of the rite of unification which said: 'The uniting Churches pledge themselves and fully trust each other that any bishop or presbyter officiating in the rite will do so with the sincere intention of placing himself unreservedly in the hands of God, to be used as He wills, as a channel of His grace, commission and authority.'[46] As Marshall puts it, the attempt was made in the fourth plan to remove ambiguity so that it cannot be interpreted in any traditional category whether that of episcopal ordination or any other.

> While the setting and the instrument of the unification act is the united Church, the agent of the unification is God. One Church does not remedy the defects in the ministry of another but it is God who unifies the ministry and supplies whatever lack there may be.[47]

The emphasis shifted to what God does through an already united Church. The separated ministries were offered to God with a prayer that He would endue each and every minister with whatever he may need of grace and authority for his future ministry within a united church, since all will

---

who do have such conscientious scruples, to recognize more heartily the unity of the Church and its ministry.' The UCNI Statement on the Unification of the Ministry. Church Union News & Views. August, 1957, p44.

[46] The Plan of Church Union in North India and Pakistan: 1965, CLS, Madras, p52

[47] MARSHALL, W.J. A United Church: Faith and Order in the North India/Pakistan Plan. ISPCK, Delhi, 1987, p93.

seek to undo the wholly anomalous situation in which the ministries of the divided churches were set in separation. The relevance of such a rite depended on the degree of mutual trust and understanding.

Conclusion

The denominational affiliation for the average Indian Protestant was not so much a matter of personal choice or conviction but an accident of geography. In the course of time with the cooperation of various Protestant missions and the rise of nationalism, the climate was conducive for the Church union movement, and for blurring the lines separating the different denominations. It was recognized and affirmed very strongly that the existence of denominational divisions was a scandal. The Church as a visible community is divided. The visible separations are the evidence of the precise opposite of unity in the Spirit. The Church is divided because of sin and this demanded a return to Christ in an act of obedience to His will.

The churches in separation had different practices such as infant or believer's baptism, and different forms of ministry. In the process of negotiation they were seen to provide an opportunity for a deeper understanding of important truths of Christian faith. For example the difficulty over baptism led to thorough examination of the church membership and the conclusion was reached that full membership should be taken as a norm in which baptism and personal faith will have equal recognition.

One obvious but profound theology of union, as Marshall said, was the Church's dependence on God. It was possible to agree on matters of difference when it was seen that God is the primary agent on the questions such as the unification of ministry and the meaning of sacraments. The Church can live only by continually receiving God's grace.

One basis of union centred on the prayer of Jesus in John 17. While the relation of the prayer of Jesus to organic union is debatable, one important implication of the discussion of John 17 as the basis of union is to recognize the importance of each person and the interdependence of all upon one another. It is the theological basis of Christian unity. This is affirmed in the belief in a God who is made known to the world through Jesus and the Spirit. The being of the same God consists in communion. The fourth Gospel tells that Jesus leads us to the Father (Jn14:9), and yet the Father glorifies the Son (Jn14:13-14), and Jesus commends the Spirit which is to come (Jn14, 15, 16, 17).

The coming together of denominational bodies on Indian soil has created a challenging situation. The Indian Christians were acquainted with a wide range of denominations but only a small proportion of Indian Christians were well acquainted with the more subtle theological distinctions. The joining together of different denominations meant that the CNI became the repository of considerable and varied groups, the diverse traditions of different denominations coming face to face within a single corporate body.

Church union in north India has at least encouraged people to join together in one koinonia instead of the many, which perhaps served to perpetuate their narrow identities. It is vital that the ecumenical identity in one koinonia be sustained against all the pressure from caste structured society and pressure from within. Lionel Caplan says that the creation of the CSI, while being recognized as a triumph of Protestant ecumenism, has itself fostered a new denominationalism. It is to be viewed in the context of attempts to control the resources both spiritual and material. The individuals and groups create allies and identify opponents by emphasizing traditional symbols of unity or division, including those of denominational attachments.[48] The challenge is to break out of those little enclosures of security and to construe an identity that could encompass the whole. The development of an ecumenical church transcending the boundaries of caste, race, regionalism or colour would be the final triumph of unity in India.

---

[48] CAPLAN, Lionel. Religion and Power. CLS, Madras, 1989, p28.

PART III
THE APPLICATION
CHAPTER FIVE
THE NATURE OF IDENTITY

An effect of nationalism was the strengthening of the Indian identity. It helped in the resurgence of Indian religions. When a national religion becomes resurgent, it might take a critical attitude to those religions which are suspected of having no roots in the native soil. Although Christianity is not new to India as proven by the presence of the ancient church in Kerala, on the whole it carries the label of foreignness in the minds of the people because of its association with colonialism.

One general assumption is that the Church in India in its organization, architecture, worship, creeds, confessions and doctrinal statements is no different from the Church in the West. It is labelled as the Latin Captivity of the Church. The Church is criticized as being alien in its environment because the form, the creeds and the confessions of the institutional church are alien to the Indian philosophical, religious and socio-cultural tradition. It is the purpose of this chapter to look at the various indigenous responses to the formation of ecclesial identity, to make an assessment of these responses in general and to discuss the nature of identity in the social and religious context of India.

Under the impact of nationalism, the questions that received serious attention were the independence of the Church from mission control and the unity of the churches by becoming free from denominational identity. It would be fair to say that in the history of Indian Christian thought, there was little serious discussion of the doctrine of the Church, whereas

Christology was one dominant theme. It was dominant among the Indian Christian thinkers because of their preoccupation with the problem of communicating the Gospel of Christ in a multi-religious society. Although there was no grappling with the doctrine of the church as such, still one can identify certain elements which point to a new understanding of the Church and its nature. In the following section the response of some Indian thinkers will be discussed under four models and then a general assessment of these responses will be offered.

Ecclesial Identity

a. Apologetic

One distinctive feature of Christian thought in India is Christian apologetic. In the words of M.M.Thomas it is in Christian apologetics in the context of Hinduism that the crucial issues of an indigenous Christian theology have become clarified and its fundamentals formulated.[1] The work of the apologists consisted largely of indigenizing the categories and forms of theological thought. Apologetic thought in India used either Sankara's advaita Vedānta or Ramanuja's Visishta advaita. For example, Brahmabandhav proposed that Vedānta thought could do the same service for Christian faith in India as scholastic philosophy once did.[2]

---

[1] THOMAS, Madathilparampil M. Toward an Indigenous Theology. In: ANDERSON, Gerald H. ed. Asian Voices in Christian Theology. Maryknoll, N.Y:Orbis, 1976, p14.

[2] Brahmabandhav (1861-1907) was a brahmin from Calcutta and his real name was Bhavani Charan Banerji. He was baptized in the Anglican church in 1891, but in the same year joined the Roman Catholic Church, and lived like a sanyasi till the end of his life. Then he became fully engaged in the

We must fall back upon the Vedāntic method in formulating the Catholic religion to our countrymen. In fact, the Vedānta must be made to do the same service to Catholic faith in India as was done by Greek philosophy in Europe. The assimilation of the Vedāntic philosophy by the Church should not be opposed on the ground of its containing certain errors.[3]

Brahmabandhav was impressed by the teaching of Thomas Aquinas especially for its coherent system with its firm philosophical grounding in Aristotle. This led him to look for something similar in Indian philosophical systems. The one that attracted him most was that of Sankara, known as 'Advaita Vedānta'. Sankara, a Vedānta philosopher, was a great exponent of the way of knowledge during the eighth century. The issue was to realize the unity of 'Ātman' or soul with the 'Paramātman', Supreme Soul or 'Brahman' by overcoming the mists of 'Māyā'(illusion). An interpretation of 'māyā' was still needed: therefore he said that 'māyā' is not mere illusion but is the result of choice.

The Sanskrit word 'advaita' means 'non-duality'and in this perspective, reality is all inclusive. Brahmabandhav recognized that while Christianity was valid for some Hindus at the level of a personal devotional theistic religion, with a personal God revealed in incarnation, yet he thought that God who is unconditioned must be higher than that. Therefore he proposed God as 'Saccidānanda'. In Sankara's Advaita, Sat-chit-ānanda points to the Supreme Being, Brahman. Brahman is Sat (Positive Being),

---

nationalist movement in Bengal. In 1907 he was imprisoned by the British and in October 1907 he died in prison after an operation.

[3] UPADHYAYA, Brahmabandhav. The Clothes of Catholic Faith, Sophia, Vol.V, No8, August 1898. p124. In Indian Journal of Theology. Vol.28, 1979, p56.

Chit (Intelligence), Ānanda (Bliss). Brahmabandhav used Saccidānanda as an analogy to the Christian doctrine of the Trinity. Sat corresponds to the absolute existence of the Father, Chit to the Logos and Ānanda to the Holy Comforter. This he thought could be understood fully in terms of the Christian doctrine of the Trinity.

In putting his view as early as 1898, Brahmabandhav tried to show that the Christian doctrines of the Trinity and of Creation are there in Hinduism, which led him to say that by birth one is Hindu and will remain Hindu till death. But as dvija (twice born) by virtue of sacramental rebirth, one is Catholic. His eagerness was for a church universal, catholic yet Indian in outlook. For him it was a practical issue which brought him into conflict with the Catholic Church. His plan to establish a sanyasi order - itinerant missionaries thoroughly Hindu in their mode of living - was nipped in the bud by higher ecclesiastical authorities.[4]

While Brahmabandhav's thought was to use advaita Vedānta, yet there is another tradition in Indian religion which equally claims to derive from the inspired Vedas. This is the bhakti religion. There are different manners in which God is present in different objects. Bhakti is man's response to God's immanence. Bhakti is also generally considered as the deep love of man for God, finding its highest bliss in union with Him.

The one who gave philosophical basis to this religion was Ramanuja during the later half of the eleventh century. Where Sankara emphasized jñāna as a means of salvation, Ramanuja stressed bhakti as a means of

---

[4] MOOKENTHOTTAM, Antony. Indian Theological Tendencies. Peter Lang, 1981.

salvation; Brahman is the conscious and controlling self of the world and individual selves are not dissolved into Brahman. It is not surprising that it became a great attraction to Indian Christian thinkers. Bishop Aiyadurai Jesudasen Appasamy (1891-1975) stated a preference for the system of Ramanuja rather than that of Sankara because he thought that the monistic idea did not provide a suitable basis for a corporate fellowship.

Appasamy laid much stress on mystic experience. The mystic derives his experience of identity with God but it is wrong when that identity is based on the assumption that like God one is incapable of sin, which is heretical. It is at the point of denial of man's sinfulness that the mystic denies the core of the Christian Gospel. Here Appasamy thought of integrating the Christian thought to build the foundation for Christian theology.

> Among the Christians in India it is being felt more and more that Christian theology and biblical exegesis taught in India follow too much the western traditions and do not take sufficient account of the problems, difficulties and the age long ideas of the problems of India. A theology of this character unrelated to the history of Indian thought, possesses naturally a foreign and unattractive character. What the Christians of India have to do is to get a real grasp of the various trends of Hindu thought and to interpret Christian documents like St John's Gospel, with these constantly in mind.[5]

One difficulty was of integrating the corporate aspect of fellowship with bhakti thought, but that is where Appasamy believed that Christianity could contribute because of the stress of bhakti on the spontaneity of

---

[5] APPASAMY, A.J. 'The Mysticism of Hindu Bhakti Literature', D.Phil Thesis, 1922, Oxford, p7.

different souls and the philosophical basis in Visishta advaita.

> The nearest approach to corporate mystical fellowship of the type in Bhakti thought and practice is the Kirtan Party, in which the worshippers of Krishna or Siva of all degrees of spiritual culture, assemble and sing together moved with devotion. Such a crowd is however too loosely knit together, too haphazard in its nature to be properly compared to the Christian church, represented by the image of the vine.[6]

The Christian idea is based on the corporate character of the experience of God as contrasted with the exclusive individual orientation of the Hindu devotee. It is through loyalty to Christ and the Church that one can discriminate from Hindu mysticism. One interesting feature of Appasamy's treatment is that of the relationship of God to the world, the most debated subject in Indian philosophy. Brahman is real and the world is māyā. Appasamy affirmed that God is not identical with the world nor the world mere illusion, but God is present and active in the world as 'Logos'. Immanence is an important element in bhakti thought, and therefore Christianity in India needs to stress the doctrine of immanence. The Bhakti idea of communion between God and man is thought to be of help in showing the intimate relationship between the inner spirit of Christianity and the inner spirit of Indian religious thought. The Christian idea is that through faith and loving surrender one can be united with Christ: but it is not a union in which one is absorbed but the believer and his Lord retain their distinct personalities.

Appasamy was determined to integrate the Gospel with Indian

---

[6] APPASAMY, A.J. 'The Mysticism of Hindu Bhakti Literature', D.Phil Thesis,1922,Oxford,p147.

culture. This is understandable from his active career in the affairs of the Church, his work on the committees for church union in south India, his bishopric in the CSI from 1950-59, his friendship with Sadhu Sundar Singh, all of which were factors in shaping his theology. This was distinctly reflected in his development of the Pramānas or norms for Indian Christian Theology. In the course of his search to settle the norms of Christian thought, Appasamy highlighted that Hinduism has three Pramānas or sources of authority. The Scripture (sruti), Experience (anubhava), and Inference (yukti). Sruti comes from the root 'sru' meaning hearing. It is applied to the Vedas which the 'rishis' were said to have heard directly from God. The derived meaning of this word is revelation. Anubhava is experience and Indian seekers after God look not for intellectual knowledge but for experience. The scientific study of religion requires reason or yukti. But from a Christian point of view there is a serious lack in the Pramānas. In setting the norms for judging the validity of religious thought, Hinduism omitted one valuable norm of religious doctrine, the Church. So Appasamy added 'sabhā' to the three pramānas accepted in India.[7]

b. Rethinking

The Christians were being charged with lack of nationalism. The charge from outside the Church and the denominational divisions within the Church induced a group of thinkers to make their views known to fellow Christians. They were Vengal Chakkarai, Pandipeddi Chenchiah,

---

[7] APPASAMY, A.J. Christian Theology in India. International Rreview of Mission. April,1949, p151.

G.V. Job, S. Jesudason, Eddy Ashirvatham, D.M. Devasahayam, A.N. Sudarisanam. They were commonly known as the Madras Rethinking group. They published a book called <u>Rethinking Christianity in India</u> in 1938 with the particular object of making their views known to fellow Christians assembled at Tambaram for the World Missionary Conference.[8] They were looking towards the frontiers of the Christian enterprise in a kind of pastoral care and making Christianity an indigenous movement.

> Enlightened Hindus acknowledge freely the service which missionary endeavour has rendered and is rendering to the country... Resentment there is against the aggressiveness of missionary propaganda. National self-consciousness has created a desire to preserve something at any rate of the ancient culture on which many potent solvents are operating with alarming rapidity. A people agonizingly conscious of long political subservience dread the possibility of their coming under the religious dominance of the west.[9]

They thought that the Indian Christian community had failed to utilize to the fullest extent the added stimulus of Indian nationalism. By its suspicion of the national struggle, the Christian community proved itself an unhelpful neighbour to the Hindus and Muslims. The Rethinking Group's object was to set the order of priority in the right context. Their contention was that denominational loyalty was not altogether absent among Indian Christians but where it was present, it was found with a spirit of tolerance and a sense of solidarity with other Christians.

---

[8] JOB, G.V and others. <u>Rethinking Christianity in India</u>.   A.N.Sudarisanam, Madras, 1938.

[9] JOB, G.V. Christian Movement in India. <u>In</u>: <u>Rethinking Christianity in India</u>. 1938, p1.

This comparative absence of denominational loyalty was the only hope for the church union movement. Where they were doubtful was that it seemed to be premature. They thought that practically none of the churches had achieved an independent life. Church unity could be achieved only by spontaneous enthusiasm resulting in an indigenous movement from within the Indian Christian community. Therefore for them an elaborate organic model of working for unity was not at all indigenous and necessary for Indians.

Their thought needs to be judged in the context of the theological climate of that period. The publication of the Laymen's report in 1932, known as the 'Rethinking Mission' had created a sensation in missionary circles, particularly for its suggestion about attitudes to non-Christian religions.[10] Commenting on the report, the Dutch theologian Hendrik Kraemer (1888-1965) said it was a total distortion of the Christian message, the suicide of mission and an annulment of the Christian faith.

> It is the product of urbane, liberal minded Gentlemen, devoid of any real estimate of the divine and the diabolic in man as conceived in the gospel, and therefore living under the illusion that the world religion is born out of benevolent consultation and unanimous agreement.[11]

Kraemer is best remembered for his controversial book The Christian Message in a non-Christian World, written in preparation for the

---

[10] HOCKING, William E. Rethinking Missions. Harper and Brothers, New York, 1932.

[11] KRAEMER, Hendrik. Religion and the Christian Faith. Lutterworth, London, 1956, p224.

188

international Missionary Conference at Tambaram, Madras in 1938.[12] He had grappled with the issue raised by the encounter of Christianity with non- Christian religions. The approach of Kraemer was a reaction to the liberal approach as represented by the Laymen's group. Kraemer acknowledges throughout his work that it is carried out by a subjective method and argues strongly that it can only be done in this way, because it seems to depend on what one believes is happening in God's revelation in Christ. But the fundamental question still remains as to whether the activity of God in Christ is so unambiguous as to provide the sort of clearcut criterion that Kraemer claims. Christ must be normative, but to insist on restrictive interpretation by rejecting non-Christian insights leads to difficulty.

The Rethinking Group saw in Kraemer a return to Barthianism.[13] The general criticism against Barth and Kraemer was their triumphalism.

---

[12] KRAEMER, Hendrik. The Christian Message in a Non-Christian World.
Edinburgh House Press, London, 1938.

[13] It is not fair to cite Kraemer with Barth for the eclipse of Indian Christian Theology because Kraemer seems to be siding with Brunner against Barth. Barth had viewed revelation as the annulment of religion because religion is a human striving for the ultimate. Kraemer felt that Barth had overemphasized divine sovereignty and grace. 'His concern to demonstrate that the sovereignty of God's grace is the Alpha and Omega of theological thinking seems to me quite legitimate - even the only legitimate method for Christian theology. However there is something in the way in which Barth elaborates this with untiring energy, and versatility that strikes one as artificial, somehow unreal, convulsive and overdone.' KRAEMER, Hendrik. Religion and the Christian Faith. Lutterworth, London, 1956, p192.

But the idea of the Rethinking Group was to preach the gospel and not to recruit for the church. They were satisfied with the idea of conversion being a change of life, but not affiliation to the church. What they looked forward to was Christianity as a movement in the Hindu social fold rather than a solid society outside. Therefore they were opposed to focusing the common life in the Lord through one central organization.

> The ecclesiastical systems evolved in the West are foreign to the Indian soil. While these systems may have rendered service of a high order in the West in their time, they cannot be claimed to belong to the essential elements of Christianity. Farther removed from the Indian spirit is the elaborate institutional conception of Christianity connected with the historic episcopate or the Papacy.... To attempt to foist this medieval system on Indian Christianity, when Hindu India is rising from its age-long slumber caused by the domination of its own medieval conceptions, is to court disaster for the Indian Church and bring Christianity into contempt in modern India.[14]

They thought of the Church as being not an instrument or foretaste of the kingdom but rather a rival to the kingdom. Therefore the recovery of the 'kingdom of God' was an essential feature of Christianity. Their contention was that in the sayings of Jesus, the idea of the church as understood now does not occur. They pointed out the absence of reference to the church but the prominence given to the kingdom of God.

> In India we are not prepared to identify Christianity with the Church, or rather to identify the Church with Christ. The separation has been made in the Indian consciousness. It knows Him apart from the church, Western or Eastern and apart from

---

[14] DEVASAHAYAM, D. M. South India Church Union Movement. In: G.V.Job & Others. Rethinking Christianity in India. Madras, 1938, p153.

civilization, in which the Church lives, breathes and has its being.[15]

The view of this group was very radical, particularly in their desire to be independent. Their plea was that the Indian churches should be given freedom. G.V. Job even went to the extent of claiming that the missionary societies should withdraw their support, assistance and guidance from the urban Indian Christian communities and let them sink or swim, and the missionaries must venture in faith into new fields for the pioneering work like their predecessors. Having been brought up in a congregational tradition, their position was independent to the core.

It would be wrong to say that the group did not want the church as part of Christianity, but their objection was that the church usurps the loyalty of the believer to herself rather than to Christ. Their contention was that the Church as an organization seeks to regulate the life of its members. That was objectionable and alien to Hindu catholicity. Solidarity in any group life is the consequence of a functioning together but this should be the result of spontaneity.[16] They objected to the view of enforced authority both by the missionaries and their counterpart Indian ministers.

> India will regard the Church as a useful human institution for the threefold purpose of worship, fellowship, and propagation. The talk of the Church being a divine society seems to be more a claim than a demonstrable fact. The claim can not add to Christian prestige, or status. Even in its utilitarian aspects, the Church may not receive the same high value as in the West.

---

[15] CHAKKARAI, Vengal. The South India Rapproachment. In: JOB, G.V. and others. Rethinking Christianity In India. 1938, Madras, p193.

[16] FORRESTER, Duncan B. Caste and Christianity. Curzon Press, 1980, pp181-184.

Church worship receives exaggerated importance because in many countries and societies, no other worship exists. The traditions in India have always nurtured family devotions. The household was a temple, the father the priest. A sad feature of Christian life is the decline of the worship at home.[17]

The Rethinking Group were not theologians by profession or training. They were engaged in secular professions. It is interesting to note that they were a powerful prophetic voice which is often neglected in the Church. They regarded both the family and the Church as being places of worship. The function of carrying the message of God to people pertained to the prophets and not the priests and the prophets can never belong to an established institution.

c. Open Community

There was a gradual shift in the discussion with the emergence of India as an independent state. The search for a modern India with an emphasis on social justice was not without effect on Christian thinking in India. The questions were raised that India has refused to take the Christian Church seriously because it announced a Gospel of justice, love and freedom, in the context of and in collaboration with a colonial and neo-colonial system of exploitation and conquest. Therefore the identity of the Church is not a question of definition of a doctrinal statement or heresy hunting but primarily orthopraxis by being open to the world and by the quality and style of its life lived as a kenotic presence in India.

In the context of nation building after independence in India, the

---

[17] CHENCHIAH, Pandipeddi. The Church and The Indian Christian. In: JOB, G.V. and others. Rethinking Christianity in India. Madras, 1938, p93.

search for a common human concern was reflected in the writings of Paul David Devanandan and Madathilparampil Mammen Thomas. Their association with the Christian Institute for Study of Religion and Society and their contribution through this Institute has been profound. Their assertion was that India is passing through a process of modernization and therefore there is tension between tradition and modernity.

Devanandan's interest in the Church is on the 'new creation' as a healing, serving and transforming koinonia. Diakonia and kerygma are the two major aspects of the transforming community, called the Church. The mission of the Church consists in going into the world of contemporary India and witnessing by proclamation and true community in action. It needs to be shared with the Hindus in such a way that they are encouraged to examine their own fundamental credal basis, because Hinduism has never thought in terms of corporate worship except in the renascent movements.

> The congregation which God uses to communicate the Gospel is a community which is constrained by the love of Christ to share this experience with each other and to draw those outside into this koinonia through the power of the Holy Spirit....only when the impact of Christian koinonia is felt on the group life of traditionally ordered society, does the outsider become inquisitive and ask questions concerning our faith.[18]

The process of new creation, inaugurated in the cross and the resurrection of Christ, moves forward to its consummation. The Gospel was essentially the Good News of new creation in Jesus Christ, which has

---

[18] DEVANANDAN, Paul D. Called to Witness: Address to the Third Assembly of World Council of Churches, New Delhi, 1961, Ecumenical Review, January 1962.

personal, social and cosmic dimensions. Devanandan saw the pledge of the new creation both within the church and without it. The Church in his thought stood for revolution. Its purpose is to proclaim God's forgiving love and redeeming purpose, and that He is concerned with what man makes of his life. He acknowledged peculiar difficulty in the Indian situation. To talk of the Indian Christian community brings reminders of electorates, offices, privileges and claims. Along with this the word 'Church' immediately evokes opposition to all that missions stand for. This is unfortunate but true. The important fact for him was that the Church should be a living, witnessing and serving fellowship as part of the new creation.[19]

The idea of a transforming community continued in the thought of M.M. Thomas. His emphasis was on 'Openness' becoming a fundamental characteristic of the Church. He argued that Christian and non-Christian share in the common human concerns. Therefore secular, political, ethical and human values, and the programme of nation building will bring together the people of different faiths. At the heart of this is the assumption of common humanity, the struggle for humanity being a preparation for the Gospel. Thomas begins with the new humanity in Christ, the humanity that responds in faith and receives the liberation of Jesus Christ as Lord and Saviour. It transcends the Church. Christ centredness is the acknowledgement of the centrality of the Person of Jesus Christ.

> Here my starting point is that the new humanity in Christ, that is, the humanity which responds in faith and receives the

---

[19] DEVANANDAN, P.D. The Church and Post-War India. The Guardian. December 9 1943,p581.

liberation of Jesus Christ as Lord and Saviour, transcends the Church.[20]

He goes on to acknowledge that the area of the struggles of societies for a secular human fellowship are within the structure of law and idealism and therefore self-defeating. But in some struggles there is a search for a new path beyond this, opening up the reality of transcendent forgiveness which may not have in it the full acknowledgement of Christ as person but does involve a partial acknowledgement. 'The Church cannot be the sign of the New Humanity unless it is present at this point, discerning the new humanity which is there.' This he thinks is possible if the Church itself is concerned with active participation in the struggle for secular fellowship on a Christ-centred basis. Apart from the quest for human dignity and human community, he also acknowledges in the adherents of other religions, especially Hinduism, the partial acknowledgement of Christ. He refers to those who consider that conversion to Christ does not necessarily imply conversion to the Christian community isolated from the communities in which they live. It implies building up of a Christ-centred fellowship of faith within the religion and society in which they live and thereby transforming the structures and values from within. The non-Christian religions and secular movements are together drawn into the orbit of the process of new creation in Christ.

It is right on the part of Thomas to identify the religious community in India as a communal group. Such a community of Christians has its own religious, social ideas and even politics integrated into one totality. For

---

[20] THOMAS, M.M. Letter to Bishop Newbigin, 21.10.71 In: Indian Journal of Theology, Vol.XIX, 1972, p69.

example if a Hindu becomes a Christian he moves from the jurisdiction of Hindu Law to Indian Christian Law, and separates from the Hindu community in the religious sense.

Conversion in this context largely becomes proselytism, and baptism becomes like circumcision, a mark of transference of communal affiliation. Thomas's point of the Church being 'an open church ' by giving up its own understanding as a communal or caste group and seeing itself as a community transcending all other groups is ideal. But the problem is not solved by just talking about Christ-centred fellowship as Thomas envisages: the issue is that acceptance of Jesus Christ involves some kind of actual solidarity among those who accept Jesus as their saviour. Therefore the issue is the nature of this solidarity. Bishop Newbigin in his reply to Thomas says:

> You express the desire for forms of fellowship which are explicitly linked to Jesus Christ but remain religiously, culturally and socially part of the Hindu community. I think this is quite unrealistic....He must have some way of expressing the fact that he shares this ultimate allegiance with others - and these ways will have to have religious, social and cultural elements. This is why I still feel that you are really docetic in your thinking about the Church. You seem to envisage a form of Christian corporate entity which never has existed and which never could exist.[21]

In his reply to Newbigin, Thomas argued that the goal he had in mind for Indian society was to provide the common political, judicial, civil and cultural framework that would be secular: secular in the sense of not controlled by any religion but within which all religions can build their fellowships of faith and inspire the spirit and ethos of total society.

---

[21] NEWBIGIN, Lesslie, Letter to M.M. Thomas, dated 17.11.1971. In: Indian Journal of Theology, Vol.XIX, 1972, p78.

> I advocate that the Fellowship of Christian faith stay within the Hindu religious community, to transform its religious and social patterns in the light of Christ and thus to make Indian society (which is largely Hindu and may remain so in many of its cultural aspects) a common framework for all religions to become truly religious without being communal. Since this secularization process is going on today in the Hindu community, it is now more possible than before for Christ-centred fellowships to remain within its framework.[22]

Thomas's argument of transforming by staying within the Hindu religious community is very much an ideal. Hinduism's response to Christianity has been to neutralize it by trying to make the church just another community. What Thomas intends is to free the Church from being just another community. But in practical terms how can it be achieved?

d. Marginalized

A vast majority of Indian Christians are <u>Dalits</u> and Tribals. The Church in India with its middle class leadership and powerful institutional structure projects the image of an oppressive church to these groups. There is a tendency to speak of the Indian Christian community as if it were a single homogeneous population and organized on the basis of egalitarian principles. The <u>Dalits</u> form one group of the marginalized in the church. They are fighting to recover their history, culture and spirituality. They have been suppressed by the dominant groups within the church and the

---

[22] Letter of M.M. Thomas. Dated 20th December 1971. <u>Indian Journal of Theology</u>. Vol XIX, 1972, p89.

society.[23] In this movement there is a search for dalit identity, born out of the feelings of alienation, caused by the oppressors of the dalits. Their aspirations need to be understood in a society which is divided into four castes - the Brahmins, the Kshatriyas, the Vaishyas, the Sudras - but the Dalits are the outcastes.

It is their non-humanness that forms the basis of the search for dalit identity, and this affirmation runs counter to Brahmanical culture and religion. Therefore the voice has been raised for the inclusion of this perspective to form a Dalit Christian Theology. It is a challenge to the dominant Hindu understanding of liberation in terms of self-realization. It is also a challenge to the search for values based on the ideology of hierarchy, inequality and the sacred-profane dichotomy in human existence.

> It will anticipate liberation which is meaningful to them. It will represent a radical discontinuity with the traditional Indian Christian Theology because the dominant tradition in Indian Christian Theology is essentially Brahmanic in character. This means that a Christian Dalit theology will be a counter-theology.[24]

---

[23] In general the 'Dalit Sahitya' movement in Maharashtra in the late nineteen sixties has tried to give expression to the feelings and experiences of the writers representing the people who are untouchables in the Indian society. It is the body of literature produced by the writers and poets belonging to the outcaste communities or the untouchables. They are the followers of the well known figure, Dr B.R. Ambedkar, himself a 'Dalit' and known as the father of the Indian Constitution. He himself embraced Buddhism in 1956 and believed that the teaching of Buddha fulfilled the aspirations for an authentic human life. NIRMAL, Arvind P. A Dialogue with Dalit Literature. In: PRABHAKAR, M.E. ed. Towards A Dalit Theology. ISPCK, Delhi, 1988, p66.

[24] NIRMAL, Arvind P. A Dialogue with dalit Literature. In: PRABHA-KAR, M.E.ed. Towards a Dalit Theology. ISPCK, Delhi, 1988, p76.

The Dalit theology stands for the sum of dalit meanings and expectations. It is a counter theology to the Brahmanical culture and religion in general. It is also against the dominance in the church of the caste converts, since the caste feeling is very much alive within the church.

The other marginalized group is the tribals defined in the fifth and sixth schedule of the constitution of India. The sixth schedule deals with the previous autonomous districts and regions of Assam and most of these have gained statehood such as Nagaland, Manipur, Mizoram, Meghalaya, Arunachal. The interesting feature is that the majority of the people in these states are Christians and the church is very much active. The situation of the tribals belonging to the fifth schedule are different. There is hardly any single state in the country which does not have a population of scheduled tribes of one kind or another. They form a community in the midst of other larger communities. They do not fit into the caste systems nor are they outcastes or Dalits. Their identity and liberation is a matter of great concern for the Government, and their place in the Christian community is equally important, like the Dalits. In his study of caste and tribe in Orissa, Deepak Behera concludes that

> The tribal Christians, consequent on their mass conversion, have retained the tribal exclusiveness to a large extent. This is also true of the low caste Christians. The upper caste Christians however, have merged their pre-conversion caste identities into a larger group; and are carefully maintaining a social distance from Christian converts of tribal and low caste backgrounds, like the Syrian Christians of Kerala.[25]

---

[25] BEHERA, Deepak. Ethnicity and Christianity: Caste and Tribe in Western Orissa. ISPCK, Delhi, 1989, p105.

The hope of the converts from these two groups for a better life free from stigma and humiliation appears not to have been fulfilled in the Church. Theirs is a search for an identity based on the egalitarian principles of Christianity. It has raised an important question why the Indian Christian theologians have missed out the wealth of evidence pointing to the aspirations and struggles of these subaltern people. The mass movement into the Indian church was a time with great possibilities for a powerful movement for social change. If part of the reason for conversion was to escape the inhuman existence under the caste system, the converted community could have become a paradigmatic fellowship.

An Assessment

An underlying assumption in the search for ecclesial identity is indigenization. In an essay Arvind P. Nirmal argues that the term indigenization is ambiguous. It is ambiguous because it reduces the task of theology to a translation of the Christian faith into a given situation and assumes a very static understanding of the Gospel and various situations. He says that something is either indigenous or is not indigenous but cannot be made indigenous. His thesis is that God is indigenous to all the nations of the world. The task of indigenous theology is not to seek to indigenize a God who is a foreigner but to understand God who is indigenous.[26]

---

[26] NIRMAL, Arvind P. Theological Implications of the Term 'Indigenous.' In: JATHANA, C. D. ed. Dialogue in Community. Karnataka Theological Research Institute, Mangalore, 1982, p169f.

Lesslie Newbigin says that those who approach the problem through indigenization see the Indian Christian community as a foreign enclave seeking its identity in something which is alien to the indigenous culture. In this process a distinction is made between the elements in the Christian tradition which concern the central revelation of God in Jesus Christ, about which there can be no compromise, and those elements which are social and cultural which are accidental.[27]

In order to work out a witnessing and convincing theology for India that can be indigenous, there is an attempt in some quarters to get rid of Western theology. One reason cited for this is its association with Western philosophy. The basis of this suggestion is that the Western theology has never been able to dissociate itself from philosophy beginning with Plato.

> Western theology has never been able to dissociate itself from philosophy, from the time of the Platonism of Justin Martyr onwards. Plato lies behind Augustine, Aristotle behind Aquinas and even Calvin; right down to the days of idealism, existentialism and logical positivism, no theologian, not even those like Barth who have tried to break free from philosophy, has succeeded in dissociating himself from the philosophical presuppositions of certain schools..So far as an Indian theologian like Chenchiah is concerned the formula of Chalcedon, with its underlying philosophy of substance and accident, is pure pagan Aristotle.[28]

---

[27] NEWBIGIN, Lesslie. Salvation, the New Humanity and Cultural-Communal Solidarity. <u>Bangalore Theological Forum.</u> Vol V, No 2, 1973, p1f.

[28] BOYD, Robin. <u>Introduction to Indian Christian Theology</u>. CLS, Madras, 1969, p3-4.

Explaining this, Robin Boyd says that what is needed for effective Christian witness is not demythologizing but rather reclothing of the underlying truth in another set of terms and thought forms which is already in existence and is as rich and vivid as the original Graeco-Roman context. If it was legitimate for the Church to use western language at Chalcedon and indeed ever since, it must be legitimate for the Indian Church to use Sanskritic language now and forever![29]

The underlying image of this approach is that of the kernel and husk theory. The basic Christian revelation is the kernel and the cultural settings in which it has been incarnated constitute the husk.[30] The basic question still remains whether it is as easy as it is assumed to make a clear cut distinction between kernel and husk. The concern for indigenization is also a concern for all humanity as to what God has done and is doing. The march towards indigenization is not just a matter of the use of Sanskritic

---

[29] BOYD, Robin. Introduction to Indian Christian Theology. CLS, Madras, 1969, p261.

[30] The National Conference, held in Poona, 1942 defined dogma as the essential element of the Christian faith, and defined doctrine as being to elucidate the dogma in terms of changing times and conditions. The Conference affirmed that God has revealed himself in Jesus Christ and this given-ness of the Gospel is what Indian Christians along with the Christians of other churches share in common, whereas the elucidation of it in a particular cultural context differs from culture to culture. DEVANANDAN, Paul D. Whither Theology in Christian India, International Review of Missions, April, 1944, p121f.

language, or the proclamation of equality of religions or the identification with the poor; that would be an over simplification. The real issue is much deeper.

Timothy Gorringe argues that in the quest for an authentically Indian theology, an obvious starting point is to reject western theology. As an example of what might be meant by western theology, the Chalcedonian Definition is often instanced, especially by Chenchiah.[31] His contention is that the hostility to Chalcedon based on the notion that it uses Greek as opposed to other kinds of philosophical ideas is mistaken. It is not possible to do Indian Theology simply by using categories taken from Sankara or Ramanuja as opposed to Plato and Aristotle. The attempt to make the theology Indian is not based on the use of the category of Advaita. He cites the example of the Chalcedonian solution which was not just a matter of identifying some Greek terminologies and their use by the early fathers, but of understanding the fathers' concerns in the context of their history.[32] Even the solution itself was not immediately suitable and intelligible to an educated Greek audience but the fathers remained faithful to the kerygma.

> In all the Christological formulas of the ancient Church there is
> a manifest concern not to allow the total demand made on one's

---

[31] BOYD, Robin. Indian Christian Theology. CLS, Madras, 1969, p162

[32] Timothy Gorringe says that the use of technical terms (ousia, phusis and hupostasis), if taken to illustrate a dependence on Greek Philosophy is highly misleading. Because at some time or other all were used as synonymous for one another. Ousia and phusis are used simply to mean really, truly, partaking of the reality of, hupostasis as a synonym for prosopon to please Leo in the West and to line up with his two persons in one substance. GORRINGE, Timothy. On Not Doing Western Theology, Indian Journal of Theology, Vol 32, 1983, p63.

faith by the person of Jesus to be weakened by pseudo-solutions. It must be handed on undiminished to all generations of Christendom. On a closer inspection the Christological heresies turn out to be a compromise between the original message of the Bible and the understanding of it in Hellenism and paganism. It is here that we have the real Hellenization of Christianity.[33]

Gorringe argues that in the history of heresy there was a desire for a one sided solution. The heretics were the great men who could not be untrue to what they had learned and in consequence moulded the kerygma to the shape of their philosophy. The Chalcedonian formula in all its implied contradictions, remained faithful to the kerygma. The concern of the fathers was that our God, involved in time, took flesh and died on the Cross. It is this blasphemy that has been preserved at the cost of logical contradictions. It was to avoid this 'blasphemy' that Arius made the Son a creature to be true to Greek attributes of impassability and unity. Therefore indigenization or contextualization is not as simple as just translating the Chalcedonian formula into the categories of an Indian philosophy and thereby making Christianity indigenous. The process of indigenization is slow and must start with the people.

> To be indigenous means to have existed in a place, in a climate, in a situation, for generations, to have adapted to that situation and also to have adapted the situation. This slow process is instructive for theology: the attempt to construct an indigenous theology overnight is by definition doomed to failure. The rule lex orandi lex credendi is dangerous but it is also a way of saying that doctrine moves at the pace of the people and c2that

---

[33] GRILLMEIR, A. Christ in Christian Tradition. Mowbrays, 1975, p555-6.

with the people it will evolve and thereby be indigenous.[34]

One indigenous attempt at construing ecclesial identity was apologetic. It made use of the thought forms that India can offer, particularly in terms of either Advaita Vedānta or Vishishtadvaita. But most of the contributors came from caste converts to Christianity. The result has been that Indian Christian theology has perpetuated within itself the philosophical traditions. It has also perpetuated an intuition-interiority oriented approach to the theological task in India. This is now being questioned on the basis that it does not and will never have a mass appeal. Therefore it is suggested that Indian theology needs to relate better to the contemporary situation, to the problems and prospects, questions and aspirations of people today.

It is true that Hinduism is a religion which rests on Vedāntic spirituality and this is a genuine element of Hinduism. But what is questioned is whether this is the whole truth. Hinduism is not just a religion but also a way of life. It is a religion and way of life of a people, seventy percent of whom live in villages. Theirs is the religion of pilgrimage and of story, and is not grounded in the reading of the Upanishadas and Gita, rather it is rooted in the harsh realities of agricultural practice, social customs, geographical and language barriers. What has happened in the attempt at indigenization is a mere cognitive comparison of a concept from the Hindu tradition with another from the Judaeo-Christian tradition; and along with this an attempt to christianize certain good and acceptable

---

[34] GORRINGE, Timothy. On Not Doing Western Theology. Indian Journal of Theology. Vol.32, 1983, p68.

elements of the Hindu tradition. Positively this theological innovation by the dedicated minority has resulted in constructing some kind of synthesis between Christian faith and the traditional philosophies of India, but does not have mass appeal.

As a reaction to this, two trends have emerged. One is Dalit Theology representing one of the marginalized groups. The basic aim of this group is to liberate the Dalits - the 'Outcastes, Untouchables,' or legally speaking the 'Scheduled Castes', through social change. The focus is on the identity of the 'Dalit' which is born out of their alienation from the society. In fact it is partly a reaction to the dominant tradition in Indian Christian thought. The other trend is the general consciousness of the urgency of finding liberation from poverty. It has made use of Liberation Theology, particularly in its creative example of the Christian response to the forces of exploitation; and in the attention it gives to the neglected themes in the biblical message taking seriously the Old Testament history and prophecy in their political and social dimensions. It appears to be entirely relevant in the Indian situation where the majority of the Indian people face the problem of poverty.

The liberation theologians have attempted to form an ecclesiology suited to the socio-political situation. For example the basic ecclesial communities in Latin America have led the way. They serve through the <u>diakonia</u> of faith, by denouncing injustice and promoting social transformation. They are seen as spontaneous gatherings of lay people under the impulse of the Holy Spirit. The focus is to establish a new way of being the Church without centralization and hierarchical domination. Institutionalization is regarded as a secondary feature of the church.

These basic ecclesial communities dating from the 1960s are usually between fifteen and thirty in number and they involve themselves in the study of Scripture, its application in daily life, mutual support and help, and some degree of social and political activism. The Church is viewed as being built up from below, from the poor, the marginalized and the exploited.

> But what is called for is not simply a renewal and adoption of pastoral methods. It is rather a question of a new ecclesial consciousness and a redefinition of the task of the church in a world in which it is not only present, but of which it forms a part more than it suspected in the past.[35]

One attraction of Liberation theology in India is the reversal of method by challenging the European theology. The interesting feature of this seems to be the replacement of the philosophical speculation with sociological analysis with a view to changing the world of injustice. The importance given to praxis and the radical involvement with the poor and the oppressed makes it challenging in the Indian context as it is derived from situations of poverty and inequality of economic and political distribution.

While the Indian situation is determined by the economic and political situation, there is also the cultural and religious tradition. The liberation motif has to hold together all these realities. The marxist analysis of the socio-economic realities of the haves and the have-nots is inadequate where the caste factor is a living reality. It does not mean that any dialogue with liberation theology is denied but that the emphasis is to take seriously particular aspects of Indian society.

---

[35] GUTIERREZ, G. The Theology of Liberation. SCM, 1975, p225.

Theology to be ecumenical needs to be contemporary and Indian Christian Theology is no exception. In developing a theology that would be Indian and Christian, it is important to look at these two aspects and integrate them. In any attempt at indigenizing, the tendency to absolutize the context in terms of a political-cultural entity needs to be avoided, because the danger could be to develop an uncritical attitude towards one's own national history and culture. What God does in one particular part of the world in one particular time in history cannot be overlooked, and this also has meaning and significance for those who live in the other part of the world. Without this commonality there cannot be any ecumenical theology.

The formation of the CNI witnessed a phase of unity of ecclesial identities. But it would be wrong to assume from this that once united the CNI became an ecumenical and indigenous church. A church neither becomes ecumenical just by taking a national name to overcome the denominational identities, nor becomes indigenous when the white faces are replaced by black or brown. An indigenous clergy is not necessarily a sign of an indigenous church. What makes a church indigenous or local is its active identification with the people at the grass roots. Christian theology has both an interpretative as well as a prophetic function. Therefore it is vital to ask the question of relationship between unity and mission within the social and religious context of India. It is also important to ask whether the CNI represents ecumenical consciousness in the local congregations, which often have an ethnic rather than Christian identity. In fact such a vision is a great challenge for the united Church. While in the next chapter a model for a provisional ecclesiology will be presented, in the following section of this chapter an attempt is made to look at the nature of social and religious identity.

Social and Religious Identity

The reform movements within Hinduism created opposition to Christianity. The usual slogan that Christianity is a religion of the foreign rulers is an unfortunate label. There is also a dichotomy that the East is spiritual whereas the West is material, and patriotism is interpreted as praise for everything Indian and denouncing everything Western. Renascent Hinduism persistently identified Christianity with Euro-American culture.

Romila Thapar in her study of the early history of India says that there were in existence multiple communities based on various identities. In pre-Islamic India, the religious identity seems to be related more closely to a sect than a dominant Hindu community. The notion of a Hindu community does not have as long an ancestry as is often presumed. Even in the normative texts of Brahmanism, the Dharmasāstras, it is conceded that there were a variety of communities, determined by location, occupation and caste, none of which were necessarily bound together by a common religious identity. The Community had one of its roots in location.[36]

Segmented identities were very much to the fore and the resultant multiple communities were identified by locality, language, caste,

---

[36] THAPAR, Romila. Imagined Religious Communities? Ancient History and Modern Search for a Hindu Identity. Modern Asian Studies. Vol.23, May, 1989, p220.

occupation and sect. The need to create the idea of a single Hindu community appears to be a concern of more recent times. The obvious temptation in recent times is for loyalty to one's own community in competition with others.

Indian society now is primarily perceived as being constituted of a number of religious communities. Communalism in the modern Indian context is primarily perceived as a consciousness which draws on a supposed religious identity and uses this as the basis for an ideology. It then tends to demand political allegiance to a religious community and supports a programme of political action designed to further the interests of that religious community. In the present socio-political context, the communities assume political importance and relations between communities are embittered by their relevance to the balance of power. Therefore conversion from one group to another means not only a change in spiritual allegiance but also a shift in political power. So the question of local Christian identity must not be confined within the supposed identity of being just another communal group, hoping to be dominant through conversion. In order to do this it has to come to terms with the full implications of the notion of church, not as a community in competition with other communities, but as a community called to serve in a particular culture.

To serve in a particular culture entails taking into account the social and religious realities of the people. The majority of people are poor and oppressed. The oppression which they suffered under colonial rule subsequently took on a different form. Any concern for the people must take into consideration the distinct social, cultural and ethnic groupings of

India. The Indian Christian community is related to a place and, in order to be a sign, foretaste and instrument of God's purpose, each church must show its own credibility amidst local realities.

The form of each local Church has been determined in the course of history by the geographical locality, language, ethnic identity and confessional traditions. In order to be relevant in its own surroundings the Church must be able to mediate to the people the signs of new creation. Newbigin says that the starting point of interpretation is God's revelation of himself in the history of mankind. This has not lost relevance as long as there is a community which lives faithfully to the call of God and continues to identify with people in their real situation.

> True contextualization accords to the Gospel its rightful primacy, its power to penetrate every culture and to speak within each culture, in its own speech and symbol, the word which is No and Yes, both judgment and grace. And that happens when the word is not a disembodied word but comes from a community which embodies the true story, God's story, in a style of life which communicates both the grace and the judgment. In order that it may do this, it must be both truly local and truly ecumenical. Truly local in that it embodies God's particular word of grace and judgment for that people. Truly ecumenical in being open to the witness of churches in all other places, and thus saved from absorption into the culture of that place and enabled to represent to that place the universality, the catholicity of God's purpose of grace and judgment for all humanity.[37]

The pioneers of the ecumenical movement in India sought to overcome the scandals of denominational identity in a particular place

---

[37] NEWBIGIN, Lesslie. The Gospel in a Pluralist Society.SPCK, London, 1989, p152.

through the church union movement. For them the Church's task was continually to reconsider the nature of its very existence. [38] If the critical question was what hinders a church in its context from hearing God's call, then it is necessary to ask in what ways it has become assimilated to the social realities of its place. But taking into account the insights of sociology involves a difficult question. To what extent can the conclusions of different branches of knowledge be made commensurable?

> On strictly methodological grounds it will be possible for the theologian to dismiss this new perspective as irrelevant to his opus proprium. This will become much more difficult, however, as soon as he reflects that after all, he was not born as a theologian, that he existed as a person in a particular socio-historical situation before he ever began to do theology - in sum, that he himself, if not his theology, is illuminated by the lighting apparatus of the sociologist.[39]

The object in taking into account the insights of sociology is not to engage in a religious market research but to take the social context seriously for an adequate understanding of local identity. An adequate assessment of the validity of identity cannot exclude the actual social factors. Christian

---

[38] Niebuhr says that the history of schism has been a history of Christianity's defeat. The Church which began its career with the promise of peace and brotherhood for a distracted world has accepted the divisions of the society it had hoped to transform and has championed the conflicts it had thought to transcend. In its denominational aspect, at least, it has become part and parcel of the world, one social institution alongside of many others. NIEBUHR, Richard H. The Social Sources of Denominationalism. New York, 1957, p264.

[39] BERGER, Peter L. The Social Reality of Religion. Faber and Faber, Great Britain, 1969, p185.

faith is not merely statements but the living expressions of commitment. One obstacle in this endeavour is to be imprisoned in one's cultural totality. For example the caste and communal structures of the Indian Christian congregations have been one of the main causes of its ineffectiveness as a Church.

> Within any village or town there are two or more religious communities - Hindu, Muslim, Sikh, Christian etc. Each of these communities is marked off from the others by distinct religious beliefs and practices and by characteristic modes of dress, behaviour and speech. Inter-marriage between communities is normally forbidden and even inter-dining is frowned upon in many localities. Loyalty to one's community is highly valued and infrequently gives rise to communalism, i.e. to antagonism between communities, often expressed in struggle for economic and political advantage.[40]

The social realities need to be taken into serious consideration for theological reflection. The Christian Institute for Study of Religion and Society made a study on caste in the Kerala churches in 1967-68. It revealed that the situation in the Church is not wholly different from society in general.

> Their study observes that the main characteristic as well as the reason for intercaste tension in the Kerala churches is the exclusiveness of the dominant section of the Christian community as a distinct caste. This exclusiveness is based on both the socio-cultural and economic factors.[41]

In Indian society food, spatial and ritual questions are not excluded

---

[40] ALTER, J.P. & JAISINGH, H. The Church in Delhi. Lutterworth, London, 1966, p4.

[41] CHATTERJI, Saral.K. Some Ingredients of a Theology of the People. Religion and Society, December, 1980, p21.

from the fabric of ordinary day to day life. For example the caste system has traditionally governed the residential distribution, spatial relationship, and economic and ritual life of Indian people. The practice of keeping the residential quarters of different castes apart by grouping them in different areas according to ritual purity and pollution has been more or less characteristic of Indian village communities. Even though the communities have been increasingly exposed to urbanization and modernization and a wide range of direct and indirect democratization, the magnitude of mobility is not so great as to dissipate caste relationship.

If the church takes seriously the reality of its place - language, ethnic identity, culture, work - then the issue is not just of accommodating to these local realities but a question of being true to its calling to be an instrument of reconciliation. To do this is to affirm its own identity in the context of the local background. Such an identity of the Church is proposed in the next chapter as the People of God, but to define this is not without difficulty in the context of religious pluralism.

Religious pluralism is a reality of Indian society. It is not entirely a new phenomenon as the people in India have witnessed and lived among major religions of the world. There will not be any problem if such a situation is accepted. In any society there is a need for community feeling - a feeling of belonging. But the recent history of India has witnessed a number of conflicts between the communities. There are various causes for eruption of communal outbursts. One is the struggle for identity. In the pre-independence period the emergence of nationalism was a powerful ideology that brought people together to fight for independence of the nation, and within the Church brought people together to fight against denominational identity. Once the goal of independence was achieved, the focus shifted to the self-consciousness of separate groups and communities in the nation.

To take into consideration the question of religious pluralism in India is to take note of Indian philosophy and religious traditions. There are six schools: Sānkhya, Yoga, Vaisesika, Nyāya, Vedānta, Mimāmsa. Some Hindu schools lie outside the above six such as Saiva Sidhānta. Vishnu and Siva are each regarded by their adherents as the supreme object of worship and around these figures grew up a body of literature distinct from revelation. One social reason for this was the exclusion of the lowest classes from participation in orthodox religion. These semi-orthodox writings enshrined a type of religion which was open to the underprivileged. The Saivite writings gave rise to their own particular theology and it was formalized by Meykānda in the thirteenth century A.D.

Orthodoxy is determined by accepting the validity of the Hindu scriptures but not subscribing to a particular doctrinal belief. It has led to diverse doctrinal interpretations of scriptures so that both atheism and theism are given a scriptural basis. Atheism in the Indian context is disbelief in a creator, but is not irreligiousness and is compatible with belief in salvation. There are also religious divergences. The Brahminical religion is counted as orthodox whereas the others such as Cārvāka school are counted as unorthodox.

The differing Indian religious traditions make it clear that there are differing perspectives on reality and human life. Co-existence of different views is encouraged and the views are left to develop. To be aware of this complex nature of different religious traditions is to face the question of truth claims. To say that all are partial and many-stranded is not to say that all are equally valid. In this context the response of Christian thinkers has been varied.

One approach (the exclusivist) maintains that Christ or Christianity offers the only valid path to salvation.[42] Another approach (inclusivist) affirms the salvific presence of God in other religions but still maintains the definitive and authoritative revelation of God in Christ.[43] A third approach (pluralism) is the co-efficacy of all religions. This view has a number of exponents. John Hick is one of the most extreme Christian representatives of this view.[44]

---

[42] KRAEMER, Hendrik. The Christian Message in a Non-Christian World. London, Edinburgh House Press, 1938. It is a classical treatment of the theme. Even in his own time Kraemer's importance was prophetically recognized. Critiques questioned Kraemer's thesis arguing that the Bible shows that God has revealed himself elsewhere although these revelations have been distorted.

[43] FARQUHAR, J. The Crown of Hinduism. Oxford, 1919, p58. Karl Rahner provided a reconciliation of the strengths of the pluralist and exclusivist approach to religion. His notion of anonymous Christian has drawn much criticism from both the groups. RAHNER, Karl. Christianity and non-Christian Religions The Theological Investigations. Vol.5, Darton, Longman & Todd, p198.

[44] Hick has won many supporters such as Paul Knitter & Alan Race. John Hick describes the present day thought as a 'copernican' revolution - the move from a christocentric view of reality to a theocentric one and then the further move to 'soteriocentric' - the common quest for salvation. HICK, John. God has Many Names. London, Macmillan, 1980. The Myth of God Incarnate. London, SCM, 1977. KNITTER, Paul. No Other Name? A Critical Survey of Christian Attitudes Towards the World Religions. SCM, 1985.

The idea of parity does seem particularly ideal in a pluralistic context like India for the peaceful co-existence of different religious traditions. It helps to avoid the scandal of particularity. But to accept the view of particularity is not to rule out the possibility of universal salvation. Critiques like Gavin D'Costa's question Hick's assumption. He argues that Hick is right in pointing out that one's religion is often determined by one's birthplace; 'However to imply that because of this, all religions are equal paths to the truth tends to make truth a function of birth.' This underlying assumption, which is required if the argument is to have any weight, runs into considerable difficulties.[45]

The issue is again the question of truth. One assumption is that truth is a matter of cultural coherence. People's axiomatic beliefs are conditioned by their cultural background. One cannot escape from the world view of one's age. But that does not mean that one ought therefore to abandon a claim to particularity in the name of cultural relativism. If abandoning the claim to particularity would lead others to do the same, then the situation would be equally damaging. The logical difficulty is that if the claim to historic particularity of Christianity is itself culturally conditioned then the formulations of relativism are likewise culturally conditioned. 'Relativism is the beginning of theological method, not its end: it tells us that we can expect to find only hints of ultimacy, not Euclidean chains of proof, in anyone's theology, our own included, but it has no power to decree that the gap between us and our predecessors shall be total.'[46]

---

[45] D'COSTA, Gavin. Theology and Religious Pluralism. Basil Blackwell, Oxford, 1986, p41.

[46] BARTON, John. Cultural Relativism. Theology May, 1979, p198.

Referring to the pluralist position as set out in <u>The Myth of Christian Uniqueness</u>, Newbigin comments that the culture in which this type of thinking has developed is one in which the most typical feature is the supermarket. One may stick to one's favourite brand and acclaim its merit in songs of praise; but to insist that everyone else should choose the same brand is unacceptable.

> Reality is not to be identified with any specific name or form or image or story. Reality 'has no form except our knowledge of it.' Reality is unknowable, and each of us has to form his or her own image of it. There is no objective reality which can confront the self and offer another centre - as the concrete person of Jesus does.....The movement, in other words, is exactly the reverse of the Copernican one. It is a move away from a centre outside the self, to the self as the only centre.[47]

It is not easy to resist the contemporary thinking in the direction of an acceptance of religious pluralism. But Newbigin defends Christianity as a cogent plausibility structure in its own right. He borrows the idea of plausibility structure from sociologist Peter Berger and the idea of knowledge as personal commitment from Michael Polanyi. Peter Berger's plausibility structure is a social structure of ideas and practices that create the conditions determining what beliefs are plausible within the society in question. The distinctive feature of modern Western culture is that there is no generally acknowledged 'plausibility structure' with respect to ultimate

---

[47] NEWBIGIN, Lesslie. <u>The Gospel in a Pluralistic Society.</u>　　SPCK, London, 1989, p169.

beliefs. Pluralism rules and each individual has to make a personal decision about ultimate questions.[48]

Michael Polanyi pleads for a post-critical philosophy.[49] His argument is that knowledge is shaped by fundamental beliefs which are 'given' or 'assumed' as an act of faith and there is a constant dialectical process between these assumptions and our ongoing exploration. The process of examining any topic is both an exploration of the topic and an exegesis of our fundamental beliefs in the light of which we approach it. Our fundamental beliefs are continuously reconsidered in the course of such a process but only within the scope of their own basic premises.

Polanyi draws attention to the fact that scientific discovery is impossible without faith in ideas which are of a purely speculative kind, sometimes quite hazy - a faith which is quite unwarranted from the scientific point of view. If knowledge was all clear and articulate, discovery would be impossible. Science is regarded as objectively established in spite of its passionate origins. The prevailing conception of science is based on the disjunction of subjectivity and objectivity. It seeks to eliminate from science passionate, personal human appraisals, and the natural science is

---

[48] Peter Berger describes three possibilities for Christian affirmation. The deductive that selects one of the given traditions and reaffirms it like Karl Barth; the reductive like Bultman's demythologization; and the inductive like Schleiermacher which Berger favours. Berger argues that the rival truth claims of the different religions are part of different values and must be grounded in comparative and historical analysis. Religious experience occurs in sanctuary but its claim to truth has to be tested in the public world of facts.

[49] POLANYI, M. Personal Knowledge: Towards a Post-Critical Philosophy. London, 1958.

defined as a set of statements which is objective in the sense that its substance is entirely determined by observation.

Polanyi refers to the faith in ideas in the course of scientific discovery as 'tacit knowledge'. He finds in it an essential element of his theory of knowledge and how true knowledge grows out of this tacit knowledge. The intuition by which a great scientist sees a new pattern in the facts is only a development of an everyday skill. The leap of imagination in a great discovery is the leap from a lot of known particulars to their joint meaning.

Polanyi showed that the science of measurements, experiment and doubt to which other knowledge was to be made to conform, in fact rests on a foundation of faith in what cannot be proved, in skills and imaginative powers that cannot be formulated and in tradition by which alone such skills can be passed on. This opens the way of accepting validity of the truths that can be explained in myth, poetry and ritual.

One important implication of the use of the thought of Berger and Polanyi by Newbigin is that communication has to begin with a particular standpoint rather than in abstraction. Newbigin draws attention to the nature of epistemological particularity - especially where it carries with it universal intent: the enterprise of making public a claim and demonstrating its right to command credence, that is, the intention to commend faith and knowledge to the reasonable consideration and acceptance of others.

There is a danger that particularity might lead to unmitigated subjectivism. This involves a tension between faith as God's gift, and understanding as a form of discovery where development is essential in order that the faith may be related to the current situations. Faith is meaningful when interpreted by a community which lives according to its truth. It is only in this context that there can be no total disjunction between the 'Gospel' and the 'Church'.

Newbigin asserts that this is always where the act of faith begins and ultimate commitments are revealed. There is no knowing without believing and believing is the way of knowing. The danger in such a view is that it might lead to subjectivism.

> What is surely obvious about all this is that it is risky business. Knowing things as they are is not something that happens automatically or that can be guaranteed against failure. .....The commitment is a personal matter; it has to be my commitment. In that sense it is subjective. But it is a commitment which has an objective reference. It is as Polanyi puts it, a commitment 'with universal intent.' It looks for confirmation by further experience. The test of its validity will be that it opens the way for new (and often unexpected) discovery. It has to be published, shared so that it may be questioned and checked by the experience of others.[50]

The tendency of the present age is to reject any form of exclusivism and this appears appropriate in the context of a global society. What is called for is a common commitment to shared values which, it is supposed, may be independent of any one tradition. This is claimed to provide the focus for unity. All this assumes that truth is ultimately unknowable, and for Newbigin, it is the final evidence of 'cultural collapse'. Total relativism provides grounds for absolutizing one's own wishful thinking.[51] Therefore

---

[50] NEWBIGIN, Lesslie. The Gospel in a Pluralist Society. SPCK, 1989, p35.

[51]NEWBIGIN, Lesslie. The Gospel in a Pluralistic Society. SPCK, London, 1989, pp156-162.

Newbigin x2particularly draws attention to the fact that the Church throughout the ages has proclaimed the Gospel as the story of God's relation with man, and this has been the beginning of the ecumenical movement.

> It is plain, therefore that to accept religious pluralism as a principle of action - to propose that theology must henceforth be centred not on Christ but in the general religious experience of the human race - would not be an extension of ecumenical movement but a reversal of it. A movement of mere theological relativism would never have developed the power that this one has done... The greatness, the finality, the absoluteness of what God has done in Jesus Christ for the salvation of the whole world radically relativized the differences between the Christian confessions of him.[52]

The nature of the Church as a historical community cannot be minimized to an ideal or code of ethical directives. The Uniting Church as a particular community in history put the doctrinal differences between the different denominations in the context of being obedient to God for mission. Therefore the unity movement could not be dissociated from the mission of the Church.

The question of identity is related to the communication of Christian faith in all sincerity. This is an important concern of the mission of the Church. Therefore any discussion about the mission of the Church cannot overlook the challenges of Indian society. Particularly the overwhelming poverty and multifaceted religiousness are inseparable realities that constitute the matrix of any theology that is Indian. Poverty is not

---

[52] NEWBIGIN, Lesslie. The Christian Faith and the World Religions. In: WAINWRIGHT, Geoffrey. ed. Keeping the Faith. SPCK, 1989, p337.

susceptible to a Marxist reduction. The specific form of the Indian social and religious systems needs to be taken into account as a causal factor. Religion and philosophy are interwoven. Philosophy is a religious vision and religion is a lived philosophy - an interpretation of a view of life and way of life. The separation of religion from culture and from philosophy is difficult in the Indian context. They are both interwoven culturally and economically to constitute the social and religious reality of India. Poverty and religiousness seem to coalesce in the context.

Conclusion

One key aspect of Indian society is its community life, but the rise of communalism is a cause of concern for the country as a whole. The Church as a community claims that in Christ God really did something decisive for the world. This is not a set of ideas that needs to be confronted with other religions. The Christian apologetics in India was carried out on the fringes of the Church by individual converts from high castes. It is not surprising that their thought is original - but it seldom bears relation to the experience of ordinary Christian people. Within that limitation, the apologetic thinkers have opened a dynamic conversation with Indian philosophical and religious tradition. This conversation is not irrelevant as an academic exercise in the context of religious pluralism.

Salvation is not just an inner change in the life of individuals but a reconciliation with God and with one another. The problem of combining faith with the religious lore of the nations is by no means new. The great orthodox Christian theologians as well as the great heretics have drawn upon the words and ideas of the world around them.

Western theology is often developed in terms of individuals saved from sin but joined together in a Church. The Church as a whole being fragmented in its fellowship and divided in its witness is nothing but a blasphemy against Him who died on the Cross to break down the barriers between humanity and God, and between people. The missionary movement as a product of this theology went along the same lines, saving souls from heathen superstition and reforming society through the spread of Christian influence. But the object of mission should be the creation of a new People not individuals. Seen from this perspective, the ecumenical movement is not just a means of promoting cooperation and unity among different denominations but a rediscovery of the true identity of the Church.

One danger in developing the identity of the Church is to identify the religion with a culture. Many Indian Christians in the Church are ignorant of Indian culture. An invisible cultural wall seems to separate Christians from their compatriots. The general idea is that anything Indian is Hindu. The reasons for this are complex but the social exclusiveness of community is an important one.

The striking aspect of the Indian Church is that it is drawn from all communities, a people where there was no people. What is needed is a concern to focus on the people as being a reconciling community. The question of identity was at the heart of the movement for a uniting Church in India. The debate has been about Indian identity and Christian identity, rich and poor, dalit and non-dalit, tribal and non-tribal. Unfortunately there has developed a dichotomy between Indian-ness and Christian-ness on the assumption that one's commitment to Christ alienates one from being truly Indian. The question is whether after giving due recognition to the historical accidents of the colonial period which often created misunderstanding, there can be an identity which is both Indian and Christian. It is not an easy one but not, I suggest, an impossible one to answer.

CHAPTER VI
A UNITING ECCLESIOLOGY

The Church of North India is a reconciliation of different Protestant traditions into organic union. It went a step further than the CSI in that union took place not only between episcopal and non-episcopal churches but the Baptists were also included. The question has been raised whether behind the ecumenical verbiage the pursuit of union was largely pragmatic. Pragmatic considerations could not be ruled out altogether. The Anglican communion had refused since 1947 to recognize the ministry of the CSI. The problems created by lack of any initial unification of ministry in the CSI made the negotiators in the north determined to seek for unification of ministry from the start. Heavy emphasis on the episcopate to be seen as the instrument for continuity of the Church led to tensions.[1]

In the organic union the principle of unity in diversity is defended as an acceptable and even essential characteristic of a united Church. Therefore the question needs to be addressed regarding the interpretation of the principle of unity in diversity, and the deeper issue of the identity of the CNI in relation to former denominational identities. The denominations were the outcome of the church's struggle for renewal. They found growing

---

[1] STEWART, William. The Lambeth Quadrilateral: Bane or Blessing? Indian Journal of Theology, 1959, p125. He criticised the 1958 Lambeth Conference for re-issuing verbatim the 1920 formula. He appealed to Anglicans to rethink their quadrilateral in the light of the history of the churches and the Gospel itself. See also Chapter IV, n.11.

convergence in their apprehension of the gospel, their expression of worship, and the ordering of church life. But when denominations enter into competition with the movement for church unity this becomes a denial of the missionary perspective, and a stumbling block for the witness of the worshipping community.

The CNI is the consequence of the attainment of selfhood in a nation, but such attainment must involve wrestling with the realities of its task in a particular geographical context. As discussed in the fifth chapter, the vast majority of Indians are Hindus and the majority of Christians in India are 'Dalits' and 'Tribals'. The inequalities and discriminatory practices found in Indian society are very much operative in the Church. In such a situation it would be much easier for the Church to cater for one particular type of social background. Perhaps this would save the Church from many painful strains and be helpful in satisfying the particular religious interests of a group. But it would not be able to stand up to proclaim the message that 'God was in Christ reconciling the world to himself' (2 Cor.5:19).

Therefore the object of this chapter is to propose a provisional ecumenical ecclesiology that would provide a framework within which the CNI could continue to witness and serve. Any ecclesiology to be ecumenical cannot but be a uniting ecclesiology because the very essence of the Church is being a community of the people who proclaim themselves to be reconciled to God and to one another, through the life, death and resurrection of Jesus. Reconciliation in the Church means living out together the reconciled life and engaging in the mission of reconciliation in order to draw others into the fellowship of those already reconciled. It is God who reconciled the world to himself in Christ. But the divisions within the

Church have impaired that mission of reconciliation. It is therefore important to ask how unity is to be expressed and realised in such a way that it is possible for it to take root in the social and cultural life of humanity.

It is proposed to consider Narrative, Doctrine and Institution as three helpful categories in construing a uniting ecclesiology. These three categories are interrelated and should be in constant dialogue with each other to give a holistic perspective. It is also suggested that the Lord's Supper (hereafter the Supper) as a focal point of Christian worship might perform the task of inter-relating the three suggested categories. The proposal is written from a standpoint within the CNI, concerned for its future, and in dialogue with a range of Western Christian debates and theologies.

Categories of Ecclesiology

a. Narrative

People identify with particular stories and the Church as a community is no exception. To exist as a church means to have a collective memory and story bears the corporate memory. The Church as a story-telling fellowship, tells the story of Israel and of Jesus Christ. The use of story as a category in Christian theology has been a subject of extensive discussion in recent decades.[2] Story is employed to describe a variety of things. In the broadest

---

[2] FREI, Hans W. The Eclipse of Biblical Narrative, New Haven, Yale University Press, 1974. Frei suggests that a realistic narrative framework for the interpretation of Scripture was the most common pre-critical way of reading the Bible until after the Reformation, when doctrinal, pietistic, and

sense it is the account by a narrator of events, and in the narrower sense, as it is used in much theological inquiry, it is described thus by Fackre: 'A story in the narrow sense is narration self-consciously controlled by narrator vision in which the flow of events become a plot, and participants become characters in a storyline marked by conflict and moving toward resolution.'[3] It will be sufficient for our purpose to note that a substantial

---

last of all historical-critical methods displaced it. Barth revived this exegetical tradition in a partly post-critical form. FREI, Hans W. The Literal Reading of Biblical Narrative in Christian Tradition: Does it Stretch or Will It break? In: McConnell, Frank. ed. The Bible and the Narrative Tradition. Oxford University press, 1986, p33-77. THIEMANN, Ronald F. Revelation and Theology: The Gospel as Narrative Promise. Notre Dame: University of Notre Dame Press, 1985. Thiemann considers the question of narrative as a literary category emphasizing the interaction of circumstances and character, incident and identity in an ordered chronological sequence. FACKRE, Gabriel. Narrative Theology: An Overview. Interpretation, Vol.37, No4, October 1983, p340f. Narrative theology as a discourse about God in the setting of a story. STROUP, George. The Promise of Narrative Theology, SCM, London, 1984. HAUERWAS, Stanley and JONES, Gregory L. Why Narrative? Readings in Narrative Theology, William B.Eerdmans, USA, 1989. MACINTYRE, Alasdair, After Virtue:A study in Moral Theory, 2nd Edition, Notre Dame, 1984. He stresses the importance of narrative in shaping the outlook of a community, in that it is able to ground the particularity of that community in history. Narrative functions as the bearer of a tradition, which illuminates the present and opens up options for the future, p223.

---

[3] FACKRE, Gabriel. The Christian Story, Eerdmans, W.B., 1984, p5. Fackre suggests three distinct but often overlapping forms of narrative theology as canonical story, life story and community story. Canonical story

part of the Bible is made up of narrative in that narrow sense. This basic form is referred to in this thesis as 'story'.

My concern in using story as a leading category is to show how the story of Israel, the story of Jesus and the early church lead to a vision of the church that can form the basis of an ecumenical identity; to gain insight for the self-understanding of the CNI; and to overcome narrow identities within the Church. In considering the meaning and content of the common story of the Church, it is proposed to incorporate the ideas proposed by George Lindbeck. Lindbeck suggests that in ecclesiology, the traditional narrative reading, in combination with historical-critical awareness, brings out more continuities between the Church and Israel.[4]

Story is a powerful category for forming corporate identity. It helps to give a community identity, and therefore helps to constitute community. It can express things for which other idioms would be inappropriate. In particular the identity of a group can be articulated by stories. People are what they tell of themselves in their story and what they make of their story. It is also true that the story is vulnerable because it could be abused by a community by becoming the bearer of an ideology like the myth of the Aryan race or of white supremacy.

The Church is called to tell a story of which it believes God to be the

---

focuses on the biblical materials, life story on human experience and community story on the classical Christian tradition.

[4] LINDBECK, George. The Story-Shaped Church: critical exegesis and theological interpretation. In: GREEN, Garrett. Scriptural Authority and Narrative Interpretation. Fortress Press, Philadelphia, 1987, p161-178; and The Church. In: WAINWRIGHT, Geoffrey, ed. Keeping the Faith. SPCK, London, 1989.

author. It is God who has reconciled the world to Himself through the death and resurrection of Jesus Christ. This is not a fairy tale but an active word which makes history. It calls into being a fellowship of people for a specific task by His grace. The story tells of God's engagement with human history. In the search for an ecumenical ecclesiology, it is vital to strive for an ecumenical perspective through this story in a context where narrow particularity is often divisive, encouraging identity as black or white, first world or third world, male or female, and in particular within India as brahmanical, dalit or tribal.

The basis of all different local theologies is the story that YHWH has chosen the people of Israel from all nations, and in Jesus Christ YHWH has chosen a people from Jews and all Gentiles. That is a regulative statement in ecclesiology for forming an ecumenical identity. It includes the unity and reconciliation between Jews and Gentiles and the overcoming of human divisions - race, class, caste, gender, colour etc.

i. The Story of Israel

The primary symbol of Israel's self-interpretation is the people of YHWH. They owe their origin and existence to YHWH's elective activity. The interpretation of this story of the people of YHWH is seen in the continuity between Judaism and Christianity in terms of promise and fulfilment. The Old Testament is seen in terms of promise and New Testament in terms of fulfilment with the church as true Israel.

The story of the Church includes a failure to recognize the historical bonds that tie it to the history of Israel. The need is to understand the story in its historical matrix as it developed. The identity of the people of Israel is based on the Covenant. This goes back to their historic experience of deliverance from bondage in Egypt (Dt.26:5f and Joshua 24).

> And you shall make response before the Lord your God, 'A wandering Aramaean was my father; and he went down into Egypt and sojourned there, few in number; and there he became a nation, great, mighty and populous. And the Egyptians treated us harshly, and afflicted us, and laid upon us hard bondage. Then we cried to the Lord the God of our fathers, and the Lord heard our voice, and saw our affliction, our toil, and our oppression; and the Lord brought us out of Egypt with a mighty hand and an outstretched arm, with great terror, with signs and wonders; and he brought us into this place and gave us this land, a land flowing with milk and honey.' (Dt.26:5f)

The concept of 'People' belonging to God is at the heart of the above confession. Once they were 'No People' but now they are 'A People'. The declaration begins in the land of Canaan then moves to Egypt and then out of Egypt. It calls into memory those events which were supposed to make 'A People'. The identity of the People was maintained by the Covenant and the Law which was important for the stability and structure of the community. Both are the acts of identification of the people. YHWH is the God of Israel and Israel is the people of YHWH. The deliverance from Egypt was systematically worked out in Deuteronomy and that idea underlies other writings of the Old Testament.

The union between YHWH and His people is based on a free historical activity of God in the history of His people. The most important aspect of the story of Israel is that it is not the people's but God's free choice, his mercy, love and faithfulness that constitute a people. Israel was only summoned to recognize that as an act of grace. Israel was repeatedly reminded of that moment when she was led out and responded to that act of grace. The story of Israel is a story of response and failures, judgment and punishment.

The discontinuity of Christianity from its own historical matrix in Israel was focused through faith in Jesus Christ. Christian tradition has characterized the discontinuity represented in Jesus as a deepening of the faith of Israel. But this does not mean that the Church as the people of God has no relation to Israel. Israel is the historical matrix. The continuity is broken in so far as Israel stands for a determinate ethnic and national way of remembering God.

ii. The Story of the Early Church

The disciples of Jesus saw themselves as Israel in the same way as other groups such as the Pharisees, the Sadducees, the Zealots and the Essenes. In the beginning the earliest Christian community in no sense felt themselves to have a new religion distinct from Judaism. There was no boundary line between themselves and their fellow Jews. They saw themselves as Israel. They met in the temple (Acts 2:46). They took the categories for self-understanding from the Old Testament. They understood their story as a continuation of the story of Israel rather than its fulfilment. It was Jesus Christ who was the fulfilment.

> Early Christian communal self-understanding was narrative shaped. The Church was in other words fundamentally identified and characterised by its story. Images such as 'body of Christ' or the traditional marks of 'unity', 'holiness', 'catholicity' cannot be first defined and then be used to specify what was and what was not 'church'. The story was logically prior. It determined the meaning of images, concepts, doctrines, and

theories of the church rather than being determined by them.[5]

The idea of the people of God was fundamental to the understanding of the self-description of early Christians. The reality from 'No People' to 'A People' finds expression in the book of Acts and the Pauline Letters. One crucial issue that triggered off changes in the continuity between Judaism and Christianity was the place of the Gentiles in the Christian community. The Church wrestled with that problem.

> The later Church, for which the separateness of the two communities was a given fact of life, could avoid the problem by ignoring the Jews altogether, or by denying their theological right to exist as Israel. For Paul that was impossible. The separation was a present necessity but ultimately a theological 'anomaly.'[6]

The letter to the Romans sets the tone of the theological debate about the story of relationship between historical Israel and the Church. Paul believed himself to have been called to be the apostle to the Gentiles but he had to work out the contrast between the old and the new, the law and the Gospel, Moses and Christ. He was aware of his own background: 'If any other man thinks he has reason for confidence in the flesh, I have more: circumcised on the eighth day, of the people of Israel, of the tribe of Benjamin, a Hebrew born of Hebrews; as to the law a Pharisee, as to zeal a persecutor of the church, as to righteousness under the law blameless.' (Phil:3.4f) Paul maintained to the end that God had been at work in the

---

[5] LINDBECK,G. The Church. In: WAINWRIGHT,G. ed. Keeping the Faith, SPCK, London 1989,p183.

[6] MEEKS, W.A. The First Urban Christians. Yale University Press, Newhaven and London, 1983, p108.

past, the law itself had been given by God and God had not abandoned his people Israel. He saw continuity and discontinuity.

In Romans 9-11, Paul reflects on the relation between the Gentiles and the Jewish people. It is the relation between two communities and their existence in the mysterious plan of God. In the course of history the Church picked up that side of Israel's 'No' to Jesus Christ. The rituals that were the identity of the Jews, particularly circumcision and sabbath observance, were abandoned by the Christians. Paul argued that the eschatological unity of Jews and Gentiles in the new household of Christ was the logical implication of one God of Israel. 'Is God the God of Jews only? Is he not the God of Gentiles also? Yes, of Gentiles also, since God is one; and he will justify t2he circumcised on the ground of their faith and the uncircumcised through their faith' (Rom.3:29).

God is one, the God of Jews and Gentiles. The bone of contention was the unexpected and unthinkable claim that the Messiah had died a death cursed by the law, and was resurrected. It posed a shock and a sharp challenge to the way in which the people of God would be constituted and bounded. The perspective began to change in the course of history with various historical circumstances and with the early Christians' experiences.

> Anyone who enjoys a good detective story knows that the author will have scattered clues throughout the pages of the book - often apparently trivial or incidental happenings - which suddenly appear significant when Hercule Poirot or Miss Marple or whoever it is starts putting two and two together; the pattern of events becomes clear only when the mystery is cleared up.[7]

---

[7] HOOKER, Morna D. Continuity and Discontinuity. Epworth Press, 1986, p42.

The first Christians had gone through this experience. When the disciples claimed that Jesus was the fulfilment, they were beginning from their experience from the past. The words of Jesus began to take on new meaning and the disciples began to take part in a new way in the story of Israel. The boundary of circumcision was broken but the Lord's Supper and Baptism provided symbolic expression of group identity.

Paul defended his belief that there is no distinction between Jews and Gentiles by appealing precisely to the unity of God and His impartiality. He had to explain the purpose of God which could encompass the crucified Messiah. But he had to struggle with the dialectical tension between Israel's past and future place in God's purpose. In the words of Krister Stendahl, Paul has often been seen through the lenses of Luther or Augustine, but in fact he was a successful Jew (Phil 3.2). Therefore Stendahl argued that the problem of late medieval piety cannot be read back into the first century and by doing that the Western Church has made the apostle in its own image.

> Romans became a theological tractate on the nature of faith. Justification no longer 'justified' the status of Gentile Christians as honorary Jews, but became the timeless answer to the plights and pains of the introspective conscience of the West. Paul was no longer seen 'among Jews and Gentiles' but rather as the guide for those perplexed and troubled by the human predicament. [8]

---

[8] STENDAHL, Krister. <u>Paul Among Jews and Gentiles.</u> SCM, 1977, p5.

Jesus was a Jew but he was also the crucified Messiah. The Christians identified the 'One God' as the God of Israel but at the same time the One who raised Jesus from the dead (Rom.4:24, 2 Cor.4:14). This belief in God who was identified with the crucified Messiah introduced a new paradigm that determined the identity of the Christian community. They were a Jewish sect but started asking questions about the death and resurrection of Jesus.

To a Jew of Jesus's time, it was not completely foreign that a man be raised from the dead, be exalted to heaven, or be a person of the past returning at the end time. Such statements might apply to Enoch or Elijah. The difference was the confession of Jesus as the Messiah. 'If he was crucified as an alleged Messiah, then - but only then - does faith in his resurrection necessarily become faith in the resurrection of the crucified Messiah. In this way the distinctiveness of the Christian idea of the Messiah, in contrast to the Jewish, was given from the outset.'[9]

The continuity of the community with the story of Israel was the belief in one God, the God of Israel, the creator of the universe and ultimate judge of all human actions. The discontinuity was that it became difficult on the part of the Gentiles to think of themselves as Jews.

> Thus not only was the synagogue excluded but one people of God was broken into two peoples, the old and new. This created the problem of how to relate them, and the solution was to read the scriptures as if Israel were the type no longer simply of the coming kingdom and of its instantiation in the person of

---

[9] DAHL, Nils A. The Crucified Messiah and other essays. Augsburg, 1974, p26.

Christ but also of the church, which thus became the antitype, the fulfilment.[10]

Both the continuity and the discontinuity are indicated through the story of Israel, Jesus and the early church, with Paul as one of the main interpreters. After the Roman empire was converted, the persecuted Christians became the persecutors, and anti-semitism became a paradigmatic problem. To go back to the story of Israel is to note the meaning of the church in the story of Israel as appropriated by the early Christians. It is to draw attention to the primacy of the empirical aspect of the church, and to the church as referring to a concrete group of people.

iii. 'The People of God': a key to the Narrative Identity of the Church.

Different images of the church have emerged over time in a variety of contexts.[11] In the history of Christianity concepts of the Church have been influenced by the form of the Church at any given time. It is possible that the Church too easily can become a prisoner of one image; an image made for itself at one particular period in history. Every age has its own

---

[10] LINDBECK, George. The Story-Shaped Church. In: GREEN, Garrett. Ed. Scriptural Authority and Narrative Interpretation. Fortress Press, Philadelphia. 1987, p171.

[11] MINEAR, Paul S. Images of the Church in New Testament. Lutterworth, London, 1961. Minear lists some ninety-six images of the Church. Brunner, E. The Misunderstanding of the Church. Lutterworth, London, 1952, p107. Brunner argues that the Church in the biblical sense is not an institution but a brotherhood. It is a communion of persons. BONHOEFFER, Dietrich. Sanctorum Communio. Collins, London, 1963, p123. Bonhoeffer argues that the Church is an interpersonal community. It is constituted by the complete self-forgetfulness of love.

image of the Church arising out of a particular historical situation. Avery Dulles in his influential work on ecclesiology has identified key models of the Church as Institution, Mystical Communion, Sacrament, Herald, Servant. His conviction is that the Church like other theological realities is a mystery. Mysteries are realities of which one cannot speak directly. If one wishes to talk about them, then one must draw on analogies afforded by the experience which provides the models.[12] Depending on the circumstances in both the Church and the culture, one or the other has indeed taken form as a response to a particular cultural context. For example the Church has challenged the culture, taking the side of the oppressed in being the servant church. It has proclaimed its identity as herald, and has acceded to the way things are conforming to culture in being an institutional church. The images are not exclusive but helpful in focusing the understanding of the Church.

For example, the image of the body of Christ is often used for organic union of the churches and was applied by the uniting churches. It is an analogy to the human body with various organs. This image of the body of Christ is predominantly Pauline. It has been used in the history of church union to represent for organic unity as it is found in Romans 12 and I Corinthians 12. But Paul's understanding which comes to expression in those two chapters is related to the local church. It is the Church in Rome, the Church in Corinth and the body metaphor refers to the Corinthian group of believers.

---

[12] DULLES, Avery. Models of the Church. Gill & Macmillan, Dublin, 1976.

The members of the body are individual members and so he does not yet speak of the universal Church. Each member within the body has some function. To each is given some charisma. Each is a member of the body in so far as the Spirit knits them into the corporate unity by the manifestation of grace through the person. All the body's functions are important to the health of the whole. The body metaphor is a classic illustration of unity in diversity, but a unity which does not emerge out of rigid conformity, rather which results out of the harmony of many different parts working together, each depending on the other.

While not denying the power and usefulness of the image of the body of Christ, the image of the people of God is proposed in order to construe an ecumenical identity. To say that the Church is the people of God is not just to name one metaphor among others, because the idea of people of God is implied in the very conception of the Church. The full implication of this can only be rightly understood within the context of the whole history of the people of God. The other metaphors applied to the Church could be said to be qualifications of the basic conception of the people of God. This image is based on the story as expressed in the story of Israel and the story of the early Church.[13] To claim to be part of the Church universal is to claim to be part of the story of Israel and the story of the early Church. That is the key to the formation of an ecumenical identity of a Church.

The concept 'People of God' is a common one for both the story of Israel and the early church. As a concept it has deep roots in the Old Testa-

---

[13] DAHL, Nils A. The People of God. Ecumenical Review, Vol.IX, 1957, p154f.

ment. To concentrate on the Hebrew-Christian legacy of early Christianity might be important in a situation when the Church is becoming more global in its understanding of itself, and also for India where much objection is made to the western nature of Christianity. The present situation in India is similar to an earlier period when the transition was made from a Jewish to a non-Jewish setting. The present period is like the Christian beginnings where the Christians are just a minority but entrusted with the task of being a sign to the whole nation.

Central to the concept of 'people of God' is the doctrine of election. Any discussion of the Church as the people of God is related to the doctrine of election. To talk about election in the context of ecclesiology is to open the wounds of division, but it also opens the way to the reality of God. Newbigin draws attention to election in the context of the debate about the church as the community of the Holy Spirit. Jesus of Nazareth crucified under Pontius Pilate is the elect of God. Election is by incorporation in Him. The source of election is the gracious will of God and the context is 'in Christ'. The visible Church is the reality within which the doctrine of the Holy Spirit is to be understood. People are related to God's saving activity by being related to the people called into being by God within a particular strand of history. This is not a privilege but a responsibility of a particular community. This is the pattern throughout the Bible.

Newbigin expounds the scandal of particularity in terms of the doctrine of election.[14] God's purpose is the blessing of all the people.

---

[14] NEWBIGIN, Lesslie. The Open Secret. William B. Eerdmans, 1978, Chapter 7.

Therefore the one is chosen for the many, and that the particular is chosen for the sake of the universal is the main theme of election. Salvation must be that which not only binds the soul to God, but each to the other and all to the world of nature. Interpersonal relatedness belongs to the very being of God. Therefore there can be no salvation for man except in relatedness.[15] The blessing is indeed for all, but the very nature of that blessing means that it must be given and received in a manner which binds each to the other. It is important for identity of mission.[16]

One of the challenges in adopting the image of the people of God in the context of the doctrine of election is the relation between the universal and the particular. The key to this relation is claimed in the story of Israel as God's way of election. The very idea of any particular community claiming to be elected by God in any part of the world, including the CNI, seems to imply exclusiveness and superiority and to be inappropriate in an age of religious pluralism.

The Church in India has at times tried to overcome this exclusive

---

[15] NEWBIGIN, Lesslie. The Open Secret. p78.

[16] The encounter of Peter and Cornelius (Act.10:1-11:18) is generally referred to as the conversion of Cornelius but it was equally the conversion of Peter. This event was not only the conversion of Cornelius - the recruitment of a Pagan household into the Church. It was also the conversion of the Church to a much fuller understanding of its nature and mission. It was that, by a sovereign action of Holy Spirit; two things happened: Cornelius and his household became part of Christ's ongoing mission, and the Church was led to a fuller understanding of the nature of that mission. NEWBIGIN, Lesslie. The Christian Faith and the World Religions. In: WAINWRIGHT, Geoffrey. ed. Keeping the Faith. SPCK, London, 1989, p339.

identity by making some compromises in order to identify with India's religious traditions. For example in the pre-Portuguese period, the Syrian Christians in Kerala were content to exist as a caste structured society on the principle of co-existence of several religious communities. It was ideal in the sense that the Church lived as a community as long as it did not disturb the Indian social structure. Religion as such was treated as entirely separate from that of social structure and institution.

Similarly in the first chapter of the thesis it was observed how the great Jesuit Robert de Nobili insisted that high-caste Indians could be Christians without breaking caste. The fruit of this was a Christian community drawn from the higher caste of Hinduism. Later on in the eighteenth century, missionaries both Catholic and Lutheran accepted caste as a social factor and never thought to contradict it. It was thought necessary to accept Christianity as a creed like any other creed such as Hinduism. In this context the Church accepted the religious practice of Hinduism to accommodate itself in a multi-religious context.

Even now in the twentieth century, the missiologists of the 'Church Growth' school insist that as a matter of missionary obedience the Church should accept and welcome the organization of congregations of different castes in the same town or city. For example, Donald McGavran's thesis is to plant churches on the caste and tribal pattern of Indian society. 'The Church in India must both "plant the church in every caste" and "press forward in establishing One church in which all Christians are brothers" -

simultaneously. The tasks are equally important.'[17]

The question is how to be a community where there is communion among the people and with God, and where all barriers are transcended. Perhaps a deeper analysis of the story as based on the image of the people of God will be helpful, without making any claim for exclusiveness or aggressiveness in a pluralistic society. The motif of 'people of God' as an identifying description of the theme of election has become increasingly common in recent doctrinal and ecumenical discussion.[18] To take this concept as a common motif for the church has a good historical and exegetical mandate.

The history of Israel was for the early church its own history. When priority is given to the story in identifying the Church as the people of God, then the concept carries with it the sense of history as a people. It is not something trans-empirical but an actual people. Lindbeck suggests that 'The primacy of narrative thus implies that exalted concepts and images such as holy, bride usually refer to empirical churches in all their potential messiness.'[19]

In suggesting story as a possible category for the ecumenical identity

---

[17] McGAVRAN, D. A. Understanding the Church in India. Gospel Literature Service. Bombay.1979.

[18] It is one of several used of the church in the documents of the Second Vatican Council and Hans Kung also speaks of the Church as the people of God. But the concept as 'people of God' in these contexts tends to be subsumed under the notion that the church is in fact the new Israel. See KUNG, Hans. The Church. Burns and Oats, London, 1967, p107f, p148.

[19] LINDBECK, George. The Story Shaped Church, p165.

of the Church, particularly as the story of 'the people of God', it is assumed that narrative is a fundamental way to express human identity. As a category it refers to the identity of the Church as contingent and historical, particularly to an actual group of people. It is worth noting that the roots of the ecumenical movement were to be found in the realization that mission was obstructed by the divisions between the Christians. The CNI as a product of this movement, is called to tell the story of God's gracious call and to be a continuation of the story.

The identity of the CNI has to some extent been shaped by colonialism because Christianity accompanied western colonialism. But positively speaking western Christianity has produced a ferment within Indian society and the Church, and to sustain that ferment is vital for the Church. Therefore Christianity in India needs to be understood within the emergence of Indian nationalism as discussed in the second chapter. Indian nationalism in general has been deeply exercised about the idea and expression of community in the context of the impact of the west. It has been seeking to fight the evils of social tyranny through religious reformation within Hinduism though it has not been able to break with it completely.

In the nineteenth century the indigenous elites adopted different views in a period when two cultures and civilizations confronted each other in the context of colonial domination. Among some there was an objective discernment of the new along with the usual defensive tendencies of a rising nationalism. In others there was a spirit of acceptance together with a genuine rational enquiry into the new but with the rejection of all that hindered a national regeneration. In others still there was a strong concern with the preservation of Hindu heritage along with a selective acceptance of western culture. In general the emerging national consciousness adopted the heritage of Indian culture as the focus of its identity, and gloried in the past.

The Indian Christian nationalists shared the nationalist milieu. The criticism of Christianity as a foreign religion affected the Christian thinkers. They saw it was necessary for the Indian church to acknowledge India's religious heritage and unite it within the Christian faith. Their concern was with the structure of Christian community in relation to the emerging national community. It contained the idea of a church in India with a new selfhood able to give spiritual and moral content to the new selfhood of the nation.

The CNI as a realization of the principle of ecumenism and of selfhood took the form of a national church. It is legitimate to fear that the restriction of the principle to a national church might lead to a situation where a dominant culture or a particular group might impose its understanding and expression of the Christian faith on the whole Church. This fear finds expression through some of the indigenous ecclesiologies.

The dalit theology criticizes Indian Christian theology for being a cultural domination. The culture and religion of millions of Indians, including the dalits and tribals, have seldom featured in the indigenization efforts of Indian theologians which mainly produced apologetic theology as the basis for dialogue in order to get rid of the charge of being western in character. A large part of these theologians' work has consisted of indigenizing the categories and forms of theological thinking. A particular preoccupation has been the thought forms of religious philosophy as a means of expressing the Christian faith.

The dalits claim that there exists a large mass of subaltern people who are the victims of the dominant culture. Cultural divisions exist within the same society. Any contextualisation cannot just ignore either these facts or the aspirations of the subaltern people. An authentic theological discourse must take these diversities into consideration. Therefore it is vital that the Church should not lose the true ecumenical dimension for the sake of maintaining ethnic or national identity.

The suggestion of incorporating a perspective of the people of God as a category, is to acknowledge that there is no division between the Jews and the Gentiles, male or female, black or white, rich or poor, brahman or dalit, tribal or non-tribal. It is to proclaim the beginning of a new humanity that gathers all human kind into one people. The coming together of different strands of denominational history and of different caste, language and regional groups within the CNI is both a challenge and an opportunity to all to share both their gifts and their life as the people of God. This is an opportunity which must be grasped.

An understanding of the Church as the people of God refers to an actual group of people. In that perspective the Church's claim to be the people of God does not indicate any superiority over other people; neither does it create any trans-empirical community. It means to grasp the meaning of election in a new perspective. The election if properly understood, is not a status but an opportunity for selfless service to humankind. The identity of the Church thus based on the free and gracious will of God is realized in ongoing relationship with God as the Lord. Only then can the Church be a witness to serve the purpose of God. Unfaithfulness within that relationship can sever the Church from its root. This has been the experience of Israel and the Church when they have been unfaithful. In the language of Revelation 'You are lukewarm, and neither cold nor hot, I will spew you out of my mouth.'(3:16).

Election is communal and a community as the people of God is marked both by blessing and curse depending on their response to Him. The prophetic element within the story of Israel entails an important challenge for the Church. The presence of this perspective has critical and decisive significance for self-understanding. The significant aspect of Israel's story was that it had the unique ability to confer meaning on the people and to sustain them in times of crisis. It also challenged through prophecy in times of drifting away from God, and reminded Israel of its relation to the rest of humanity.

The Church in claiming to be the people of God cannot escape from the prophetic note as was applicable to Israel. The same argument will be equally applicable to the Church as the people of God, which means the Church in any place must avoid seeing its identity on the basis of any ethnic, national or social unit. It must be prophetically self-critical so that the story of the Church now can be a sign of the kingdom of God.

The CNI as a united and uniting church should aim to find its identity in terms of nothing else but the people of God. Therefore the question must be asked, is the CNI as the people of God functioning as a true sign and instrument of God's purpose? The Church is called by God to be a sign and challenge on the way to freedom for all people. Any attempt to be indigenous on the basis of separating India and the West using the antithesis of spiritual and material, individual and corporate, atomised society and natural community is an over-simplification. However to deny the antithesis is not to deny the particularities. For example when the Church moved into Europe, it was obviously deeply affected by the ideas of Greek philosophy, Hellenistic culture, Roman law and government. Western Catholicism was shaped in its intellectual formulations by men trained in Greek philosophy, either in the Platonism of early scholars like Augustine, or the Aristotelianism of the later scholars like Thomas. Even so to deny the antithesis is to acknowledge that it is not that simple to divide in terms of clear dichotomies.

The CNI as a uniting Church cannot just ignore the past history of the Church as it is an heir to the inherited traditions of the Church and is part of the One, Holy, Catholic and Apostolic Church. From the beginning it was recognized that the division in India can never be resolved by homogenizing the various strands of history. Unity must be achieved by retaining diversity because the CNI is not a melting pot but a mosaic to which all can contribute their gifts. It is that part of the Body of Christ which God is building up out of all generations and races. Therefore the CNI rightly acknowledges the stories of other traditions which are the fruit of the continuous working of God's Spirit in history. It is traced from the Apostolic time through the Reformation and down to our own day.[20]

In acknowledging that it is part of the common story, one crucial issue is to retain all the effective resources of the story. A point which is often raised in the context of mission in India is the place of the story of the

---

[20] THE CHURCH OF NORTH INDIA. Constitution of the CNI. ISPCK, Delhi, 1987, p1.

Indian people prior to the coming of the Gospel. An often-cited example is the people who have gone beyond the recognition of Christ as the ideal and responded to him in faith. Keshub Chandra Sen's Church of the New Dispensation in the nineteenth century and the Subba Rao Movement in the twentieth century are two examples of this approach. 'There is in Keshub Chundra Sen an affirmation of the distinctively Asian heritage in religion, metaphysics and culture, not merely as a medium of communication of the meaning of Christ but as containing truth and value which should find fulfilment in Jesus Christ and his universal Church.'[21]   Subba Rao's devotion to Christ never finds any need for baptism or fellowship of the visible Church. Having been baptized by the Spirit, there is no need of water baptism. His outstanding feature of faith is his complete devotion to Christ. One of his vulnerable points is his attitude to the Bible. His prayer meetings include reading and exposition of passages from the New Testament, but never from the Old Testament. Even his claim to direct realisation and unity with Jesus makes the witness of the written word unnecessary.

Going beyond the recognition of Christ as the ideal to the faith response still remains an issue in the context of the debate about the place of the story of the Indian people prior to the coming of the Gospel. The Church as part of her story claims to share in the story of Israel and of Jesus. But to become part of this story is not to lose one's own story and substitute another one for it.

---

[21] THOMAS, M.M. <u>The Acknowledged Christ of the Indian Renaissance.</u> CLS, Madras, 1970, p71.

The importance of this is that to convert is not, as Gandhi thought, to lose my story and substitute another one for it; it is to add another chapter to an already immensely complex story. To become Christian is to put my Celtic, Germanic, African, Dravidian or Aryan story into another perspective, to recognize that 'roots' are not primarily a matter of blood and soil but of the story which makes me what I am. Story is far more fundamental than nation as the problem of minorities all around the world very clearly illustrates.[22]

A narrative identity of the Church rooted in the story of Israel, Jesus and the early church is one where God is seen as the author of the story; the one who elects Israel and the Church. This is a particular identity with universal implications which are focused through the climax of the story of Jesus, in which he dies for all. The Resurrection and Pentecost mean the formation of a missionary community that relativizes all social, racial and religious divisions and looks forward to the culmination of the story in the realization of the kingdom of God. The Church is called to be a sign and instrument of the kingdom of God, celebrating in word and sacrament the God who is identified in the story.

Most apparent in this conception of the church is the issue of the nature of identity. Like Israel, the calling is to be a faithful people but it is the whole people who are called to such faithfulness. Their election and mission is communal.[23] The context in which God's promises are received and his story continually interpreted anew requires the creation of

---

[22] GORRINGE, Timothy. Redeeming Time. Darton, Longman and Todd, London, 1986, p165.

[23] LINDBECK, George, The Church, p193.

2community. Such a community is shaped by the Christian story which contrasts with the characteristically modern perversion of ecclesia which has been spoken of as individualism and privatism.[24]

The primary framework for ecclesial identity that is being proposed for the CNI is that of the story of God's involvement with His world, as focused especially on Israel, Jesus and the Church. There are of course many issues which would need to be dealt with if this were to be developed fully, but what has been said has indicated the broad advantages of this approach. This approach is a more widely accessible ecclesiology for ordinary Christians. It allows a healthy balance between individual and community which are both interwoven. Thus it will be able to counter not only liberal individualism but also the individualism of Hinduism and the ideas reflected in the writings of the Rethinking ecclesiology. The authority in this perspective resides neither in society itself nor in the individual, but in God. The implication of this would be that the church is constituted in the movement and power of the Spirit. It is oriented towards an eschaton which continually acts as prophetic critique of the present.

b. Doctrine

The Church as a community not only tells a story but it is a form of historical existence and has a corporate identity. So it is marked by certain social features. Therefore communication in the Church requires linguistic expression in various forms. One aspect of the linguistic expression besides story is the need for ongoing interpretation. It arises due to the inevitable

---

[24] FARLEY, Edward. <u>Ecclesial Man.</u> Fortress Press, 1975, p182-85.

passage of time. To the degree that linguistic expression constitutes the church's very existence, it contains an impetus to make its story contemporary through doctrine.[25] Interpretation of story within a community of faith is important and doctrine plays a critical role in the interpretation of story.

Therefore it is not enough that a community is a collection of individuals who point to a series of past events in history. The past needs to be appropriated in order that the present members participate in the vision of the future. The category 'narrative' suggests that a particular literary 'genre' is of decisive though by no means exclusive importance for the self- understanding of the Church.[26] The task of the theologian is to provide criteria or what Ritschl calls 'regulative sentences' for making critical judgments about and comparisons among the different narratives.

Doctrine plays a critical role in the interpretation of a story and in defending the meaning in case of threat from outside. Its purpose is to refine, formulate, and clarify the story of the Christian community and to communicate the reality of God in human language. In theological statements the truth of being part of a story takes a determinate form.

---

[25] RITSCHL, Dietrich. <u>The Logic of Theology.</u> SCM, London, 1986, p14f.

[26] David Ford suggests that Barth had acute sensitivity to narrative parts of the Bible, especially the logic of crucifixion and resurrection, and developed the possibilities of the stories as pointers to the nature of God and humanity. Yet there is, he argues, an overstraining of the stories by generalizing and typologizing in order to arrive at conclusions which seem to require other modes of argument besides those appealing to biblical narratives. FORD, David. Assessing Barth. <u>In</u>: SYKES, Stephen. <u>ed.</u> <u>Studies of Theological Method</u>. Clarendon Press, Oxford, 1979, p199.

Obviously it has its dangers. The tendency could be to integrate a story into a contemporary framework which is dominant and to integrate it into institutional structures whose interest is in their own preservation and perpetuation.

The ways of handling doctrine in the course of history have been various. In particular one modern feature is the loss of reality in contemporary christendom.[27] Doubt is raised as to whether there is any reality at all revealed in the language of the historical faith. George Lindbeck refers to the modern trend as antidoctrinalism.[28] He notes this as the loss of confidence in the possibility of finding common meaning and communal norms. David Ford identifies a feature of post modernity in the impossibility of getting beyond language to reality. The notion of a common humanity is seen as illusory.[29] It creates an atmosphere where doubt is raised whether doctrine functions as a witness to divine reality. Various r;2esponses could be noted in the attempt to grapple with the handling of doctrine. In the following section these responses have been identified under three sections: Classical, Experience and Rule. While the preference is given in this thesis for the 'rule' theory of doctrine, in the fourth section a critique of 'rule' theory is added in order to make it relevant as a category of ecclesiology.

---

[27] FARLEY, Edward. Ecclesial Man. p12.

[28] LINDBECK, George A. The Nature of Doctrine. SPCK, London, 1984, p77.

[29] FORD, David. ed. The Modern Theologians, Vol.ii. Basil Blackwell, 1989, p292.

i. Classical View

The classical response is the propositional view of doctrine. The proponents of this view adopt a realistic approach to theological statements as informative propositions about objective realities. It is based on the assumption of a one to one correspondence between word and object. The revelation is thought of chiefly as the communication of propositions or of eternal truths in the form of statements to the human mind. This makes it possible to conceive of doctrinal formulations as directly continuous with revelation as summaries of deductions from revealed truths. These formulations are supposed to be permanently valid. Once a doctrine is properly stated and explained, there is no need ever to change the mode of expression.

The identity of the Church within this classical framework is the hierarchical institution of salvation, human and divine. It funnels down from the supernatural level the grace which individual people need in order to rise upward. For example any identification of the Church with the 'City of God' leads to an immense exaltation of the ecclesiastical institution. The mission in this context is primarily the saving of individual souls. While the Roman Catholic view is easily identified with the exaltation of ecclesiastical institution, the Protestant view is also not free from this tendency.

One consequence of the classical view for identity of the Church is its difficulty to account for the complexities of doctrinal development. Lindbeck notes that the difficulty of this view is how it is possible for historically opposed positions in some cases to be reconciled while remaining in themselves unchanged. Doctrinal reconciliation without capitulation is for him a coherent notion. Lindbeck's view is questioned by

Alister McGrath as accusing the classical view of having a crude correspondence theory of truth. McGrath says that such crudity is neither a necessary
consequence nor a precondition of the cognitive approach to doctrine. The
criticism of the classical view is right where it is assumed that the
supernatural revelation transmits conceptual knowledge by means of
propositions. His contention is that it is possible to give a cognitive account
of experience without in any sense reducing experience to propositional
form or degenerating into literalism.

> Lindbeck has provided a valuable corrective to deficient
> cognitive models of doctrine. Nevertheless, not all cognitive
> theories of doctrine are vulnerable in this respect. It is necessary
> to make a clear distinction between the view that an exhaustive
> and unambiguous account of God is transmitted conceptually
> by propositions on the one hand, and the view that there is a
> genuinely cognitive dimension, component or element to
> doctrinal statements on the other. Doctrinal statements need not
> be - and, as I shall argue in the following chapter, should not be
> -treated as purely cognitive statements.[30]

McGrath's contention that doctrine has a genuinely cognitive
dimension, component or element would not be denied by Lindbeck.
Lindbeck asserts that a religious utterance acquires the propositional truth
of ontological correspondence only so far as it is a performance, an act or
deed, which helps that correspondence[31]. It is not the lack of a cognitive

---

[30] MCGRATH, Alister. The Genesis of Doctrine. Basil Blackwell, Oxford,
1990, p20.

[31] LINDBECK, George. The Nature of Doctrine. SPCK, London, 1984,
p65.

dimension, as objected to by McGrath, that is the problem but the preference for performance.[32]

ii. Experience

A response trying to overcome difficulties in the classical view of doctrine is that doctrines are not important propositionally in themselves, but are only symbols of deeper experience which could be articulated in other contemporary ways. This approach is said to be most prominent in Western theology from the time of Schleiermacher. The location of faith according to this trend is within the realm of human religious subjectivity. One result of this response is to see doctrine as human reflection, a secondary activity. Therefore doctrine is not crucial for religious agreement or disagreement which are constituted by harmony or conflict in underlying feelings, attitudes or practice rather than by what happens on the level of symbolic objectifications.[33] Thus doctrine can alter without change of meanings, and conversely religiously significant meanings can vary while doctrines remain the same.

The departure point of Schleiermacher from the classical position was the refusal of the cognitive element in revelation. Revelation according to Schleiermacher is present in immediate self-consciousness. Christian doctrine is the expression given to the self-consciousness and derived from

---

[32] Lindbeck's view of truth has been criticised for its purely pragmatic signification of propositional truth, and for a failure, according to some modes of thought, to adequately resolve the issues of relativism and fideism. See O'NEIL, Colman. The Rule Theory of Doctrine and Propositional Truth and TRACY, David, Lindbeck's New Program for Theology, The Thomist, Vol.49, No3, July, 1985, p417-442, and 460-472.

[33] LINDBECK, George. The Nature of Doctrine. p17.

the self-proclamation of Christ. This view of doctrine is classified by Lindbeck as experiential-expressivist theory of doctrine.

The 'experiential-expressive' theory of doctrine is grounded in the context of modern western thought. It is fostered by the social pressures of the period and today in addition seems more compelling as it provides a rationale for interreligious dialogue. Interreligious dialogue is considerably assisted by the suggestion that the various religions are diverse expressions of a common core experience.

Lindbeck argues that the assertion that various religions are diverse symbolizations of one and the same core experience of the ultimate, is ultimately an axiom - an unverifiable hypothesis. This hypothesis could be credible if it were possible to isolate a common core experience from religious language and behaviour and demonstrate that the latter two are articulations of, or responses to, the former[34].

Lindbeck's criticism of doctrine referring to private prereflective experience underlying all religions appears to be fair. The principle is that insofar as doctrines function as non-discursive symbols, they are polyvalent in import and therefore subject to change of meaning [35]. But McGrath points out the weakness in Lindbeck's criticism of the experiential view of doctrine as being that it does not discriminate between two different experiential approaches to doctrine.

> Christian doctrine according to Schleiermacher does not concern some 'prereflective experience' common to all religions but concerns the distinctively Christian experience of Jesus of Nazareth. Schleiermacher draws a clear distinction between

[34] LINDBECK, George. The Nature of Doctrine. p128.

[35] LINDBECK, George. The Nature of Doctrine. p17.

human religious consciousness in general, and the specifically Christian consciousness. It is this specifically Christian 'feeling' or 'apprehension of an immediate existential relationship' deriving from Jesus of Nazareth, that Schleiermacher identifies as the referent of Christian doctrine.[36]

Schleiermacher relates doctrine not to private but corporate Christian piety. Christian piety never arises independently and of itself in an individual but only out of the communion and in the communion. The communal takes priority over the individual in Schleiermacher because the doctrine expresses an experience which has been constituted by the language of the Christian community. Such a distinction is lacking in the experiential-expressive approach as expounded and criticized by Lindbeck. It is, on the other hand, in line with the position of Stephen Sykes.

At a time of religious controversy or change, the tendency appears to be towards what Stephen Sykes calls the imperial instincts of the intellectual tradition[37]. This has led to a definition of Christianity in terms of external verbal criteria, the permanence and durability of a specific quantum of 'hard matter'[38]. To insist on an identity in external formulae is unhistorical and ignores the inside dimension of Christianity[39]. Therefore he concludes:

> I should want, therefore, to defend the threefold expression of the ground occupied by Christianity in the following way: it is, necessarily, a series of propositions, constituting an external

---

[36] MCGRATH, Alister. The Genesis of Doctrine. 1989, p25.

[37] SYKES, Stephen. The Identity of Christianity. SPCK, London, 1984, p32.

[38] SYKES, Stephen. The Identity of Christianity. p133.

[39] SYKES, Stephen. The Identity of Christianity. p50.

expression in story, myth and doctrine. But this external expression is interrelated with the internal experience of new life inseparable from the story, myth and doctrine....It is in the process of interaction between this inward element and the external forms of Christianity that the identity of Christianity consists.[40]

One insight in Sykes's proposal is that the identity of Christianity is not to be sought in uniformity. The inherent ambiguities in Christianity reflect the different strands of tradition and can be appealed to for different views. Conflict is to be expected because of maintaining the purity of Christian faith but unity can be achieved by containment of conflict within bounds and not by elimination.[41] It is vital to understand the complex nature of doctrine to sustain the identity of Christianity.

Doctrine in Schleiermacher had its ground in the emotions of the religious self-consciousness and it was derived from one source: the self-proclamation of Christ. What was given for consciousness was the work of Christ inwardly appropriated. The purpose of continuing conceptualization of faith within a community was to filter out impure statements of Christian piety. The difficulty with Schleiermacher's approach is the failure to provide an adequate account of doctrine as response to God by rejecting the cognitive as a constitutive element of revelation. Within this context the doctrine became the symbolization of the development of human consciousness.

In the light of the above two responses, it is important to ask how the uniting churches, after years of negotiation, did reach agreement that can

---

[40] SYKES, Stephen. The Identity of Christianity. p261.

[41] SYKES, Stephen. The Identity of Christianity. p212.

be theologically justified on matters of disputed doctrines. It could be argued that the agreement involves self-contradiction. The issue is constancy and change, unity and diversity. For example the comprehensiveness envisaged by the negotiators in India through the two union schemes is said to be a kind of synthesis of the divergent post-Reformation traditions of the West.[42] The scheme appears to be the mere juxtaposition of views, and mirrors the impact of Hinduism, because doctrinal disputes are not of great interest to Indian Christians. The example often cited is that within Hinduism any doctrine is tolerated and the same is true about the CNI.

The underlying idea behind such criticism is that the idea of doctrinal purity ought to be the deciding factor for theological justification for union. This obviously implies that unity in India is by compromise and not by adherence to truth. Therefore there is a lack of depth and dynamism in the union. It is important to show how the church can avoid laying itself open to the charge of providing a refuge for intellectual dishonesty and ecclesiological hypocrisy. In the light of difficulty of doctrinal reconciliation on the basis of two theories of doctrines, as discussed above, it is worth considering an alternative theory of doctrine as suggested by George Lindbeck. He suggests that his account of doctrine approximates a pattern of reasoning often found in ecumenical agreements. Therefore in the

---

[42] The Derby Report commented that the South India scheme should have been more Indian and more radical. THE DERBY REPORT: THE SOUTH INDIA CHURCH SCHEME. A Report of a Committee of Theologians appointed by the Archbishop of Canterbury to consider the Proposed Basis of Union and Constitution of the future Church of South India. London, 1946.

following section the 'Rule Theory' is considered as a possibility for theological validation of the principle of plurality of doctrine within limits.

iii. Rule Theory

In contrast to the classical and experiential view of doctrine, George Lindbeck has proposed a regulative theory. He argues that a functional view helps to accommodate plurality of doctrine. Doctrine according to Lindbeck is not generally a set of first order propositions but a set of second order rules of speech. The doctrines have a regulative function like rules of grammar determining the manner in which first order statements about reality are made but without being themselves the first order statements.

The rule theory locates the abiding and doctrinal significance not in propositionally formulated truths or inner experience but in the story it tells and in the grammar that informs the way the story is told and used. The change in experience is not opposed to continuity but is a mark of vitality. In Lindbeck's terms, truth is considered as the intelligibility of the categories in terms of which a particular vision of reality is framed. Intrasystematic truth is the structural coherence of a symbol system, coherence being determined by the system's ability to order the experience of life. The structural coherence of any system of meaning is defined largely by the rules which govern its functioning.

A fundamental element in this understanding of doctrine and its attendant theory of truth is the concept of intrasystematic consistency. The doctrine regulates religions in much the same way as grammar regulates language. Lindbeck illustrates this with reference to Shakespeare's Hamlet:

the statement 'Denmark is the land where Hamlet lived' makes no claim to ontological truth or falsity but is simply a statement concerning the internal ordering of the elements of Shakespeare's narrative.

To become Christian involves becoming skilled in the language, the symbol system, of a given religion. It also involves learning the story of Israel and of Jesus well enough to interpret and experience oneself and one's world in its terms. The supposition is that different religious systems produce fundamentally divergent depth experiences of what it is to be human. The story and doctrine of a religion are the medium in which one moves, a set of skills that one employs in living one's life. In this context the doctrine functions as the abiding grammar which informs and shapes a community's faith. In effect prior socialization into a social and cultural setting is the necessary prerequisite for even having something entitled to the rank of inner experience.[43]

Lindbeck has made an attempt in Rule Theory to reverse the relation between inner and outer experience. Instead of deriving external features of a religion from inner experience, it is inner experiences which are viewed as derivative. It is understandable if it is noted that Lindbeck's concern is that the liberal tradition has surrendered the distinctiveness of Christianity, and his cultural-linguistic model can provide grounding for self-identity of Christianity. While the over-emphasis distorts the complementarity between inner and outer experience in any particular truth claim, one implication of the Rule Theory is attention to the rôle of doctrine in shaping the religious

---

[43] LINDBECK, George. The Nature of Doctrine. p37.

orientations of the communities and the understanding of doctrine for interdenominational dialogue.[44]

The rule theory gives a non-reductive framework for discussion among those who disagree. Such a view of doctrine is consistent with a wide range of particular theological positions, just as a vast variety of specific sentences may be generated within the grammar of one language. It has this advantage over the propositionalist view. The presupposition of the latter is that if doctrine is once true, it is always true, and if it is once false, it is always false. Therefore agreement can be reached between two parties if one or both sides abandon their earlier positions. Lindbeck's proposal is that doctrines function as rules. The rules retain an invariant meaning under changing conditions of compatibility and conflict.

> Rules, unlike propositions or expressive symbols, retain an in-variant meaning under changing conditions of compatibility and conflict. For example, the rules 'Drive on the left' and 'Drive on the right' are unequivocal in meaning and unequivocally opposed, yet both may be binding, one in Britain and the other in the United States, or one when traffic is normal, and the other when collision must be avoided....There is no logical problem in understanding how historically opposed positions

---

[44] McGrath discusses the social function of doctrine. The doctrine of justification was a criterion of social cohesiveness in 16th century Lutheran-ism in its formative stage but it has that function no longer as that which was essential to the self-definition of Lutherans. To engage in dialogue is not to bargain on concessions but to look for insights that may be veiled by historical or cultural forms and to recognize certain specific contingent historical circumstance that led to the perception that a given doctrine is of normative importance for the self-definition of a community in that situation. The doctrine does not cease to be true but only assumes a different social function. MCGRATH, Alister. The Genesis of Doctrine, p46.

can in some, even if not all cases, be reconciled while remaining in themselves unchanged. Contrary to what happens when doctrines are constructed as propositions or expressive symbols, doctrinal reconciliation without capitulation is a coherent notion.[45]

One helpful implication of the functional view of doctrine is the possibility of holding a plurality of doctrines within an agreed framework. The method of approach during the negotiation in north India seemed to be in line with a functional view of doctrine without being aware of such a view as a theory of doctrine. The method was to note the different beliefs, to wrestle with differences, and then to agree on fundamentals. For example the CNI distinguishes the two practices of infant and believer's baptism. It firmly recognizes the difference of conviction. Some believe that the baptism of infants is in harmony with the mind of the Lord and others believe that only those who are consciously aware of their faith may properly be baptized. Both are recognized as alternative practices in the CNI, but in relation to both a Christian upbringing is visualized as a common ground and vital for the Church. And again it is categorically admitted that the dedicated child before being baptized and the baptized child before being admitted as a communicant must give evidence of repentance and of faith and love towards Jesus Christ, and at their baptism/confirmation make profession of faith before the congregation. Similarly the Lutheran-Catholic dialogue. The opposed parties engage not in compromise but in a common search. Most of the documents might be construed as embodying the 'grammar' of Christianity divided between opposed parties during and after

---

[45] LINDBECK, George. The Nature of Doctrine. p18.

the Reformation, and showing that what is at stake are distinct but doctrinally compatible models of growth and change.[46]

A functionalist view of doctrine as second order is true in the way that allx2 human life and creation is derived from and refers to God. But the language is a rich medium of God's relation to creation. If doctrine is the language of the Christian community, Lindbeck appears to treat the Christian language as something given whereas the language develops and is partly susceptible to historical analysis. While the rule theory is provocative and useful, it is unable to account for the subtlety and the range of ways in which doctrine can be handled. Lindbeck seems to acknowledge this by identifying both propositional and modified propositional theories, and by recognizing the significance of two dimensional theories of doctrine espoused by Karl Rahner and Bernard Lonergan which combine both cognitive and experiential elements.[47]

The Rule Theory has advantages over the conventional objective approach to doctrine and also the views which trade on the relativity of all theological efforts, but the weakness of rule theory is the stress on the theological intelligibility coming from skill, not theory, and credibility coming from good performance, not adherence to independently formulated

---

[46] LUTHERAN-ROMAN CATHOLIC CONVERSATIONS. The Malta Report 1972. The Eucharist 1978. Ways to Community 1980. All Under One Christ 1980. The Ministry in the Church 1981. In: MEYER, Harding and VISCHER, Lukas. Eds. Growth in Agreement: Reports and Agreed Statements of Ecumenical Conversations on a World Level. WCC, Geneva. 1984, p167-276.

[47] LINDBECK, George. The Nature of Doctrine. p79f, p16f.

criteria.[48] His insistence on doctrine being reflective and second order activity plays down its capacity to affirm first order truth claims.

> To say that doctrines are rules is not to deny that they involve propositions...These are however, second-order rather than first-order propositions and affirm nothing about extra-linguistic or extra-human reality. For a rule theory, in short, doctrines qua doctrines are not first-order propositions, but are to be construed as second-order ones: they make, as was said in the final section of the previous chapter, intrasystematic rather than ontological truth claims.[49]

iv. Critique of the rule Theory

Lindbeck's theory is concerned with the question of the 'function' to the neglect of the 'whence' of doctrine. He does not adequately address how these two might be related. Therefore David Ford suggests that Lindbeck's preference for rules might need to be corrected in the direction of a more thorough integration of rules, categories and content. He comments that the one-sidedness lies in its suggested downgrading of the knowledge content in Christian worship and life, and the displacement of the ontological truth question into a practical question as to 'how well it organizes the data of Scripture and tradition with a view to their use in Christian worship and life'. He criticizes Lindbeck for transcending the relativistic limitations of the cultural-linguistic approach in one-sidedly practical terms and suggests a correction of this would involve a locus-oriented theology involving the coinherence of system, story and performance.

> In this there would be no neat distinction of first-order from second-order, and no avoiding of the challenge of contingent

---

[48] LINDBECK, George. <u>The Nature of Doctrine.</u> p131.

[49] LINDBECK, George. <u>The Nature of Doctrine.</u> p80.

particularity. Death is above all the contingency which is the end of all internalizing and externalizing of language and behaviour...In Christian theology the resurrection of Jesus informs and transforms systematic conceptions of ontology, of God, and of other doctrines; it establishes and illuminates the primacy of the story witnessing to Jesus; it liberates an explosion of new worship, community-building and prophetic speech and action, generating new particularity.[50]

One possible temptation that must be avoided in stating the faith in linguistic form is a commitment to any simplistic view of doctrine. David Tracy notes two major difficulties. The first is an overestimation of doctrine which seems to hold that doctrine's 'explicitness' and 'clarity' renders unnecessary any further concern with the concrete symbolic language upon which doctrine reflects. The second is to hold that doctrine is either an abstract or impoverished 'genre', or the assumption that a community does not need any explicitness or clarity to express its shared judgements on matters of belief.[51] Provided that the complex nature of doctrine is acknowledged then doctrine can be seen as a medium through which faith is expanded and the strength of the one-in-Christ bond is actualised in the Church. From this perspective one important aspect of doctrine is communication. Communication is to be understood not as a secondary or pragmatic matter but a necessary intermediate form. Doctrine as a mediated form of communication is a network of regulative statements.

The task of ecumenical ecclesiology is to track down the regulative

---

[50] FORD, David. System, Story, Performance: A Proposal about the Role of Narrative in Christian Systematic Theology. In: HAUERWAS, Stanley and JONES, Gregory L. eds. Why Narrative? Eerdmans, 1989, p 215.

[51] TRACY, David. Analogical Imagination. SCM, London, 1981, p293.

statements of ecclesiology without being too rigid in fixing the boundaries[52]. Therefore any attempt at over-formalization in fixed linguistic forms or relativization of doctrine represents a distortion of the complexity of doctrine. In the classical view the danger was a drive to eliminate the contribution of contingency and human subjectivity; and in experiential theory the tendency is to infer that the doctrines do not refer to an objective personal God.

Stephen Pickard in his doctoral dissertation argues for the role of doctrine or fundamental articles as a necessary intermediate form.[53] His inquiry is in search of foundations that are rooted in God. The foundations that are rooted in God have the capacity continually to disrupt what is stable and conventional in favour of fresh and surprising orderings of reality. The fundamental articles are a specialized form in which the general character of doctrine receives its most focused and determinate form as a maximal concentration of the truth of the ecclesial bond.

Pickard notes that doctrinal concentrations which are maximally economic in their informativeness are also subject to ossification when the truth stated in such concentration is obscured. This can occur when pragmatism intrudes into all areas of communication in the Church. So great care needs to be taken to avoid reductionism. Therefore he argues that the Rule Theory as a grammar of faith does not clarify how the life of the

---

[52] RITSCHL, Dietrich. The Logic of Theology. SCM, London, 1986.

[53] PICKARD, Stephen. 'The Purpose of Stating the Faith: An historical and systematic inquiry into the tradition of Fundamental Articles with special reference to Anglicanism'. Ph.D. dissertation, Durham University, 1990.

Church is energized in relation to the presence of God, and he has proposed an understanding of statements of faith as communications through which the strength of the one-in-Christ bond is actualized in the Church.

According to Pickard communication is not a secondary matter because such a view betrays a lack of confidence in identifying the rationale for theology in the Church. Theological discourse operates within a relation of proximity to what is given and is directed towards its appropriation at the level of language. The supposition here is that there is a fundamental form of relation between God and human beings which is not readily expressible.

> Doctrine grasps this form, not at some 'remove', but from within this relation. That such grasping is inadequate or rather incomplete, is not simply a result of distortion caused by human refraction. Rather, incompleteness arises precisely because theology can only ever mediate with the same quality as those other intermediate categories for God's presence.[54]

The underlying idea in the suggestion of Pickard is that theology involves response from within a relation to God. The nature of this relation is difficult to specify as the mediation of the relation is the mediation of plenitude concentrated in Christ and experienced by humankind as God's superabundance of grace. It has recurred as the Trinitarian concept in the history of Christian theology.

One interesting aspect of Pickard's suggestion is that the genre of doctrine is intended to have the quality of being a maximally economic and informative communication of truth. When doctrine is over-formalized or relativized, it leads to distortion. It is distorted as the attempt is made to fix

---

[54] PICKARD, p316.

it in particular formulae or to transpose it altogether into the region of consciousness. Therefore to generate variety, spontaneity and openness to function as a genuine intermediate form is possible if doctrine has a mediating function in relation to God, human beings and the world.

It could be said in line with Barth that there is the affirmation of correspondence between what is real and its linguistic forms. For Barth, correspondence is derived from the action of God as Trinity. Theological statements have their truth from Him and not in themselves. It is a linguistic overflow of God's presence.

> There is no point in dogmatic thinking and speaking if in it all systematic clarity and certainty is not challenged by the fact that the content of the word of God is God's work and activity, and therefore God's free grace, which as such escape our comprehension and control, upon which, reckoning with it in faith, we can only mediate, and for which we can only hope.[55]

Doctrine thus construed with a correspondence to the Trinity represents a compressed linguistic form which Pickard calls 'maximally economic communication of information'. It operates as both summary of narrative and as catalyst for extended discourse. The narratives provide the raw material for more discursive theological programmes. It is exemplified in the writings of Karl Barth. David Ford refers to Barth's doctrine of God as a metaphysics of the Gospel story.[56] The doctrine in such endeavour is aimed at a better understanding and recollection of story. It is the story that

---

[55] BARTH, Karl. Church Dogmatics. Vol.1/2, T & T Clark, Edinburgh, p868.

[56] FORD, David. Barth's Interpretation of the Bible. In: SYKES, Stephen W. ed. Karl Barth: Studies in his Theological Methods, Clarendon Press, Oxford, 1979, p55-87.

provides the criteria for doctrinal formulation to decide between alternatives. Thus doctrine can be understood as a network of regulative statements. As Ritschl says, the regulative statement for the doctrine of the Church is 'YHWH has chosen the people of Israel from all the nations and in Jesus Christ has chosen the church from Jews and all Gentiles.'[57]

An excessive concern for definition in the interests of fixing boundaries for acceptable belief for institutional stability might ignore the directional thrust of Christian faith. But where directional thrust comes into focus, the doctrine functions as a medium through which the plenitude of God's own being could be expressed. Such a thrust does not obliterate boundary making activities but significantly modifies how boundaries ought to be conceived. The boundaries could no longer operate as barriers to communication but as facilitators of communication, the necessary precondition for further enlargement of understanding. Then doctrine becomes a medium through which God's creating and redeeming love is witnessed to, and functions as a genuine intermediate form through which the bond of being one in Christ is communicated.

v. The Place of Doctrine in the CNI

Christian doctrine is what the Church believes and teaches. It takes the form of a statement of faith. But it would be wrong to identify doctrine with a statement of faith because there is no common agreement about what the fundamentals are even though contemporary ecumenism invokes the notion of fundamentals. A fine example of this is the formulation of the

---

[57] RITSCHL, Dietrich. The Logic of Theology. p124.

Chicago-Lambeth Quadrilateral, adopted by the house of Anglican Bishops in Chicago in 1886 and by the Lambeth Conference of 1888. The four elements of this statement were Scripture, the Creeds, two Sacraments and the Episcopate; and these were reiterated throughout the negotiation period in north India. On the surface such a statement was highly desirable and was even helpful for negotiation among the churches. But the fact is that there is no precision in the content of the fundamentals. It can have many meanings when applied to Christian doctrine.[58] To evoke the notion of fundamentals for the unity in essentials but freedom in all matters non-essential is good, but difficult, since it is not easy to draw the line between essentials and non-essentials.

When doctrine functions as an intermediate form to communicate the bond of being one-in-Christ, then the question is to inquire into those ways in which people are held together. This is a life which makes a total claim upon the believers in a community. In that community consensus is the ideal and is to be pursued to the end through a basic core of beliefs. This idea found general agreement among the negotiating churches of North India. In the course of negotiation the concept of consensus was construed with minimal orientation to the past and with maximum openness towards further determination.

This implies two perspectives: 'actual' and 'ideal'. The latter means

---

[58] SYKES, Stephen and BOOTY, J. eds. The Study of Anglicanism. SPCK, London, 1988. p232. Sykes quotes the comment of William Palmer of Worcester College, Oxford, 1838, that the term 'fundamental' is capable of so many meanings as applied to Christian doctrine, and it actually is, has been, and must continue to be, in so great a diversity of senses, that it is morally impossible to avoid perplexity while it is employed in controversy.

belief in fundamentals which are eschatological, being open to the future. This is a vital element for the doctrinal identity of the Church because the bond of being one-in-Christ is not a disembodied spirituality, but life in a visible fellowship; and this corporate belief is constituted in the expectation of God's future salvation. While the roots of this expectation lie in the past and are reflected in the actual consensus, the resurrection of Jesus draws the Church into the future. This makes demands on God's pilgrim people and points to the fact that the Church is a social reality. The social reality of the Church is significant in so far as it is the locus of redeemed sociality.

The former perspective - 'actual' - means belief in actual agreement by the negotiating churches expressed through the statement of faith. This statement acknowledges that the fellowship of the life of the Church is grounded in Christ. But Christ is in close fellowship with God the Father and the Holy Spirit - the Comforter. Here was the assumption of the doctrine of the church being rooted in the unity of the Godhead, which is expressed in the redemption achieved in Jesus Christ and sustained in the activity of the Paraclete. This implied doctrine of the Trinity in the statement of faith of the CNI is the basic grammar of Christian unity. It arose in the past as a way of explicating the language of the Christian community which is expressed through the biblical story. The Trinitarian conception of God is depicted within the overall context of history and creation. The Church's identity can only be conceived within the overall mission of the Son and the Spirit through the Father.

This primary constitutive element of the doctrine is related to the activity of the Father, the Son and the Holy Spirit. It is a particular confession but includes what God has done for the world in creation. In other words the united church acknowledges in its statement of faith the worship of one God - Father, Son and Holy Spirit. An acknowledgement of the doctrine of the Trinity in the statement of faith of the CNI does not necessarily solve the divisions in the Church but is a pointer to reconsider the traditional images of communion. For example,

> 'Father-only' images are associated with power-lust and domination; 'Jesus-only' images with moralistic activism or individualistic pietism; 'Spirit-only' images with introspective escapism or charismatic excess. The conceptions of the Church derived from attention to one person of the Trinity only do tend to give rise to a variety of spiritual ills. In the being of God, Father, Son and Spirit are what they are only by virtue of their relations with each other; does not our ecclesiology equally require attention to trinitarian perichoresis?[59]

By asserting that relationship is based on the nature of a God who is triune, it is confessed that disunity is a sign of failure of relationship within the Church. The call is to be a reconciling community on the basis of living the life of God. Relationships in the churches often reflect those in societies - impersonal, broken, self-centred. The need to reconcile should arise from the image of self-giving, which is the essence of the triune God. One important question is: if the doctrine of the Trinity is the basis then how is God the three in One related to the actual historical and visible community?

> We ground the being of the Church in the source of the being of all things, the eternal energies of the three persons of the Trinity as they are in perichoretic interrelation. The primary echoes of that being are to be heard in the ways of God to the

---

[59] BRITISH COUNCIL OF CHURCHES. Report of the British Council of Churches Study Commission on Trinitarian Doctrine Today. London, 1989, p28.

world in creation and the perfection of that creation in both Jesus and the Spirit.[60]

To relate the triune God to the historical community is to uncover the presence and action of God in an ongoing relationship with human life. That would require a need to reconsider the fundamental theoretical and normative conceptions frequently used in theology. For example in the Christian notion of God, there has been a tendency to monarchianism by stressing the unity and sovereignty of God. The result of this is that the norms for the performance of life are closely determined. Focusing attention on the Trinitarian life of God is to realize the complex dynamic order which constitutes God's unity. This is His active self-structuring relationship with human social life in a world which is complex, changeable and contingent.

c. Institution

The Church, having a historical existence, bears in itself an impetus towards institutionalization. The impetus toward institutionalization exists in any group which desires any kind of permanence. In remembering the story of Israel and Jesus there is brought to mind the sequence of events which establish a community in history, but which at the same time break all attempts to confine the presence of God to rigid institutional conditions. On the one hand the tendency to an excessive claim for institutionalization leads to an institutional sacralization and enforces uniformity; on the other hand excessive concern for individualism creates the spirit of anti-

---

[60] GUNTON, Colin E. The Church on Earth. In: GUNTON, Colin E. and HARDY, Daniel W. eds. On Being the Church. T&T Clark, Edinburgh, 1989, p78.

institutionalism which distorts the image of the community.

Therefore an adequate theological view of institutionality would have to take into account both its indispensability and its relativity. Institutionality is necessary to maintain order, but it ought to move beyond the purely pragmatic level. It should manifest the creating work of God, and so order the life of the community as to guard against threatening activities.

The Church as a historical institution displays characteristics and institutional problems similar to other social groups. The idea of being content with a story and doctrine of being one in Christ without insights into the institutional aspect, would lead to indulgence in ecumenical docetism. The Church possesses forms in which it expresses some of the essentials of faith. The form is always in interaction with its environment. The kind of interaction which takes place exerts influence on the internal structure. For example, the conversion of Constantine in 312 led to an organisational merger with immeasurable effects on the future of the Church. The Church came to terms with the Roman empire which was highly centralized and bureaucratic after the reform of Diocletian (284-305). The old loose organisation of the Church had to accommodate itself to political realities. Similarly the Reformation brought a crisis to the medieval church by stressing the priesthood of believers and justification by faith.

The form of church order has been shaped by various cultures. For example, the eighteenth century English Bishop who stayed in London for nine months of the year to fulfil his duties in the House of Lords by supporting the party that had appointed him to his see, is not easily recognizable as a successor of the apostles.[61]

The Church as a social reality is subject to the contingencies, limitations and influences of the society in which it lives. The structure of the Church must provide those dimensions and opportunities to participate in the mission of the Church in the contemporary world that are demanded by faith. What is needed is a positive appraisal of the institutional identity of the church that should be true to the story. My object in the following section is to consider both the indispensability and relativity of institutionality drawing attention to two institutional aspects of the Church: 'ministry' and 'management'.

i. Ministry

The church union negotiators had to come to grips with the emergence of different forms of order in the history of Christianity. They had to cope with the different terms such as bishop, minister, pastor, priest, presbyter, elder, deacon. In the New Testament one can trace different words expressing different forms of ministry. The word <u>hiereus</u> (priest) is used once of a pagan priest, many times of Jewish priests, and in the Epistle to the Hebrews, of Christ (Heb.4:14,5:6). Hebrews draws attention to the fact that there is but one perfect Priest.

Another common word is <u>episkopos</u> (supervisor). It is a very loaded word. All the major denominations have <u>episkopoi</u> including the Baptists who call them superintendents. The word itself does not provide any

---

[61] MACQUARRIE, John. <u>Theology, Church and Ministry</u>. SCM, London, 1986, p155.

support for diocesan bishops or the Baptist superintendents. But all can bring their presuppositions to supplement the facts. Yet another word is presbuteros which is commonly rendered in English as 'elder' or 'presbyter'. In view of the Jewish background and the general tendency in society to give respect and honour to the older men, the word may mean the senior people in the community.[62]

The negotiators also had to cope with the feature of ambivalence in the Indian situation. On the one hand the institutional expression of Christianity was viewed in circles like the Rethinking Group as artificial. That view is accompanied by the opinion that the Church has failed both in proclaiming and living the Gospel. The vision of a non-institutional Church was not new in India but acceptance of such a view would have been a failure to take historical existence seriously.

On the other hand the Church is a body, a community and therefore an institution. An institution ensures the identity and continuity of a community in history. This can take different forms. It could be preserved either by fixing forms of life as good and permanent ones, or by adapting those forms to new conditions of life or even replacing them by new ones to serve the purpose of the common good.

The negotiators tried to weave three forms of church government into its institutional structure. They were episcopal, presbyterian and congregational. The guiding factor was the Chicago-Lambeth Quadrilateral. The inclusion of the historic episcopate in the Chicago-Lambeth

---

[62] HUDSON, D.F., Diakonia and Its Cognates in the New Testament. Indian Journal of Theology. April-June, 1965, Vol.14, No.2, pp138-147.

quadrilateral meant that episcopacy was an issue in any negotiation where Anglicans were involved. In the course of time a consensus among the negotiating churches in north India was developed; that the historic episcopate in a modified form was a desirable element in the ordering of Church life.

The CNI accepted a centralized, hierarchical and bureaucratic structure. Its Constitution placed power in the hands of the Synod and its executive committee.[63] The Report of the Evaluation Commission of 1990 confirms this:

> Planning for Church Union was a good opportunity for the Indian Church to find an alternative organizational and administrative church structure suited to Indian conditions. But unfortunately, the church leaders took the easiest course by borrowing the concepts and thought-patterns of the West.... By rapidly changing the structures, it would have been possible for the CNI to set the pace and become independent of the West in terms of action and thought.[64]

In the light of this report the CNI must take seriously the question of the meaning of the church as an institution. Being a community in history, the Church cannot avoid some form of order and organisation. The purpose of order is to fulfil a particular task in a particular time and is meant to

---

[63] The organ of the whole Church, comprising all Dioceses is the Synod, which is the supreme, supervisory, legislative and executive body of the Church and final authority in all matters pertaining to the Church. THE CHURCH OF NORTH INDIA. Constitution of the CNI. Clause I, ISPCK, 1987, p92.

[64] THE CHURCH OF NORTH INDIA. Profile of A Christian Church: Report of the Evaluation Commission To Study The Life and Work of the CNI. Institute for the Development of Education, Madras, 1990, p73.

serve rather than to rule. Therefore it can be altered and or replaced. Nobody can doubt the question of authority within 'a community of faith' if the guiding principle is: 'whoever wants to be first must be the slave of all' (Mk.10:44). The validity of authority in the church lies in serving. Those who give themselves in service have authority because they do so, and such service has the ability to awaken trust within a community.

The key issue is not the order itself but the authority implied and expressed through its different forms. In the present united context, the renewed sense of the priesthood of the laity transcending different confessional barriers has the opportunity to grow in strength. The uniting churches laid down, in conformity with the teaching of the New Testament, that the Church is a royal priesthood of believers. No individual and no one order can claim exclusive possession of this priesthood. 'The Church is a royal priesthood of believers, all its members have direct access to God, and all the members have their share in the commission and authority of the whole church.'[65] To the whole church and to every member of it belong the duty and privilege of spreading the Good News, and to share in that service of God which is the church's ministry.

The great characteristic of all Christian diakonia (ministry or service) is that it is a responsibility laid upon every baptized member of His body. In the New Testament two principal terms are used to speak of the servant of Christ, doulos (slave) and diakonos (servant). The former refers to status and the latter refers to function. Christian ministry as doulos or diakonos

---

[65] THE CHURCH OF NORTH INDIA. The Constitution of the Church of North India and Bye Laws. ISPCK, Delhi, 1987, p20.

is something that is not accidental to the Christian but essential.

The dominance of sociological factors over theological has often led to the obscuring of the servant function in the development of order in the Church. While nobody in theory would disagree with this, in practice its application in the real context of ministry is often the opposite as when the attention is given to the title 'Reverend' or 'Most Reverend'; this is somewhat incongruous when seen in the context of diakonia.

Basically diakonia is concerned with doing things for other people. It could be sharing with them with the gift of the Gospel or giving food or providing counselling. Diakonia is grounded in the earthly Jesus (Mk.10:42-45, Mt.20:25-28, Lk.22:25-27, Jn.13:1-17). The ministry of Jesus was one of service. John Macquarrie suggests that one of the ancient orders of ministry in the Christian church was the diaconate, and it symbolizes for us the obscure unspectacular service that is very much at the heart of Christian ministry. Then he says that it is our unwillingness to be merely obscure servants that has led to the decline of the diaconate and its reduction to a temporary stage in ministry.[66]

In the context of ministry the word which has great content and which is not only derived from the words of Jesus but also from his own action is diakonos (servant). The secularization of society, and the stress on the responsibility of the laity has led to the radical questioning of the present form of ministry. One positive aspect of this is that it has forced us

---

[66] MACQUARRIE, John. Theology, Church and Ministry, SCM, London, 1986, p160.

to look beyond the sociological accidents of ministry to its theological essence.

The content of ministry is derived from the self-giving of God Himself. Diakonia is unique because the Lord Himself has come in the form of a servant. The famous hymn in Philippians 2:5-11 presents a challenge to those who aspire for power in the ministry. Jesus being on equal terms with God, assumed the role of a servant. Such a picture means self-emptying rather than the grasping of authority. Jesus pursued his mission to the point of self-giving. This is a testimony to God's action in Jesus of Nazareth. The fact is that it was in lowliness that God revealed himself as God. It implies that in being prepared to be lowly, the Church can be a witness to the majesty of God.

From the beginning of negotiations the distinctive calling of the diaconate was emphasized; but the continuing of this form of diaconate as a step to the ordained ministry still prevails. One answer to this seems to be in the direction of restoring diaconate as a permanent state. One example is that the Second Vatican Council in 1964 decreed a permanent diaconate. The ordained deacon is not merely a probationer under training for office but a proper and permanent member of the hierarchy. The permanent diaconate is a restored intermediate order between the higher ranks of the Church hierarchy and the rest of the people of God. But diakonia is to be seen as embracing church efforts in service to the community and the world, and neither as a step toward clerical status nor a permanent diaconate of intermediate order. All service (whether of) ordained ministers or the laity is of equal importance before God.

The ministry as servanthood is unique in Christianity and not necessarily connected with any formal religious office. As long as servant remains the primary model for Christian ministry, then the question of status remains awkward. This brings into focus that corps of commissioned people of God who exercise their servanthood in their vocation. So the ministry cannot be construed in the context of a hierarchical order but as a parallel order exercised according to its respective calls. This is to adopt a doctrine of parity. But the doctrine of parity of ministers must not be confused with there being no difference in function. The people will be set apart and commissioned to exercise their function with the understanding that no ministry is higher than any other. Function to act as commissioned by the Church is a solemn act within the grace of God. The continual temptation to associate function with hierarchy must be avoided.

A further difficult task is how to render service within the power-structures of society. On the one hand the Church is tempted to use worldly power in order to secure the success of its service. The Church is and needs to be aware that the needs of people are bound up with the injustice inherent in the national and international social, economic and political structures of the society. The Church is tempted to build up power structures to exert pressure to attain its ends. On the other hand it has to face the temptation to restrict itself to the ministry of Word and Sacraments. The Church can retreat into an area where it would not come into conflict with the power-structures of society. Service would then take the form of inward religious concern. But in either case the Church would deflect the real force of Christian witness.

Thomas Torrance in discussing this says that difficult though it is, there is two-fold ministry which is 'the service of the Word' and 'the service of response to the Word.'[67] The service of the Word is the ministry of Word and Sacrament and the service of response to the Word is the ministry of divine mercy, but both are a <u>diakonia</u>. These two ministries are complementary and mutually dependent. A recovery of authentic <u>diakonia</u> would require a theological reconstruction of the organizational and administrative structure of the CNI.

Paternalism was supposed to be the basis of missionary ideology that had shaped the institutional identity of the Church in India. The frequent criticism of paternalism was that it served the purposes of church authority and assumed that it knew what was best for the other. There was no reciprocal interchange between the missionary and the people. Therefore autonomy became one of the slogans of the church union movement in India. The dream was for an autonomy that would command respect. It was achieved through the formation of a united and autonomous Church, but the gradual ascendency of autonomy over paternalism within the CNI must take into account the voices of the laity, the marginalized and the women of Indian society.

The Church as a community has an active part to play in the formation and development of the institution. It was discussed earlier that story is essential to the formation of ecclesial identity, and that there needs to be a visible form in which the community's remembering of the story of Israel, Jesus and the early Church could be expressed. Formation of the Institution is a creative process for which human beings are responsible.

---

[67] TORRANCE, T.F. Service in Jesus Christ.<u>In:</u> McCORD, J.I. and PARKER, T.H.L. <u>eds.</u> <u>Service In Christ</u>. p1-16, Epworth Press, 1966.

Institutions are not merely there to be encountered but to take into account the dynamics of institutionality. Effectiveness of the mission is dependent on the degree to which it can work within the culture of the society it serves. Management theory and practice are one cultural aspect of contemporary society and as such an inescapable element in the administration of the Church.

ii. Management

In any organization, people are involved, leaders emerge, decisions are made. The Church as an institution frequently squanders the full potential of human resources available to it because it appears to lack vision and to fail to utilize creatively research findings from the social sciences. The effectiveness of the mission of the Church is not separable from the degree to which it can work within a culture of the society. One weakness on the part of the Church lies in its supposed attitude that 'we have always done it in that way before'.

Management as one cultural aspect of the contemporary society needs to be taken seriously by the Church for the effectiveness of its mission. There are different theories of management.[68] But these have to be judged

---

[68] McGREGOR, D. The Human Side of Enterprise. McGraw Hill Company, 1960, p33. Theory X: It is the traditional theory of management. Douglas criticizes this theory as it adopts a carrot and stick theory of motivation and the new strategies of decentralization, democratic leadership are usually but old wine in new bottle because of inadequate assumptions about human nature. Theory Y. p47: It is the management by integration and self-control, the creation of conditions such that the members can achieve their goals. It places the problem squarely on the lap of management. In contrast to theory X and Y, WILLIAM, Ouchi G. has proposed a

according to how far they are appropriate for the churches. The classical view of management (Theory X) is the view of direction and control. It is the principle of control and manipulation of people in order to accomplish the goals of the organization. Implicit in this theory is a world view that the average man has an inherent dislike of work and will avoid it if he can.

Since the classical theory the focus of attention has shifted to the behaviour of people in working situations and relationships. The instinctive reaction of the people has been turned upside-down so that decision makers are many rather than one. Participation by all (Theory Y) is an attempt to integrate the needs of the individual and the goals of the organization to produce a model of cooperation for management. Implicit in this theory is a view of man which is more optimistic and gives a sense of responsibility.

The search for an acceptable approach to management is not complete but some important signposts are evident. The aim is to take a favourable and personal view of human nature. This emphasis matches the way in which people see the church as a human fellowship - a free and open gathering of believers. But it is also true that most church bodies have well developed bureaucratic agencies, controlling such functions as publication, mission, education, social service, investments and property. Implicit in this structure is the hierarchical order which refers to a regular system of

---

theory of management. Theory Z: How American business can meet the Japanese challenge. New York: Avon Books, 1981. It is team work. It emphasizes a participation approach to management with a holistic orientation that incorporates the involvement of people in all facets of the organization which looks for the long-term view of the workers.

subordination and rank within the organization. In a pejorative sense bureaucracy implies excessive formalism and rigidity.

Bureaucracy is unavoidable to some extent in a visible structure like the CNI as an organization. But what is important is to look at the structure and be ready to change it if such structure becomes obsolete. For example a managerial mode of authority has crept in some form into the praxis of the ministry and management of the Church. It can be discerned in the relation between the ministry of the people of God as a whole and the minority within the whole. The minority may be those who exercise an office either by ordination or through some form of authority within the hierarchy. In some quarters the minority seem to have taken the role of the managers who then go for authority on the basis of the traditional principle of control and manipulation of people (Theory X). Such a group of leaders fails to fill the rôle of the servants of Christ.

A right attitude to management is to try to create such conditions that members of the organization at all levels can best achieve their own goals by directing their efforts towards the goal of the organization. Since the emphasis in Christianity is on the salvation of the people, the management of people is a prime concern of the Church. The biblical basis of management can be defined on the principle of the priesthood of all believers. It involves belief in the abilities of the people and trust in their interdependence.

Leadership based on this principle creates trust between leaders and the people. For example, the disciples were trained first to be servants. They were servants long before they became leaders in the community. The scripture reminds us that the servants do not exalt themselves (Mt 20:25-27,

Lk 14:11). The bishops and pastors are not to be modern chief executive officers who sit at the apex of the hierarchical organization. They are supposed to be participants, one with the other. Jesus desired that his disciples be servant-leaders among the people equipped and trained, with the authority to fulfil the tasks of preaching, teaching and healing.

Legitimate authority is defined as the right of decision and command that one person has over others. It is approved by those in the organization; but power is a force which can be used to extract compliance and when used in this way ignores the psychological relationship that exists between persons. Authority should be granted to leaders through support from followers. It is exercised by virtue of the person's position in leadership but his power should be used to determine the goals of the organization as well as those of the people.

Pastoral authority is not a coercive authority such as a policeman or a judge. It is based on a leader's servant spirit which must manifest the compassion of Christ. The concept of the servant leadership could be abused if the leader sees himself as the servant of the people rather than the servant of God. The leader should look for the growth of the members as the people of God.

The Church as a theological institution is often at odds with its practices. There is a tension between polity and practice. In such a situation it is important to understand the nature of the controls imposed to ensure coherence throughout the organization. The challenge is to strike a balance between uniformity and legitimate diversity. To suggest that just introduction of a management model would solve the problem is far from the truth. Yet structures shape communities and management methods change the nature of organization. What is needed is a self-assessment.

The CNI is hierarchical and centralised in its structure. No organization is perfect and all are evolved over time. Right functioning is related to right leadership and right structure. The inherited structure of the CNI is rigid and there is a large amount of duplication in the function of Synod and the diocese.

> The diocese is a territorial unit under supervision of a bishop, and under the Synod as its sub-unit. Administratively, the diocese has been made autonomous. That is a good move but not adequate. It should be autonomous enough to develop its own identity. The diocese does not have a separate identity of its own apart from the identity of the Synod.[69]

It was inevitable that the Church union negotiation involved conflicts of institutional interests. A written constitution, formulated in the context of atomized western societies made up of individual families with experience of democracy, seemed irrelevant to a group like the Rethinking Group. While the episcopacy seemed to imply an image of power to the non-episcopalians in the matter of church polity, it is also equally true that the groups with non-episcopal polity could be dominated by 'unconsecrated bishops'[70] with unlimited power. Some churches do have well-developed bureaucratic agencies controlling such functions as publicity, mission, education, medical care and investments. Bureaucratic structure is generally

---

[69] THE CHURCH OF NORTH INDIA. Report of Evaluation Commission to Study the Life and Work of the Church of North India. The Institute for Development Education, Madras 1990, p80.

[70] People exercising wide informal influence which could sometimes be more dangerous to the health of the people of God than those appointed formally within an ecclesiastical constitution.

related to a hierarchical order of organization.

A restructuring of an organization would have to take into consideration the needs and resources of the people. India has moved from colonialism towards capitalism despite its socialistic outlook. In a parallel manner the CNI has moved from missionary control to a national control, but one difficulty in this transition has been the tension between dependency, originating in missions, and retaining a self-supporting structure.

One problem within the CNI under national identity has been that on the one hand there is a dominant class, small in number but powerful, and on the other, a subordinate class which is predominantly rural and more numerous but in practice powerless and marginalized. This has brought a cleavage within the Church similar to that in the society in general. One section of the Church consists of the urban middle class which is ideologically close to the dominant class, and the other consists of the popular rural mass, the outcastes whose voice is barely heard in the organization despite the fact that they are in the majority.

One crucial issue is to understand the connection between the leadership and a broad-based participatory community. It is the question of dialectics, of give and take between leadership and the wider community. The rationale behind the 'theory X' approach for leadership is to control people and to meet their spiritual needs. On the contrary a 'theory Y' approach requires the fostering of an integration of the needs of people and the goal of the church as an organization. It would need a climate where cooperation and trust can grow. The end result would be the accomplishment of a goal through a cooperative effort. While the theme of cooperation is ideal, the Church cannot be content with merely handing out suggestions for implementation. Participation in the decision-making process requires a 'communication' flow between leaders and people where people are valued, trusted and mainly respected.

Looking at the inherited structure of the western church, it is obvious that the concept of hierarchical order was modelled on Roman ideas of civil order. Hierarchy within the Church flows from the belief that those who lead are chosen and sealed by the Holy Spirit and this is recognized through the consensus of the people of God. Later in the medieval period the pattern corresponded to late feudal/monarchical ideas of government.

The traditional pattern of church structure is hierarchical with power for decision making at the apex. Implicit in the participatory approach to management is a view of organisational structure which would equitably disperse responsibilities and concentrate on shared power in the decision making process. But the issue is not simple because there is always the possibility of adopting a principle in theory which is far from reality. It could become a new form of domination in the name of sharing power. For example it is possible to confuse the principles behind the slogan that the Church is democratic, and the forms that are adopted to express what it means to be democratic. Thus the Church as an institution is only deemed to be democratic if the people within it have voting rights. This may appear to be the case on the surface but in reality it could be quite different. Economic and social factors play a strong role in determining the meaning of democracy and this is too easy to dismiss as irrelevant.

The Church constituted by the story of Israel and of Jesus is a Church constituted by the movement and power of the Holy Spirit. This perspective brings into focus the conception of ministry and management as a dynamic process entailing mutuality. A 'story-shaped Church' has a communal aspect which has strong implications for ministry and management. Ministry arises out of the recognition of its nature as a community under the reign of God. Therefore the Church as an institution should be managed in accordance with its vocation as the people of God.

Authority is exercised by the missionary and eschatological perspective of the story. If the church wants to be true to the story, then its ministry needs to be open to new forms in which diakonia may find expressions appropriate to the needs and conditions of the people. Open communication prevents the perpetuation of a structure that exploits people. Communication is partly a question of language. The administration speaks one language and the people another. Several schisms have their roots in deficient communication.

The Christian conception of authority requires as its critique a theology of the cross and resurrection which is the climax of the story. This perspective always serves to lead all churches into continuing repentance and change. Change is a basic tenet of Christian faith. However this is usually identified with spiritual change, and Christians are often no better at accepting other forms of change than anyone else. If the source of all authority is God who is at once powerful, as well as crucified and risen, then a church of the cross must be ready to ensure the willing support of its people.

In the following section it is suggested that the three categories of ecclesiology, story, doctrine, and institution, need to be interrelated in a coherent whole. The presupposition behind the argument is that a community cannot exist as a recognizable, distinctive and collective entity unless it has some practice by which it can be identified.

Performative Identity of Koinonia

One activity of the community which is vital for interrelating the above three categories as the koinonia (fellowship) of the people of God is worship. The importance of worship lies in it being that activity which seeks to evoke the fundamentals and induct the worshipper into the heart of the story of the Creator.[71] Stephen Sykes suggests that the phenomenon of Christian worship makes a vital difference to the conditions under which vigorous argument of a radical kind may be regarded as a constructive contribution to the performance of Christian identity.[72]

The centrality of worship has been an emphasis more evident in the recent theological discussions irrespective of different traditions. This is evident in the World Council of Churches publication Baptism, Eucharist and Ministry (hereafter referred to as BEM). The document BEM was formulated by the Faith and Order Commission of the World Council of Churches at its meeting held in Lima, Peru in 1982. The text is one of the most important documents of the ecumenical movement.[73]

---

[71] Discussing the relation between 'the law of praying: lex orandi', 'law of believing: lex credendi', Geoffrey Wainwright suggests that the balance of the two 'laws' enables one to construe them together as not meaning the dominance of one over the other. WAINWRIGHT, Geoffrey, Doxology. London, 1980, p218.

[72] SYKES, Stephen. The Identity of Christianity. SPCK, London, 1984, p265, p278.

[73]Baptism, Eucharist and Ministry. Faith and Order paper No 111. WCC, Geneva, 1982.

At the heart of Christian worship is the recognition of the story of the triune God, celebrated in the act of thanksgiving. Daniel Hardy and David Ford draw attention to praise as a central fact of Christian life. All creation is a work of God's love and Jesus Christ is God's giving of Himself in love to restore and fulfil all creation. The Holy Spirit is the pouring out of this love in endless fresh creativity. Praise of God recognizes, enjoys and celebrates it. Their thesis is that such a category opens a new vision of the other because it is an activity related to God and to other people in the context of creation. They have identified the category of 'suspicion' in its common sense and more sophisticated forms (Freud, Marx, Nietzsche) as one of the major threats to the praise of God in contemporary life. Suspicion of God as the object of human worship represents the logic of Feuerbach's reduction of the notion of God to that of merely human projection.[74]

Worship is central in that life where the identity of God is witnessed to by a people in praise, confession, repentance, hearing the word and breaking bread. Worship is that activity which Christians engage in together where the community remembers and expresses the Christian story. The worship of the Christian community celebrates and anticipates the glory of God that will be consummated in the eschatological renewal of all creation. In the following section it is suggested that the Supper incorporates different elements of worship and that the story, doctrine and institutional identities are evoked in the performance of the Supper.

---

[74] HARDY, Daniel and Ford David. Jubilate: Theology in Praise. Darton, Longman and Todd, London, 1984, p1, p11-13, p54.

i. Story of the Supper

Stephen Sykes proposes that the notion of story remembering itself coheres closely with major elements of eucharistic theology. He notes that there are four components in story grammar: a setting, a theme, a plot, and a resolution. These four align with thanksgiving to the Father (creation), memorial of the Son (redemption), communion of the faithful (church), meal in the kingdom (eschatology). There is an extrinsic as well as intrinsic relationship between the eucharist as sacrament and the performance of a public narrative memorial.[75]

An important implication of his proposal is to recognize that the eucharist theology which uses the idea of story is not open to the same objections as can be brought against some traditional doctrines. From the beginning the Christians have focused their concerns in the Supper as seen in Paul's first letter to Corinth. The early Christians gathered at the Table to break bread and drink wine. This coming together in brotherly love was certainly not a Christian innovation. The Jews who lived in those days used to gather at the table in brotherly love. The Romans also used to assemble in brotherly love in associations, and there was need for special laws concerning such associations which were called 'Collegia'. They used to address each other in the association by the title 'brethren'. The Jewish gathering was on the basis of race and the Roman gathering was on the basis of profession. The Christian gathering was based on the declaration that in Christ there is neither Jew nor Greek, male nor female, rich nor poor, master nor slave.

---

[75] Sykes, Stephen W, The Story and Eucharist, <u>Interpretation</u>. October 1983, p365.

The central aspect of the Supper is praise. It has its root in the Jewish berakah ('Blessed art Thou, O Lord Our God ...'). God is blessed and thanked for his goodness in creation and redemption. In that blessing, the plea is that God will extend his graciousness into the present and also to the future. Through the blessing, a proclamation is made about the Lord's death and his resurrection. An understanding of the nature of God is displayed at the Supper. This culminates in grateful praise of God for his marvellous work in Christ. The decisive fact of this aspect of praise is that it tells a story and an invitation is extended to come to the Table.

The Supper relates to a story of a great feast.[76] Jesus looked to the feast in the final kingdom of God when many will come from east and west, north and south, and sit at the Table with Abraham, Isaac and Jacob (Mt8:11, Lk13:29). The story is retold again and again during the Supper. In telling this story, it needs to be remembered that it cannot be understood unless it is placed in the right context.

There are two major roots to the story of the Supper. One was Jesus' table-fellowship. The table fellowship of Jesus was a matter of great importance. Jesus had extended the meal across social boundaries, even to those who did not keep the Law. There were some who could not understand this; it was offensive and difficult for the Scribes and the Pharisees. They questioned Jesus' dining with the tax collectors and sinners (Mk2:16-17). The Lucan account of the story of a meal with Zacchaeus is an example of the

---

[76] GORRINGE, Timothy, Redeeming Time, DLT, London, 1986, pp150-174.

table fellowship of Jesus which he used as a sign of forgiveness and acceptance (Lk.19:1-10).

The other root of the story of the Supper was the meal which Jews celebrated, and still celebrate each year at the Passover.[77] The Passover meal was a celebration of the way in which God had brought the people of Israel out of their bondage in Egypt and set them on the road to the promised land. It was an occasion for reminding themselves of the gracious act of God. The book of Exodus, which records the institution of the Passover, states that 'This day shall be for you a memorial day, and you shall keep it as a feast to the Lord; throughout your generations you shall observe it as an ordinance for ever.' (12:14)

The word memorial gave the Jewish paschal meal its whole meaning as an actualization of the deliverance of the people of God. It is not a subjective remembrance, but a strong power in forming the identity of the Jews. 'And when your children say to you, "what do you mean by this service?" you shall say, "It is the sacrifice of the Lord's passover".' (Ex.12:26, 27). The Jews as a people of God recall what God once did so that He may continue it today. It involved also a thanksgiving to God, a praising of God. Psalm 116 was sung during the meal - 'What shall I render unto the Lord for all his bounty to me? I will lift up the cup of salvation, and call on the name of the Lord' (116:12,13).

---

[77] Whether the Last Supper was indeed a Passover meal, and if so whether it was held at the time when others would be eating the Passover meal or a day earlier. In Synoptics the Last Supper is itself a Passover Meal (Mk 14:12f, Mt 26:17f, Lk 22:7f). while in John this Supper comes 'before the feast of the Passover' (13:1, 18:28, 19:14).

298

The Supper in the context of passover is a blessing for the wonderful deeds of God, a sacrifice of praise and thanksgiving. The Church in continuation with the story of passover celebrated the Supper with praise and by recalling the death and resurrection of Jesus. The story is told that it is God who has reconciled the world to Himself. This story of reconciliation gives the worshipping community its identity at the Table. The Church gathers around the Table to hear the story of what God has done for all mankind in Jesus, and goes out to tell the story. Jesus is a crucial part of that story but it begins with the call of Adam. That call sets the agenda of God's engagement with human history.

The table fellowship background of the story of the Supper reminds one of the importance of the meal. 'We for whom a meal is often a rushed cup of coffee and a piece of toast, or a hamburger taken on the run from a station buffet, need to realize afresh the importance of meals in the ancient world, and still today in other cultures. The meal is an expression of friendship and hospitality. To break bread with another was to share something of that person's life.'[78] Jesus accepted many invitations to meals and much of his teaching was also given in the context of a meal. Quite a number of parables featured a meal or banquet theme. The Passover background of the Supper is a reminder of the Jewish antecedents of the Christian Supper.

---

[78] DUNN, J.D.G. Whatever happened to the Lord's Supper? Epworth Review. Vol.IX, No.1, Jan, 1992, p35.

In both cases the background of the Supper is a meal. The significance of the meal lies in the fact that it was a sharing of food and drink together. 'In one case, a meal eaten in company as an expression of the character of Jesus' mission and the fellowship of the kingdom of God. In the other, a meal re-enacting Israel's history of salvation as focused in the exodus.'[79] They both give reminders that in essence the Supper is a celebration. It was celebrated on the first day of the week. He who was crucified, was expected to come and was experienced in the power of the Spirit.

One failure on the part of the Church is to treat the Supper as just a matter of individual piety rather than a corporate community celebration in anticipation of a meal in the kingdom. The perpetuation of individual piety in a caste society like India becomes again a barrier to communion where eating together with the outcastes is still a problem.

The Supper narrates the fundamental event of the Christian community and gives substance to the values and aspirations of that community, and enhances its sense of unity and purpose. It is maintained that the existence of the community is derived from the tradition concerning the death and resurrection of Jesus Christ. The Supper evokes the memory of this narrative.

The retelling of this narrative affirms values and beliefs of central importance to the community of faith. It tells a story and thereby generates values. A narrative identity of the Supper makes a minimum of presuppositions and thus is ideally suited as a starting point for exposition of the

---

[79] DUNN, J.D.G. Whatever happened to the Lord's Supper? Epworth Review, Vol.IX, No.1. Jan, 1992, p36.

nature of the meal. In this way it is capable of functioning as a point of entry for those who experience difficulties in making sense of the Supper, on account of a multiplicity of difficult ontological assumptions.

A narrative account of the Supper provides the community of faith with a sense of historical location as does the table fellowship of Jesus and the 'Passover'. They narrate the fundamental events. The story of the death and resurrection of Jesus is affirmed to be the story of the community of faith, inviting hearers to correlate their situation with the pattern of death and life disclosed in the narrative of the Supper.

The Supper as a story is vulnerable to abuse or misinterpretation. George Stroup refers to those Protestant traditions which insist that celebration of the Lord's Supper and baptism should always be accompanied by the sermon. The theological presupposition for this position is that the spiritual presence of the Word in the sacraments should not be separated from the appearances of the Word in Scripture and sermon.[80] The Word is present when the Spirit enables personal and community identity to be fused to the narrative history of God's grace. Sacraments without narratives are vulnerable and this is what Sykes means when he speaks of the extrinsic relation between eucharist as sacrament and the performance of public narrative memorial. The intrinsic relation between the eucharist as sacrament and performance of public narrative memorial is to link the sign character of the eating and drinking to the sign character of the public recitation of the narrative. The ritual of eating and drinking of

---

[80] STROUP, George, The Promise of Narrative Theology. SCM, London, 1981, p253.

eucharist elements and the performance of narratives are together indicative of an interior intention; it is by means of both that the proclamation of the meaning of Christ's death is constantly made.

ii. Doctrine of the Supper

The origin of different denominational identities that went into the formation of the CNI goes back to the conflicts of sixteenth century Europe. The Reformers emphasized the importance of a visible Church. The intention of the Reformers was to reform in order to preserve the true identity of the Church. They felt that the identity of the early Church had become distorted by the late medieval Roman Church. They were engaged in rediscovering the Biblical perspective. According to them the Church is nourished by the Word of God. It is the community or fellowship of believers, anchored in a common faith in a common Lord. This community meets together to hear God's word preached and to participate in the sacraments. The identity of the community is determined by the preaching of the Gospel of Christ and by the correct administration of the sacraments.[81] The reformers placed word and sacrament at the centre of

---

[81] a. 'The sure mark by which the Christian congregation can be recognized is that the pure Gospel is preached there. For just as the banner of an army is sure sign by which one can know what kind of Lord and army have taken to the field, so, too, the Gospel is the sure sign by which one knows where Christ and his army are encamped. We have sure promise of this from God in Isaiah 55:10-11), "my word" (says God) "that goes forth from my mouth shall not return empty to me; rather, as the rain falls from heaven to earth, making it fruitful, so shall my word also accomplish everything for which I sent it".' (Luther), Gritsch, E.W. ed. Luther's Works. Fortress Press, 1970, Vol.39, p305.

the ministry of the church. The Lord's Supper was the bond of charity that united the faithful community. Communion was a function of community by which all were joined in one body.

The story of the history of the Supper is one of controversy. The division between the churches has centred upon the question of the nature of the 'real presence', and 'sacrifice'. In this respect the eschatological aspect has been undermined, which ought to be a celebration, an act of praise, in anticipation of the coming reign of God. Much doctrinal difference centres on the word <u>anamnesis</u> (memorial). Scholars give different nuances to their explanations. There have been arguments between Catholics and Protestants, and among Protestants, concerning both the eucharistic sacrifice and the presence of Christ; and between East and West about the relation between the roles of Christ and the Holy Spirit in the eucharist.

The doctrinal dispute over the centuries has led to the mutual alienation of the traditions of East and West; and within the Western tradition, to alienation between Rome and the Reformation. It has also caused difficulty in understanding the meaning of the Supper for those entering the Church from other religious traditions. For example the theology of the Eastern churches has stressed the divine liturgy as a reflection of the heavenly liturgy before the throne of God. In the West the

---

b. 'Where ever we see the Word of God purely preached and heard and the sacraments administered according to Christ's institution, there, it is not to be doubted, a church of God exists. (cf.Eph2:20) For this promise cannot fail: "where ever two or three are gathered in my name, there I am in the midst of them" (Mt.18:20)'. (Calvin), McNeil, J.T. ed. <u>The Institutes of Christian religion</u>. Westminster Press, 1960, p1023.

emphasis came to lie on the words of institution as relating to the representation of Jesus' sacrifice on the cross, and the significance of Jesus' words over the giving of bread and wine.

Within the ecumenical movement, a wide-ranging consensus has come into being over the doctrine of the Supper. One widely accepted multilateral document is BEM. In BEM, the doctrine of Eucharist is treated under five headings. They are Thanksgiving, Memorial, Invocation of the Spirit, Communion, and Anticipation of the Meal in the Kingdom. One important category of all these is the anticipation of the Meal in the Kingdom. To achieve consensus in this respect one fundamental error into which the church is prone to fall is that of subordinating the eschatological to the historical.[82] The Church is treated as having, for practical purposes, the whole plenitude of God's grace in itself now. God has, as it were, deposited His grace with the Church and left it to her to administer. The fact is that the Church is not there to administer grace; rather it is a worshipping community of men and women who celebrate the reign of God. At the heart of that celebration is a rehearsing of His words and deeds. A congregation which believes and lives by the Gospel is characterized by its eschatology.

The Supper points to an inclusiveness because it is rooted in the story of the Table Fellowship of Jesus and the Passover. Jesus shared a meal with tax collectors and sinners and the Passover with his disciples. The Supper in itself is a redemptive act, an effective sign that also creates the possibility for an openness to the future. Seen in this perspective it depicts what is

---

[82] See also ANGLICAN-ROMAN CATHOLIC INTERNATIONAL COMMISSION. The Final Report 1981. SPCK, London, 1982.

needed to remove all that hinders fellowship, and incorporates the idea of the coming reign of God, giving rise to a new vision. Eschatological belief points to the possibility of a new order based on faith that in the incarnation the word of God entered into His own disordered world. The divine economy entered into historical and creaturely existence. This is what Paul spoke of when he referred to the gathering up of all things into Christ, things visible and invisible. It is an ordering within the eternal purpose of divine love and fellowship. The celebration of the Supper is anchored in the adoration of God. In celebration the ultimate essence of catholicity lies not in doctrinal controversy but in the transcendence of all divisions in Christ. It covers all areas and all dimensions of life.

iii Institutions and the Supper

The Supper as a church doctrine is essential to the identity of the group. It helps to constitute faithful adherence to a community. But disagreement on the matter of doctrine constitutes one of the main reasons for refusing to resume table fellowship between different denominations. There is a glaring discrepancy between the theological character of the Supper as a sacrament of fellowship and the historical situation of mutual excommunication. In the present ecumenical context the debate centres on the question of inter-communion.

Some believe that it is Christ present in the Supper who invites all to His Table. This cannot and should not be thwarted by ecclesiastical discipline. Others believe that there cannot be inter-communion between separated Christians as it implies full unity in the wholeness of his truth. All Christians wish to overcome this gap. Ecumenists have differed on ways and means. Some think that communion at the Supper should be the final goal of Christian unity, and others think that intercommunion should be seen as an effective step on the way to fuller unity.

> The common participation in one Eucharist will allow the Lord creatively to bring us closer to the perfect peace and unity that will mark the final kingdom, for such a Eucharist will be the occasion for Him to exercise the three eschatological functions of casting out from us in judgement what is amiss in us, of uniting us closer to Himself in divine fellowship, and of joining us together in common enjoyment of His presence and gifts.[83]

The Church as a koinonia cannot live except as a visibly defined body with a structure. But that does not indicate continuation of one structure. It means repudiations of tradition are to be followed by reassertions when a break occurs; then a new structure is formed. Order is the co-ordination of the life of the Church.

In the biblical story the concept of order is viewed over against disorder and chaos. The beginning of the story is that the world was without form and void except for the creative word of God. Sin entered into the ordered cosmos and brought chaos. The story ends with the point that the covenant of God contains the promise of a new order, a new creation when all things will be restored to order. So order is part of the story which must be reflected in the institutional identity of a community.

Intercommunion is associated with the ordering of the institutional life of the Church. Substantial agreement on doctrine does not automatically lead all churches to intercommunion, because intercommunion involves the

---

[83] WAINWRIGHT, Geoffrey. Eucharist and Eschatology. Epworth, 1971, p143.

issues of ministry and authority. In most churches the celebrant at the supper is normally an ordained minister. The general recognized responsibility of the ordained ministry is to proclaim the word of God, and to celebrate the Sacraments. The ordained ministry becomes a visible focus of institutional identity in the celebration of the Supper as well as a cause of dispute for intercommunion.

Being one of the concerns of the ecumenical movement, the missionary witness of the Church is vital. Ministerial order must be ancillary. Saying this is not to discredit the role of the ordained ministry, but to draw attention to the concept of the priesthood of the people of God. The minister is a representative of the people and thus is understood to represent the priestly people.[84]

In the community celebration of the Supper, the minister is to be seen as seeking the response and acknowledgment of the community. It is by committing his life to the community that a minister has the authority to celebrate. This authority is governed by mutual love within the community and is exercised with respect to the community. It is shared by all, and not exclusive to any group within the people of God.

The goal of ecumenism is the ordering of the Household of God, where He is the Head. The word oikonomia is the ordering of a house. God came into the world to take control of His household and it is He who will gather everything to Himself. His oikonomia is not an imposition on the world but operates from within. Reordering of the household is done

---

[84] SCHILLEBEECKX, Edward. The Church with a Human Face. SCM, London, 1985.

through Jesus in the form of a servant. In the course of that reordering the Church is called to obedience through the Spirit. In that calling the Church on earth shares all historical contingents. The question of management of the household as a concern of the present is wide ranging. One contemporary set of questions is concerned with liberation and social justice.

The Church as a <u>koinonia</u> means fellowship with God as well as with fellow human beings. Therefore <u>koinonia</u> is not a cover for individualism in which each looks out for himself or for herself at the expense of others; neither is it a cover for toleration, to maintain harmony among free individuals. The Church as a <u>koinonia</u> speaks of the manifestation of the love of God. Therefore the prophetic role in <u>koinonia</u> is essential; that also constitutes one element in the institution of the Supper. The church always requires a contemporary prophetic ministry like that of Paul's to the Corinthian congregation. Alongside the narration of the events of the Supper, Paul needed to elucidate what it meant to discern the true nature of the Church as the body of Christ (1 Cor.11:33). In Corinth's case there was failure of discernment that led to the persistence of social division in the congregation.

The Supper is a challenge to the Church when it remains static and unquestioning with regard to injustice within the life of the community. If hope rests on God, then the Church must endeavour to leave behind any tendency towards stabilization and go on with readiness to be open to the future. That means to be in constant dialogue with the present, maintaining hope in God for a new situation. Such an aim cannot consist in adaptation or preservation of the status quo but in readiness to be the instruments for the reconciling purpose of God.

India is not by tradition individualist. The family and the community play a great part in Indian life. In the east the family has a much wider significance than in the west since it consists of not only husband and wife but parents, brothers, sisters, children and grandchildren. The Christians in India have also learnt from the Bible that God the Father cares for individuals and society, and that the individual has his own worth in society. It is possible to see in the Church that type of life which perfectly reconciles the individual and community.

The community that celebrates the Supper is reminded of a divine relationship where there is a correspondence between human rights and dignity, and the place of every human being in the eternal will of God. It is the place where God is the Father, Jesus Christ is the brother, and the Spirit is the counsellor. Every human being is a person whose rightful place is within the divine relationship.

The individual person emerges within the community in the free giving of himself or herself in surrender to the other. In such an act of surrender to each other the personhood becomes real and there arises a community. When several persons surrender to each other in this way there arises a community in which 'Love finds communion without seeking it, or rather precisely because it does not seek it.'[85]

The historical character of Christian faith demands that the Bible as a witness to the integration of individual and community must be taken

---

[85] BONHOEFFER, Dietrich. <u>Sanctorum Communio.</u> Collins, London, p125.

seriously. The socio-cultural background of the Old Testament and the New Testament is a witness that confessions of faith are not theoretical statements but are based on God's redemptive acts and his message as applied to particular situations.

Individual conversion is not complete outside of a reconciled community. The ideal is a community which has a vision to transcend the divisions of society. The inclusiveness of community consists in recognition of the importance of the family in society and the humanity of all, and the acceptance of sick, weak, outcastes, poor and rich. Implicit in this recognition is a risk-taking love for others which is proclaimed and celebrated in the act of the Supper. The question of self-emptying when applied to the community is ultimately based on Christ's self-giving obedience unto death.

Therefore one fundamental feature of self-emptying for the community is an activity: a performance. It is found by the persons in the community in participation within divine relationship. This community is composed of those people who have their place within it not by virtue of their capacity to love but by virtue of the reality of the gift of the Holy Spirit. So the community is helped to be free from introversion of love which could work as a fragmenting force and lead to a tyrannical collectivism.

The community constituted by the love of the triune God is neither a continuing self-perpetuating institution in which God does nothing new, nor simply a momentous event which happens ever anew when a group of Christians meet together. The community constituted by the love of God is visited by the Lord in both love and judgement as it praises, listens to His word, prays for the world and breaks the bread together. Therefore worship constitutes an important element in shaping the identity of the Christian community. It is a fact that the majority of Indian Christians are from the outcastes but are excluded from receiving any privileges such as are afforded to scheduled castes by the Government. The Mandal Commission reported that:

> In view of this the Scheduled Caste converts to Christianity, Islam, Buddhism etc, should not be denied the benefits extended to Scheduled Castes and the same should hold good in respect of Other Backward Classes. At some places it was also contended that all Muslims and all Christians should be included in the list of Other Backward Classes as these communities were really very backward.[86]

It is also argued in some circles that a communal church is ideal on the basis that the churches drawn from homogeneous caste or tribal groups are among the strongest in India. They have carried over some of their old social cohesion intact. But the question is whether that ought to be an ideal for the Church in India with regard to dealing with the issues of justice, and witnessing to the reconciling power of the gospel.

The compartmentalization of India into different religious communities has the effect of isolating Christians from being a part of the ferment in the life of the nation. 'India deals with foreign elements much as an oyster deals with a piece of grit. The invader is allowed to become a part of India, but he is prevented from contaminating the national life by a

---

[86] Mandal, 1980, p47. The Second Backward Classes Commission (known as Mandal Commission) under the chairmanship of the late Mr B.P. Mandal, was appointed on 1 January 1979 and the report was submitted on 31 December 1980.

protective wall of social distance.'[87] Any new religions that enter India have a good chance of survival, but they often become in effect a new caste. The religion is accepted as a recognized component of Indian society, but in return it is expected not to disturb the existing pattern. For example the Jews and Parsees have long been accepted on this basis.

BEM in the section on eucharist draws attention to the communion of the faithful. The ecclesiological section particularly emphasizes the socially reconciling character of the relationship in the new community, and the challenge of the eucharist to social separation and injustice. Section 'E' Meal of the Kingdom, continually affirms the vision of the renewal of creation and mission to the whole world. The bread and wine is offered in a setting which transcends the social as well as natural divisions. In that setting the offering of bread and wine speaks of the goodness of the created order, the offering of One life for many, and the sharing of that blessing by all.

The very act of sharing embraced in the Supper questions the oppressive structure of the society and the division of the community between rich and poor, male and female, black and white, high caste, low caste and outcaste. As a celebration it incorporates both aspects of remembrance, the past as well as the future. Suggesting the interrelation of the three categories: 'narrative', 'doctrine' and 'institution' through the performance of the Supper as an act of worship, is to draw attention to the basis of Christian identity.

---

[87] GRANT, John W. God's People in India. London, 1959, p21.

It is the human tendency to cling to the past and to a structure that makes them insensitive to the Lord's active visitation of His people in judgment and renewal. Institutional blindness could be one important factor in the persistence of divisions among Christians, and therefore has led to continued celebration of the Supper in mutual isolation. The eschatological dimension of worship assists in challenging a community. It contains a polarity of the 'already' and the 'not yet'. The most obvious thing regarding the Supper is that it was instituted during the course of a meal and it has to do with food and drink. Yet its nature as a real meal has hardly been prominent in the popular conception of the Supper. A rethinking of the importance of the Supper in the life of a united Church would bring the different perspectives of ecclesiology to the whole.

Conclusion

One dominant feature of the debate during the negotiation in north India was the question of unification of ministry and right practice of baptism. The debate continues about a valid form of baptism and its place in the socio-religious context of India. The issue of baptism is debated in the context where the Church has to take into account the question of conversion because in India conversion has never been a strictly individual matter.[88]

---

[88] GORRINGE, Timothy. Redeeming Time. Darton, Longman and Todd, London, p150. Gorringe talks about a reversal of the usual practice where baptism is treated only after the eucharist, as a matter of the arcanum, the secret discipline which is primarily the concern of the gathered Christian community. The eucharist, on the other hand, is understood as rooted in a practice for which the paradigm is as much Jesus' meal with Zacchaeus as

Baptism as well as being a personal acceptance of Christ, includes a social aspect, that is, the need to take into account the significance of a religious community as a social unit. Pressure from without and an ingrained attitude from within compel the Church to operate as a religious community like any other. The converts leave behind one set of personal relationships and accept another and this involves shifting the delicate balance of communal power.

The new loyalty in the community does not abolish the old. For example while rigid retention of caste is not general in the Church, the underlying attitude is very powerful in the relationships between the members of the Church. Conversion from one group to another means not 8only a change in spiritual allegiance but also a shift in political power. Therefore communalism has been a fertile source of political and social tension. Today in India it shows itself in the rivalries of different castes, language groups, and in some cases the threat of secession from the Indian Union.

To suggest replacing <u>koinonia</u> with an individual piety would be the end of the ecumenical movement. Rather the need is for a right understanding of the social identity of Christian <u>koinonia.</u> Being with God is fundamentally interpersonal. Discussing social identity based on the triune God is to focus on the sociality of being within God. As Barth says, human inter-relationship is derived from the relationship which is within

---

it is the 'last' supper. It is the sign of the gracious messianic invitation to 'the nations', an invitation extended to all, and as such takes place in the economy of redemption.

God's own being. Human community is thus grounded in the community of God's own being. So the human being created in correspondence with God's own being is not solitary but a being in relation.[89]

Inter-relating the three categories of ecclesiology through the Supper draws attention to an intermediate category for remembering God's presence in the world. It does not mean that such a category is exhaustive but that it is a particular category through which the bond of being one in Christ could be realized in the community.

The identity of the church as a community is shaped by the story. In a world where people feel lost, there is a powerful urge for individuals and groups to reaffirm their distinctiveness, doing this perhaps in racial, national, tribal and local ecclesiastical terms. It is feared that consensus would lead to a disappearance of identities, which would be in danger of being swallowed up in the uniformity.

Christians have always tried to maintain their identity amidst differences of geographical area, language, lifestyle, belief systems, and programmes of action; and Indian Christians are no exception. But it is vital to ask how the CNI as a community incorporating different former ecclesial, caste and language identities, could sustain its own identity without falling into uniformity or chaotic diversity.

One fundamental challenge to the CNI is to sustain the multiform identity of Christianity in a coherent way. The object in depicting the

---

[89] BARTH, Karl. Church Dogmatics. Vol.111/2, T & T Clark, Edinburgh. p220, p324.

identity of the Church in terms of story, doctrine and institution is to focus on the corporate nature of the Church as the people of God. The way this has been described suggests that it is not an invisible people of God but an actual people on a journey.

CONCLUSION

The impact of the Christian mission on the churches of India and the awakening of the Indian people to nationalism were two important events of great historical significance. The Christian missions corresponded with the period of colonialism. It was the elite oriented to western education who became the leaders of Indian national awakening. In this context the Christian missions and churches were faced with a complex reality.

The Church in India had to face the post-independence situation for its identity and mission. One daunting task was to dissociate itself from its colonial image and to identify with the mainstream from which it was alleged to have separated itself by not being involved fully in the national struggle for freedom. The Indian Christian elites have spared no effort to conscientize the Christian community in India to join the mainstream of the nation after independence and to emerge from a period of western mission identity to a national church.

The Indian Christians are a minority community, only 2.43% of the total population according to the 1981 census. The Christians since independence have tried to be part of the nation-building process, and as a minority community have claimed a legitimate share in the governance of the country. The Church has been successful in building an image of itself like other religious minority communities. The minority concept has given legitimacy in the attempt to survive and to raise its own grievances.

The Church has often been a minority in many parts of the world. The power of the Church lies in its obedience to its call even unto death on the Cross. The Church therefore does not establish itself in final form at any given time but functions as the pilgrim people of God on the way to liberation. To recognize this minority dimension of the Church is to recognize the reality of God's power; and to realise God's power is not to play with number games in mission strategy but to proclaim God's love and justice through the reconciled community.

The success of the church union movement is seen in the formation of two united churches: the Church of South India and the Church of North India. This thesis has drawn attention to the story of negotiations that led to the formation of the Church of North India. The historical continuity of the church's faith and life are embodied in the inherited diversities of ecclesial traditions. In bringing together people from different denominations, castes, languages, cultures into one koinonia, the CNI could become the avant garde of a new age in the kingdom of God. The CNI is transconfessional and committed to manifesting the unity of the Church by gathering Christians together in a given place while not giving up the vision of the universal koinonia. It involves a tension by being local and at the same time not losing sight of the wider communion which transcends national and cultural boundaries.

Losing one's specific denominational identity brought fear and reason for opposition to church union. The denominational stories did indeed play a great role in the formation of the united Church. A plausible explanation of the advent of ecumenism in India includes the mixture of two factors - the theological and non-theological. But ecclesiology is not a static concept. It grows out of a complex interaction of national, cultural and confessional heritages. In the context of the church union movement it was a question of identity and relevance. The issue was not just a change from denominational identity to an ecumenical identity. It was how to respond creatively in forming a new identity and be relevant in the social and religious situation of India.

This thesis has proposed that narrative, doctrine and institution are three helpful categories for forming an ecumenical identity and revealing the sign and servant character of the Church. The identity of the worshipping community sustained through the Lord's Supper is not an identity over against or in competition with other religious communities, but a mediational identity to bring closer the different narrow identities. The object is not a power game but service to the people.

The inquiry has provided a strategy for exploring a range of issues to do with the development of mission and the national identity of the CNI. By developing this more general issue through the story of the Christian missions and church union movement in north India, attention has been drawn to the essentials of ecclesiology. Important matters concerning the nature of ecclesiology, its social form and function have repeatedly surfaced in the course of the thesis. The relevance of some of them is particulary specified in the third part of the thesis.

Ecclesiology, its social function and indigenization are a broad field of complex and nuanced study. An evaluation of a critical comparison of different streams would be a thesis in itself. This thesis has only identified as matter of passing reference the questions of caste, class, culture and poverty. More than this the issue of the diaconate, the place of women in the society and the church, the question of parity of ministers and lifestyle, and an appropriate structure of the church as an institution are questions of vital importance which need detailed analysis and study.

This thesis points to the fact that the identity discussion in ecclesiology is significant and that it needs to be understood constantly afresh if the Church is to be a witnessing community. The development of doctrine in the CNI includes a dialectical relation between the central Christian affirmations and the varying historical contexts in which these affirmations find expression in the statement of faith. The strategy has included compiling a common statement of faith to express the bond of union. This is generated from the early Church's experience that God was in Christ reconciling the world to himself. This oneness of faith has crystalized in various semi-credal and local statements of faith. While an ecumenical ecclesiology needs to take this into account, it is affirmed in the thesis that God, the Trinity, is the unifier. The task has been to determine how the one-in-Christ bond operates within the fellowship.

This thesis has argued that constructing an identity was an important part of the Church union movement in North India and in doing so, it has shown more specifically how this significance ought to be understood in the context of a uniting Church. In undertaking the description of the formation of the CNI, the perspective of a critical ecclesiology is presented in the sixth chapter. Having established the story of the mission and the story of negotiations, attention was then given to aspects of an ecumenical ecclesiology which were found lacking in the CNI.

There is a stress on the importance of narrative, doctrine and institution, particularly through the performative identity of worship in the Lord's Supper. The Supper as a meal is powerful in shaping the ecclesial identity for witness and could also be seen as indigenous as well as ecumenical. It is indigenous in that it avoids systematic abstraction and is particularly relevant in the social and religious situation of India where food, spatial and ritual questions are not excluded from the fabric of ordinary day to day life. It is ecumenical in that the identity and continuity of the community is preserved in the framework of biblical narrative, rather than seeking it in other frameworks of belief in the name of religious harmony in the context of religious pluralism.

This obviously involves the scandal of particularity but it is argued that this does not imply either any superiority or a narrow view of God. It is argued that to accept Christian particularity, rooted in specific historical events, is not to exclude the activity of God in other ways. Affirming particularity is to question any practice within the Church as well as society that tries to monopolize the activity of God. Such a questioning has deep roots in the prophetic tradition both in the story of Israel and the Church.

In worship the identity of the <u>koinonia</u> is maintained through praise, confession, ministry of the word, intercession and breaking bread. One focal point is remembering and expressing the story. It has been argued that the Church's identity is made manifest through its <u>diakonia</u> and therefore, although ministry is an integral part of ecclesiology, the threefold ministry of the CNI does not constitute the full view of the ministry. The CNI lacks a proper form of diaconate expressing the true nature of the ministry.

The union of the churches is based on an organic model. It is a useful concept through which union was achieved. But a dialogue with the description of God's relationship with the people is vital. This thesis emphasises the category 'the people of God' to open up new horizons. One important idea of 'the people of God' is the theme of community and this is an intrinsic aspect of Indian society. An acknowledgement of this perspective helps the church to have a dynamic vision.

To focus on the Lord's Supper as the centre of community worship is particularly relevant if India wants to make any contribution to theological thinking. An indigenous ecclesiology closely related to nationalism has to safeguard itself against narrow nationalism. Resurgence of Hinduism owes a great deal of its vigour to the feeling that an independent nation ought to cultivate its own religion. The Church through the ages has had unhappy experiences with its attempts to identify Christianity with the cause of the nation. For example the German Christianity of the 1930's was not Christianity at all but Nazi racism in Christian guise. So the Church has a prophetic role in relation to the nation, and in the future, if certain trends in Indian politics continue, this may be a costly and unpopular vocation.

Any indigenous ecclesiology cannot overlook the fact that India has played an active role in the whole ecumenical movement and has established its own two united Churches. A united church cannot retreat into isolation from other churches. It also cannot be a witnessing community if it continues to present itself in the same way as any other religious community in India. It will be unfortunate if in its enthusiasm for an indigenous theology, it makes compromises for survival. Breaking down barriers is an important part of the mission of the Church. The striking character of the Indian church lies in its potential for breaking down barriers between the people, and making 'a people' out of 'no people'. It is here that there lies not only potential but a great challenge to construct an indigenous ecclesiology.

The history of the ecumenical movement is informed by a spiritual movement which constitutes a challenge and aims at manifesting the real nature of an institution. One positive aspect of the movement for union is not the rediscovery of principles or rules but of a new spiritual impetus. Sometimes a rigidity aiming to preserve the accuracy of theological discourse and concentration on precision of formulas might run the risk of extinguishing the desire for renewal in the Spirit. The Church cannot overlook the past, as it has to refer back to the events of its foundation, but at the same time the need is to engage in a more intensive and discerning way with the present, moving beyond immediate issues of ecclesial pragmatics and attempting to open up and articulate the issues concerning the truth of God's presence in the world. From this perspective the Church as the people of God is only a means and a form through which God's creating and redeeming love is witnessed to. It also points to the contingent status of the church as well as to the dialectical concerns not to obliterate boundary making activities. Boundaries in a dialectical concern do not operate as strategies for exclusion or opposition to others, rather as facilitators of communication, the necessary precondition for further enlargement of understanding, harmony and perfection of life.

Much ecumenical discussion concerns boundaries, and much of this thesis has therefore been about them too. The complex transition from separate church identities to shared CNI identity has been set in the context of other important boundaries - between East and West; various religions, castes, classes, tribes and localities; diverse stories and their varied interpretations; laity and clergy; past, present and future. Through all the divisions, enmity, misunderstandings, failures and ambiguities, the faith is that in its own small way the CNI can help to transform those boundaries into a sign of hope in the kingdom of God.

ABBREVIATIONS

BMS   Baptist Missionary Society

CLS Christian Literature Society

CNI Church of North India

CMS Church Missionary Society

CSI Church of South India

CUP Cambridge University Press

OUP Oxford University Press

CISRS   Christian Institute for the Study of Religion and Society

LMS London Missionary Society

RTC Round Table Conference

NC   Negotiating Committee

SPCK   Society for Promoting Christian Knowledge

ISPCK   Indian Society for Promoting Christian Knowledge

WCC   World Council of Churches

APPENDIX I

THE CONSTITUTION OF THE CHURCH OF NORTH INDIA
SECTION III - THE DOCTRINES OF THE CHURCH[1]

Clause 1. The Church of North India holds the faith which the Church has ever held in Jesus Christ the Redeemer of the World, in whom alone men are saved by grace through faith, and in accordance with the revelation of God, which He made, being Himself God Incarnate, it worships one God, Father, Son and Holy Spirit.

Clause 2. It accepts the Holy Scriptures of the Old Testament and the New Testament as the inspired word of God as containing all things necessary to salvation, and as the supreme and decisive standard of faith, and acknowledges that the Church must always be ready to correct and reform itself in accordance with the teaching of those Scriptures as the Holy Spirit shall reveal it.

Clause 3. It accepts the Creeds commonly called the Apostles' and Nicene as witnessing to and guarding that faith, which is continuously confirmed by the Holy Spirit in the experience of the Church of Christ.

Clause 4. The use of the Creeds in worship is an act of adoration and thanksgiving towards Almighty God for His nature and for His acts of love and mercy, as well as joyful affirmation of the faith which binds together the worshippers.

Clause 5. The Church of North India is keenly aware of the fact that divergence of conviction on certain other matters of faith and practice is something which can only be borne within one fellowship by the exercise

---

[1] See <u>The Constitution of the Church of North India & Bye-Laws.</u> ISPCK, Delhi, 1987, p4-15.

of much mutual forbearance and charity. Nevertheless, it believes that it is called to make this act of faith in the conviction that it is not the will of the Lord of the Church that they who are one in Him should be divided even for such causes as these. It further believes itself to be called to this venture in the confidence that in brotherly converse within one Church those of diverse convictions will be led together in the unity of the Spirit to learn what is His will in these matters of difference.

Clause 6. For the confession of its faith before the world and for the guidance of its teachers and the edification of the faithful, it shall be competent for the Church of North India to issue its own statements, provided always that such statements are agreeable to the Holy Scriptures.

Clause 7. The Church of North India furthermore acknowledges the witness to the catholic faith contained in the confessions of faith adopted both at the time of the Reformation and subsequently, and formulated by the uniting Churches or their parent Churches. In particular, the Church of North India accepts the following statements as consistent with the doctrinal standards of this Church.

A. Declaration (i) of the Constitution of the Church of India, Pakistan, Burma and Ceylon.
B. Confession of the Faith of the United Church of Northern India.
C. The Doctrinal Standards of the Methodist Church (British Conference).
D. The Baptist Church Covenant of the Council of the Baptist Churches of Northern India.
E. Declaration of Principle of the Baptist Churches.

APPENDIX II
AN AFFIRMATION OF FAITH AND COMMITMENT:
A STATEMENT FOR USE IN THE CHURCH OF NORTH INDIA

Introductory Note

This statement may be used by members of the Church of North India as an expression of their faith and commitment in response to the contemporary Indian context from the perspective of the Gospel of Jesus Christ. The affirmations in this statement are securely rooted in the biblical faith in general and in the Faith and Order of the Church of North India in particular. The affirmations may be recited by members of the Church of North India and especially by its Committees, Commissions, Boards, and planning bodies not as a substitute to the classical Creeds (the Apostles' Creed and the Nicene Creed) but as their faith-response to the contemporary Indian context. In practical terms this statement of affirmations and commitment must inform and determine the priorities, policies, decisions, actions and programmes of the Church of North India at all levels.

An Affirmation of Faith and Commitment

I. We the members of the Church of North India, believe and affirm that as members of this Church we are a part of the one, Holy, Catholic and Apostolic Church, a people of God, which he is building up out of all generations and races of men and women. The Church of North India is what it is by reason of what it has received from God in Christ through bringing together into one living body the several traditions of the Churches that have united. This our heritage is the fruit of the continuous working of the Holy spirit in the Church from apostolic times down to our own day.

II. We affirm and uphold the historic faith of the Church universal. We believe in one God -Father, Son, and Holy Spirit. We believe that God has acted in Christ to transform the whole creation which he loves and continually renews.

III. We believe that in the long history of our country Christ, the Eternal Word, has been at work drawing the people of our land from untruth towards Truth, from darkness towards light, from death towards life. Christ has been present in the Indian people's deep longing and search for God, in all that is noble and true in the diverse religious scriptures, traditions and cultures of our land.

IV. We rejoice in this our rich religious and cultural heritage and are one with the generations of the people of our land who have developed it. We believe that Christ calls us to affirm this heritage with the people of diverse religions and cultures. We also believe that the Gospel of Christ exposes and corrects whatever is oppressive and dehumanising in all cultures and religious traditions, including our own.

V. We believe that Christ, breaking the walls that divide people, unites them across divisions of race, language, class, culture and religion, and calls us to be instruments of love, reconciliation, justice and peace.

VI. We believe that God desires that all people be liberated from all demonic and enslaving powers and sin, and that they may have the fullness of life as God's free children. The Bible also reveals that God has a special concern for the liberation of the powerless, the poor and the oppressed from all that hinders their full development as God's free children. We believe that at the present time God calls us to strive for justice and freedom to multitudes of the poor the oppressed, the outcasts and the powerless in our own count8ry and in the world.

VII. We believe that in obedience to Christ Crucified and Risen we are called to suffer with God's suffering children and strive towards the fulfilment of His promise of fullness of life for everyone.

VIII. We affirm our commitment to unity, witness and service in the name and for the sake of Jesus Christ.

So help us God.

APPENDIX III

STATISTICS

Census of India 1981

Population of India 665,287,849 excluding Assam.

Percentage of	Hindus	82.64		Muslim	11.35
	Christians	2.43	Sikhs		1.96
	Buddhists	0.71	Jains	0.48	
	Other religions	0.42	Religion not stated		0.01
	Scheduled Castes	15.75%	Scheduled Tribes		7.76%

Provisional Population Total of Census 1991 - 843, 930, 861 excluding Jammu and Kashmir. Census was not conducted in Assam in 1981 and yet to be held in Jammu and Kashmir.

Church of North India

Dioceses	23
Congregations over	3,000
Membership over	9,000,000
Ordained Ministers	1,000

All the states of Indian Union, except for the four states of South India, are within the bounds of the CNI. This means that it covers 80% of the area and 75% of the population of India. Nine regional languages as well as Hindi and English, along with a further six major tribal languages are used within the CNI area. All the cultural differences of India's people are to be found within the CNI with congregations dispersed throughout the cities, villages and towns.

APPENDIX IV

A MAP OF THE CNI

331

BIBLIOGRAPHY

ALLEN, Roland <u>Missionary Methods: St Paul's or Ours?</u>
World Dominion Press, London 1912, reprint 1960.
ANDERSON, Benedict <u>Imagined Communities: Reflections on the Origin and Spread of Nationalism.</u> Verso Editions and NLB, London, 1985. ISBN 0860910598/7592.
ANDERSON, Gerald H. <u>ed.</u> <u>Asian Voices in Christian Theology.</u> Maryknoll, NY: Orbis, 1976.
ANDERSON, Rufus <u>Foreign Missions and their Relations and Claims.</u> Charles Scribner, New York, 1869.
ANDY, Pulney S. <u>Are Not Hindus Christians: An Address before Madras Native Christian Literature Society on 22.3.1888.</u> Madras, 1894.
APPASAMY, A.J. <u>Church Union: An Indian View.</u> CLS, Madras, 1930.
"   'The Mysticism of Hindu Bhakti Literature.'
D.Phil Thesis, 1922, Oxford.
ARRANGADEN, A.J. <u>Church Union in South India.</u>
Basel Mission Press, Bangalore, 1947.
ASIRVATHAM, E. <u>Christianity in Indian Crucible.</u> Calcutta, 1957.
AVIS, Paul D.L. <u>The Church in the Theology of the Reformers.</u> Marshall Morgan and Scott, London, 1981. ISBN 0551008520
"   <u>Ecumenical Theology and the Elusiveness of Doctrine.</u>
SPCK, London, 1986, ISBN 0281041857
BAAGO, Kaj <u>A History of the National Christian Council of India 1914-1964.</u> National Christian Council, Nagpur, 1965.
"   <u>Pioneers of Indigenous Christianity.</u> CLS, Madras, 1969.
"   First Independence Movement Among Indian Christians. <u>Indian Church History Review.</u> Vol.I, No.I, June, 1967, pp65-78.
BANERJEE, K.M. <u>Truth Defended and Error Exposed.</u> Calcutta, 1841.
"   <u>Claims of Christianity in British India.</u> 1864.
"   <u>Arian Witness to Christ; Jesus Christ the True Prajapati.</u>
Calcutta, 1875
"   <u>The Relation between Christianity and Hinduism.</u> Calcutta, 1881.
<u>Bangalore Theological Forum.</u>
BARBER, B.R. <u>Kali Charan Banerji.</u> Madras, 1912.
BARNETT, J.M. <u>The Diaconate.</u> Seabury Press, 1981.

BARRETT, Lee C. Theology as Grammar: Regulative Principles or
Paradigms and Practices. Modern Theology. IV/2,
January 1988,p153-172.
BARTH, Karl Church Dogmatics. Vol.1/2, II/I, III/2, IV/2.
T. and T. Clark, Edinburgh, 1956, 1957, 1958.
"   The Protestant Theology in the Nineteenth Century.
SCM, London, 1972. 334-01335-6
BASSHAM, Rodger C. Mission Theology. William Carey Library, Pasadena,
California, 1979. ISBN 0878083308.
BAYNE, S. ed. Ceylon, North India and Pakistan. SPCK, London 1960.
BBC Recordings and Transcripts of Interviews: Tales from the Raj.
Oral Archives, India Office Library, London.
BEASLEY-MURRAY, G.R. Baptism in the New Testament.
William B.Eerdmans, Grand Rapids, 1962, reprinted 1985.
ISBN 080281493X
BEAVER, Pierce R. ed. American Mission in Bicentennial Perspective.
William Carey Library, California, 1977.
"   The Ecumenical Beginnings in Protestant World Mission:
A history of Comity. Thomas Nelson and Sons, 1962.
BELL, G.K.A. Documents on Christian Unity. 4 Vols, OUP, London, 1924,
1930, 1948, 1958.
BERGER, Peter L. The Social Reality of Religion.
Faber, London. 1969. ISBN 0571088651
BEVAN R.J.W. ed. The Churches and Christian Unity. OUP, London, 1963.
BOAL, Barbara M. The Konds: Human Sacrifice and Religious Change.
Warminster: Aris and Phillips, 1982.
BOFF, Leonard Church: Charism and Power.
SCM, London, 1985. ISBN 33401946X
BONHOEFFER, Dietrich Sanctorum Communio: A Dogmatic Inquiry into
the Sociology of the Church. Collins, London, 1963.
BOYD, R.H.S. An Introduction to Indian Christian Theology.
CLS. Madras. 1969.
"   India and the Latin Captivity of the Church.
CUP. Cambridge. 1974. ISBN 0521203716
BRASS, Paul R. Language, Religion and Politics in North India.
CUP, Cambridge, 1974. ISBN 0521203244
BRASS,Paul R.Ethnicity and Nationalism.
Sage Publication, Delhi, 1991. ISBN 0803996942

British Council of Churches The Forgotten Trinity : Report of the British
        Council of Churches Study Commission on Trinitarian Doctrine
        Today. BCC, London. 1989. ISBN 0851691145/1196
BRUNNER, E. Christian Doctrine of Church, Faith and Consummation.
        Lutterworth, London, 1962.
    "   The Misunderstanding of the Church. Lutterworth, London,
        1952.
BUCKLEY, James J. Doctrine in the Diaspora.
        The Thomist. Vol 49. No.3, July 1985, pp443-459.
BUHLMANN, Walbert The Coming of the Third Church.
        St Paul Publications, England, 1974. SBN 854391193
CAPLAN, Lionel Class and Culture in Urban India: Fundamentalism in a
        Christian Community. Clarendon Press,
        Oxford, 1987. ISBN 0198234023
    "   Class and Christianity in South India: Indigenous Response to
        WesternDenominationalism. Modern Asian Studies.
        Vol.14/2, October 1980, p645-71.
CAPLAN, Lionel Religion and Power. CLS, Madras, 1989.
CAREY, William. An Enquiry into the Obligation of Christians to use
        Means for the Conversion of the Heathens. Leicester, 1792.
        New Facsimile Edition 1961. Reprinted 1991,
        BMS, Didcot. ISBN 0901733091
CEYLON   The Scheme of Church Union in Ceylon.
        United Society for CLS, Madras, 1949
CHADWICK, H. The Early Church. Penguin, 1967.
CHAMPION, L.G. Baptists and Unity. Mowbrays, London, 1962.
CHATTERJEE, Partha Nationalist Thought and Colonial World:
        A Derivative Discourse. Zed Books, London, 1986.
        ISBN 0862325528
Church Missionary Intelligencer: 1850-1906
Church Missionary Review: 1907-1927
Church of England Believing in the Church: The Corporate Nature of Faith.
        A Report of the Doctrine Commission of the Church of England.
        SPCK, London, 1981.
    "   ARCIC The Final Report.
        London, SPCK, 1982. ISBN 0281038597

Church of England <u>Deacons in the Ministry of the Church: A Report of the House of Bishops of the General Synod of the Church of England.</u> London, 1988. ISBN 0715137182

CHRISTENSEN, T. and HUTCHISON, W.R. eds. <u>Missionary Ideologies in the Imperialist Era - 1880-1920: Papers From the Durham Consultation: 1981.</u> Denmark. 1982.

Church of North India <u>Forward to Union.</u>
      ISPCK & LPH, Delhi & Lucknow, 1968.
"   <u>The Constitution of the Church of North India and Bye-Laws.</u> ISPCK, Delhi, 1987.
"   <u>Plan of Church Union in North India.</u> 1951, 1953, 1957, 1965. CLS, Madras.
"   <u>Profile of A Christian Church: Report of the Evaluation Commission to Study the Life and Work of the CNI</u> Institute for Development Education, Madras, 1990.

<u>Church Union News and Views.</u> New Series. Organ of the Negotiating Committee for Church Union in North India and Pakistan. Feb 1956- March 1970.

Church of South India <u>Proposed Scheme of Church Union in South India.</u> CLS, Madras, 1942.
"   <u>The Constitution of the Church of South India.</u> CLS, Madras, 1983.

<u>Church Union News and Views 1930-1947.</u>

CLEMENT, Keith <u>Friedrich Schleiermacher.</u> Collins, 1987. ISBN 0005999804

COLLINS John C. <u>Diakonia: Re-interpreting the Ancient Sources.</u> OUP, Oxford, 1990. ISBN 0195060679.

<u>Concilium.</u>
      Sociology of Religion: The Church as Institution. <u>Concilium.</u> Vol.1, No 10, January 1974.

DAHL, Nils A. The People of God.
      <u>Ecumenical Review.</u> Vol.IX, No.2, 1957, pp154-161.

DAVID, Immanuel S. History of Christianity in India: Changing Perspective.<u>Indian Church History Review.</u> Vol. XXX, No.1, June 1986, p5-12.

DAVIES, Rupert E. <u>Methodists and Unity.</u> Mowbray, London, 1963.

DAY, Lalbehari <u>Searching of Heart - An Address.</u> Serampore, 1858.
"   <u>The Desirableness and Practicability of Organising a National Church inBengal.</u> Calcutta, 1870.

DAY, Lalbehari Recollection of Alexander Duff. T. Nelson, London, 1879.
Decennial Missionary Conferences:
    Allahabad 1872-73.
    Calcutta 1882-83.
    Bombay 1892-93.
    Madras 1902.
D'COSTA, Gavin Theology and Religious Pluralism. Basil Blackwell,
    Oxford,1986. ISBN 0631145184
DILLISTONE, F.W. The Structure of Divine Society.
    Lutterworth, London, 1951.
DONOVAN, V.J. Christianity Rediscovered : An Epistle from the Masai.
    SCM, London, 1982. ISBN 334019354.
DOUGLAS, Mary How Institutions Think.
    Syracuse University Press, New York, 1986. ISBN 0815623690.
DUBOIS, J.A. Letters on the State of Christianity in India. London, 1823.
DUFF, Alexander India and India Missions. J. Johnstone, Edinburgh, 1839.
DUNN, James D.G. Unity and Diversity in the New Testament. SCM,
    London, 1977. 334024048.
DULLES, Avery Paths to Doctrinal Agreement: Ten Theses.
    Theological Studies. XLVII, 1986, pp32-47.
    "   Models of the Church. Gill and Macmillan, Dublin, 1976.
DUSSEL, Enrique Ethics and Community.
    Burns and Oats, 1988. ISBN 0860121623.
EBRIGHT, Donald F. The National Missionary Society of India 1905-42.
    Chicago, 1944.
Ecumenical Review.
EHRENSTROM, N. and MUELDER, W.G. Institutionalism and Church
    unity.SCM, London, 1963.
ELWOOD, J.D. ed. Asian Christian Theology: Emerging Themes.
    Westminster Press, Philadelphia, 1980.
FACKRE, Gabriel Narrative Theology: An overview.
    Interpretation. Vol. 37, No.4, October 1983, pp340-52.
FACKRE, Gabriel The Christian Story.
    W.B. Eerdmans, Grand Rapids, 1984.
FARLEY, Edward Ecclesial Man: A Social Phenomenology of Faith and
    Reality. Fortress Press, Philadelphia.1975. ISBN 0800602722
FARLEY, Edward Ecclesial Reflection: An Anatomy of Theological Method
    Fortress Press, Philadelphia. 1982. ISBN 0800606701

FARQUHAR, J.N. The Crown of Hinduism. OUP, London, 1913.
FEY, H.E., ed. A History of the Ecumenical Movement 1948-68.
    Vol.2. WCC, Geneva, Second Edition 1986. ISBN 2825408727.
FINDLAY, G.G. and HOLDSWORTH, W.W. History of the Wesleyan
    Methodist Missionary Society Vol V. Epworth, London, 1924.
FIRTH, C.B. An Introduction to Indian Church history. CLS, Madras, 1961.
FORD, David F. Barth and God's Story.
    Verlag Peter Lang, Frankfurt am Main, 1981. ISBN 3820459677
    "   ed. The Modern Theologians: An Introduction to Christian
    Theology in the Twentieth Century. 2 Vols.
    Basil Blackwell, Oxford, 1989. ISBN 0631153721/68087
    "   System, Story, Performance: A Proposal about the Role of
    Narrative in Christian Theology. In. HAUERWAS, S and
JONES, L.G. Eds. Why Narrative? Eerdmans, W.B. Grand Rapids,
    1989, pp191-215
FORD, David and HARDY, Daniel Jubilate. Darton Longman and Todd,
    London, 1984. ISBN 0232515506
FORRESTER, Duncan, Indian Christian Attitudes to Caste in the Nineteenth
    Century. Indian Church History Review.
    Vol.VIII/2, December, 1974, pp131-147.
FORRESTER, Duncan, Indian Christian Attitudes to Caste in the Twentieth
    Century.Indian Church History Review. Vol.IX, No.I,
    June,1975, pp3-22.
    "   Christian Theology in a Hindu Context.
    South Asian Review. Vol.8, No4, July-October, 1975, pp343-58
    "   Caste and Christianity: Attitudes and Policies of Anglo- Saxon
    Protestant Mission in India.
    Curzon Press, London and Dublin, 1980. ISBN 070070129X
FREI, Hans The Eclipse of Biblical Narrative:A study in Eighteenth and
    Nineteenth Century Hermeneutics.
    Yale University Press, New Haven, 1974, ISBN 0300016239
GARRISON, Winfred E. and DE GROOT, Alfred T. The Disciples of Christ
    A History. Bethany Press, St. Louis, Missouri, 1958.

GELLNER, Ernest Nations and Nationalism.
    Basil Blackwell. Oxford. 1983. ISBN 0631129928
GIBBARD, M. Unity is not Enough. London, 1965.

GIBBS, Mildred E. The Anglican Church in India 1600-1970.
    ISPCK, Delhi, 1972.
GORRINGE, Timothy Redeeming Time.
    Darton Longman and Todd, London, 1986. ISBN 0232517010
GRANT, J.W. God's People in India. CLS, Madras, 1960.
GRANT, J.W. The Canadian Experience of Church Union.
    Lutterworth, London, 1967.
GREEN, Garrett. ed.Scriptural Authority and Narrative Interpretation.
    Fortress Press, Philadelphia, 1987.
GUHA, Ranjit ed. Subaltern Studies. 5 Vols. OUP, Delhi, 1982-87.
GUNTON, Colin and HARDY, Daniel Eds.On Being the Church: Essays on
    Christian Community.
    T and T Clark, Edinburgh, 1989. ISBN 0567295019
GUSTAVO, Gutierez A Theology of Liberation.
    SCM, London, 1974. ISBN 0334023564
HANSON, R.P.C. Ground Work for Unity. London, 1969.
HANSON, A.T and R.P.C. The Identity of the Church.
    SCM, 1987. ISBN 033400683X
HARGREAVES, Cecil Asian Christian Thinking. ISPCK, Delhi, 1979.
HARINGTON, D.J. God's People in Christ. Fortress Press, 1980.
Harvest Field: A Magazine Devoted to the Interests of Missionary Work in
    the Indian Empire.
HAUERWAS, Stanley and JONES, Gregory L. Eds. Why Narrative ?
    Readings in Narrative Theology.
    William B. Eerdmans, Michigan, 1989. ISBN 080280439X
HAYWARD, Victor E.W. ed. The Church as Community.
    Lutterworth, London, 1966.
HEADLAM, Arthur C. Doctrine of the Church and Christian Reunion:
    The Bampton Lectures for the Year 1920.
    John Murray, London, 1923.
HENDERSON, Ian Power Without Glory: A Study in Ecumenical Politics.
    Hutchinson, London, 1969.
HENNELLY, Alfred T. Liberation Theology: A Documentary History.
    Orbis Books, Maryknoll.N.Y. 1990. ISBN 0883445921.
HICK, John God has Many Names. Macmillan Press, 1980. ISBN 0333277473
HICK, John, Problems of Religious Pluralism.
    Macmillan, London, 1985. ISBN 0333394860/879

338

HICK, John and KNITTER, Paul eds. The Myth of Christian Uniqueness.
SCM, London. reprint 1988. ISBN 0334010667
HICK, John and HEBBLETHWAITE, B. eds. Christianity and Other
Religions. Collins, 1980.
HOCKING, William E. and others Re-Thinking Missions: A Layman's
Enquiry After One Hundred Years.
New York/London; Harper Brothers, 1932
HOEFFER, H.E. ed. Debate on Mission: Issues from Indian Context
Gurukul Lutheran Theological College, Madras, 1979.
HOGG, Alfred G. Karma and Redemption: An Essay Toward the Interpreta-
tion of Hinduism and Restatement of Christianity.
CLS, Madras, 1909, reprinted 1923 and 1970.
"   The Christian Message to the Hindu. SCM, London, 1947
HOLLIS, Michael. The Significance of South India. Lutterworth, 1966.
"   Mission, Unity and Truth. London, 1967.
"   Paternalism and the Church: A Study of South Indian Church
History. OUP, London, 1962.
HOLLISTER, John N. The Centenary of the Methodist Church in Southern
Asia. Lucknow Publishing House, Lucknow, 1956.
Ingham, K. Reformers in India:1793-1833. CUP, Cambridge, 1956.
Indian Church History Review
Indian Journal of Theology.
International Review of Mission.
JOB, G.V. and Others eds. Rethinking Christianity in India.
A.N.Sudarisanam. Madras. 1938.
JOINT COUNCIL The Plan of Union Joint Council. 1940
Baptist Mission Press, Calcutta.
"   The Plan of Union Joint Council. 1942
The New India Press, Calcutta.
Journal of Theological Studies.
Journal of Ecumenical Studies.
KADOURIE, Elie. ed. Nationalism in Asia and Africa.
George Weidenfeld and Nicolson. ISBN 0297003577/3585
KAMENKA, Eugene ed. Nationalism: The Nature and Evolution of an Idea.
Edward Arnold, London, 1976.ISBN O713158743/751
KASEMAN, Ernst The Testament of Jesus According to John 17.
Fortress Press, Philadelphia, 1968.

KAYE, John William Christianity in India: An Historical Narrative.
London, 1859.
KEE, Howard C. Christian Origins in Sociological Perspective.
SCM, London, 1980. 334019338
KELLOCK, James Break Through for Church Union in North India and
Pakistan. CLS, Madras, 1965.
KELLY, J.N.D. Early Christian Doctrines.
Adam and Charles Black, London, 1965.
KELSEY, D. The Use of Scripture in Recent Theology. SCM, London, 1975.
KENNEDY, D. The History of the Church of North India.
Indian Church History Review.
Vol.VI. No2. 1972, pp101-45, Vol.VII, No.I, 1973, pp1-27.
KENNEDY, Gerald S. British Christians, Indian Nationalists and the Raj.
OUP, Delhi, 1991. SBN 0195627334
KILPATRICK, G.D. The Eucharist in Bible and Liturgy.
CUP, Cambridge, 1983. ISBN 052124675X
KOHN, Hans The Idea of Nationalism: A Study in its Origin and
Background. Macmillan. New York, 1945.
KRAEMER, Hendrik The Christian Message in a non-Christian World.
Edinburgh Press. 1938.
KUNG, Hans. The Church Burn and Oates, 1968.
KUNG, Hans. Christianity and the World Religions.
Collins, London, 1987. ISBN 000217619X
KURIEN, C.T. Mission and Proclamation. CLS, Madras, 1981.
LAIRD, M.A. Missionaries and Education in Bengal 1793-1837.
Clarendon Press, Oxford, 1972.
LAMBETH The Six Lambeth Conferences: 1867-1920. SPCK, London, 1929.
The Lambeth Conference 1948. SPCK, London, 1948.
The Lambeth Conference 1958. SPCK, London, 1958.
The Lambeth Conference 1968. SPCK, London, 1968.
LATOURETTE, Kenneth S. A History of the Expansion of Christianity.
Vol.VI 1800-1944. Eyre and Spottiswoode, London, 1943.
LEEUWEN, Vak G. ed. Searching for an Indian Ecclesiology.
ATC, Bangalore, 1984.
LINDBECK, George The Nature of Doctrine: Religion and theology in a
Postliberal Age. SPCK, London, 1984.ISBN 0281041334
LINDBECK,George The Story-Shaped Church, In GREEN, G. ed. Scriptural
Authority and Narrative Interpretation. Fortress Press, 1987.

LINDBECK, George,The Church, In WAINWRIGHT, Geoffrey. ed. Keeping
        The Faith. SPCK, London, 1989. ISBN 0281043922
LOVETT, Richard The History of London Missionary Society: 1795-1895
        2 Vols. 1899, Henry Frowde, London.
LUKAS, Bernard Our Task in India. Macmillan, London, 1914.
LUKAS, Vischar ed A Documentary History of Faith and Order Movement.
        1927-63, Bethany Press, 1963.
MACPHERSON, G. Life of L. Day. Edinburgh, 1900.
MACQUARRIE, John Faith and People of God. SCM, London, 1972.
    "   Christian Unity and Christian Diversity. SCM, London, 1975.
MALATESTA, Edward ed. St John's Gospel:1920-65: A Cumulative and
        Classified Bibliography of Books and Periodical Literature on the
        Fourth Gospel. Pontifical Biblical Institute,Rome,1967
MANSON, T.W. Ministry and Priesthood. Epworth, 1958.
MARSHALL, W.J. 'Church of North India/Pakistan:A Theological
        Assessment of the Plan of Union', Ph.D Thesis,
        Trinity College,Dublin, 1975.
    "   A United Church: Faith and Order in the North India/Pakistan
        Unity Plan. ISPCK, Delhi, 1987.
MARSHALL, Howard I Last Supper and Lord's Supper.
        Paternoster Press, Exeter, 1980. ISBN 0853643067
McGAVRAN, Donald Understanding the Church in India.
        Gospel Literature Service, Bombay, 1979. ISBN 0878081682
McCONNELL, Frank ed. The Bible and the Narrative Tradition.
        OUP, New York, 1986. ISBN 0195036980
McGRATH, Alister E. The Genesis of Doctrine.
        Basil Blackwell, Oxford, 1990. ISBN 0631166580
McGREGOR, D. Human Side of Enterprise.
        McGraw Hill University, New York, 1960.
MEYER, Harding and VISCHER, Lukas eds. Growth in Agreement: Reports
        and Agreed Statements of Ecumenical Conversations on a World
        Level. WCC, Geneva, 1984. ISBN 2825406791
MEEK, W.A. The First Urban Christians:the Social World of Paul.
        Yale University Press, New Haven and London, 1983.
Mid-Stream.
MINEAR, Paul S. Images of the Church in the New Testament.
        Lutterworth, London, 1961.
Minutes of the Round Table Conferences 1929-48.

Minutes of the All India Conference on Church Union 1931.
Minutes of the Continuation Committees of the RTC 1935-48.
Minutes of the Negotiation Committees 1955-70.
Minutes of the Working Committees 1967-70.
Minutes of the Special Committee July 1970.
Minutes of the Negotiation Committee 1951-54 are missing.
Minutes of the Inaugural Committee 1970.
Ref. Microfilm. No 1179. Bodleian Library, Oxford.
Modern Asian Studies.
MINOGUE, K.R. Nationalism. B.T. Batsford, London, 1967.
MOLLAND, Einar Christendom: The Christian Churches, Their Doctrines,
        Constitutional Forms and Ways of Worship.
        Mowbray, London, 1959.
MOLTMAN, Jurgen The Church in the Power of the Spirit.
        SCM, London, Fourth Impression 1985.
MOLTMAN, Jurgen The Open Church: Invitation to a Messianic Life Style.
        SCM, London, 1978. ISBN 334011779
Modern Theology
MOOKENTHOTTAM, A. Indian Theological Tendencies.
        Peter Lang, Berne-Frankfurt-Las Vegas. 1981. ISBN 3261046139
MORGAN, Robert and BARTON, John Biblical Interpretation.
        OUP, Oxford. ISBN 0192132571
MORGAN, Robert. ed. The Religion of The Incarnation: Anglican Essays in
        Commemoration of LUX MUNDI.
        Bristol Classical Press. 1989. ISBN 1-85399-064-7 pbk.
MUNDADAN, Mathias A. History of Christianity in India: From the
        beginning to the Middle of Sixteenth Century. Vol.I
        Theological publications in India, Bangalore, 1984.
MYERS, J.B. ed. Centenary Volume of Baptist Missionary Society 1792-1892.
        London, 1892.
National Church Collection of Papers Connected with the Movement of
National Church of India, Madras, 1893.
National Christian Council Review: Organ of the National Council of
        Churches in India.
National Missionary Intelligencer.
NIEBUHR, Richard H. The Social Sources of Denominationalism.
        World Publishing, New York, 1957.
NIEBUHR, Richard H. Christ and Culture. Faber and Faber, London, 1952.

NEILL, Stephen C. A History of Christianity in India: From the beginning to 1707. CUP, Cambridge, 1985.ISBN 0521243513

NEILL, Stephen A History of Christianity in India: 1707-1858
CUP, Cambridge, 1985, ISBN 0521303761
" Colonialism and Christian Missions. Lutterworth, 1966.

NEILL, Stephen A History of Christian Missions.
Penguin, London, 1964, Revised 1986.
" The Church and Christian Union. OUP, London, 1968.

NEILL, Stephen and WRIGHT, Tom The Interpretation of the New Testament 1861-1986 OUP, Oxford, 1990.ISBN 0192830570

NEILL, Stephen C. and ROUSE, Ruth eds. A History of the Ecumenical Movement:1517-1948.Vol.I
WCC, Geneva, 1986.ISBN 2825408719

North India Churchman: the Official Magazine of the Church of North India.

NEWBIGIN, Lesslie The Reunion of the Church.
SCM, London, 2nd Ed.1960.
" The Household of God. SCM, London, 1953.
" The Gospel in a Pluralistic Society.
SPCK, London, 1989. ISBN 028104435X
" The Open Secret.
William B. Eerdmans, Grand Rapids, 1983. ISBN 0802817521
" Unfinished Agenda: An Autobiography.
WCC, Geneva, 1985. ISBN 2825408298

NILES, D.T. Upon the Earth. Lutterworth, London, 1968.

NORRIS, R.A. The Christological Controversy.
Fortress Press, Philadelphia, 1980. ISBN 0800614119

ODDIE, G.A. Social Protest in India: British Protestant Missionaries and Social Reformers. Manohar, New Delhi, 1979.

ODDIE, G.A. Indian Christians and the National Congress 1885-1910.
Indian Church History Review. Vol.II, No.1, June 1968, pp45-54.

O'NEIL, Colman The Rule Theory of Doctrine and Propositional Truth.
The Thomist. Vol.49, No.3, July 1985, pp417-442.

PADEL, Felix J. 'British Rule and the Konds of Orissa: A Study of Tribal Administration and its legitimacy Discourse.'
D. Phil Thesis, Oxford, 1987.

PALMER, E.J. Great Church Awake. Longmans, 1920.

343

PANIKKAR, R. Unknown Christ of Hinduism.
Darton Longman Todd, London, 1981.
PANNENBERG, W. Christian Spirituality and Sacramental Community.
Darton Longman Todd, London. 1984.
PARKER, Kenneth L. The Development of the United Church of North
India.University of Chicago Libraries,Chicago, 1936.
PATHAK, Sushil M. American Missionaries and Hinduism: 1813-1910
Munshiram Manoharlal, Delhi, 1967.
PATON, David M. Anglicans and Unity. Mowbray, London, 1963.
PELIKAN, Jaroslav The Christian Tradition: A History of the Development
of Doctrine. 5 Vols. University of Chicago Press,
Chicago and London,1971, 1974, 1978, 1983, 1989.
ISBN 0226653706/722/749/765/781.
PERUMALIL, H.C. and HAMBYE, E.R. eds. Christianity in India.
Prakasam Publications, South India, 1972.
PHILIP, T.V. Krishna Mohan Banerjea: Christian Apologist.
CLS, Madras, 1982.
PHILIP, T.V.Search for an Ecclesiology in Asia In: Essays in Celebration of
CISRS Silver Jubilee. CHATTERJEE, Saral K. ed.
CLS, Madras, 1983. pp211-241.
"   Ecclesiological Discussion in India During the Last Twenty Five
Years. Indian Journal of Theology. July-December,
Vol.25, No.3 and 4, 1976, pp172-187.
PICKARD, Stephen 'The Purpose of Stating the Faith: An Historical and
Systematic inquiry into the tradition of Fundamental
Articles with special reference to Anglicanism'.
Ph.D , Dissertation. Durham, 1990.
PICKETT, Waskom J. Christian Mass Movements in India.
Abingdon Press, Cincinnati, 1933.
PIERIS, Aloysius An Asian Theology of Liberation. T and T Clark,
Edinburgh, 1988. ISBN 0567291588
PLACHER, William C. Revisionist and Postliberal Theologies and the Public
Character of Theology.
The Thomist. vol.49, No.3, July 1985, pp392-416.
POLANYI, Michael Personal Knowledge: Towards a Post-Critical
Philosophy.Routledge and Kegan Paul.
London. 1958, Revised 1973. ISBN 0710076916

344

POTTS, Daniel E. British Baptist Missionaries in India 1793-1837.
        CUP, Cambridge, 1967.
PRABHAKAR, M.E. ed. Towards a Dalit Theology. ISPCK, Delhi, 1988.
RACE, Alan Christian and Religious Pluralism.
        SCM, London, 1983. ISBN 334020921
RAWLISON, A.E.J. The Church of South India.
        Hodder and Stoughton, London, 1951.
REID, J.K.S. Presbyterians and Unity. Mowbrays, London, 1962.
        Religion and Society.
REUMANN, J. The Supper of the Lord. Fortress Press, 1983.
RICHTER, Julius A History of Missions in India. Translated by Moore,S.H.
        Oliphant Anderson and Ferrier, Edinburgh and London, 1908
2RITSCHL, Dietrich The Logic of Theology.
        SCM, London. 1986. ISBN 0334009235
ROUTLEY, Erik Congregationalists and Unity. Mowbrays, London, 1962.
ROWLAND, Christopher Christian Origins: An Account of Setting and
        Character of the Most Important Messianic Sect of
        Judaism.SPCK,London, 1985. ISBN 0281041105
ROYLE, Trevor The Last Days of the Raj.
        Coronet, London. 1990. ISBN 0340517417
RUDGE, P.F. Ministry and Management. London, 1968.
SAMARTHA, Stanley J. Hindu Response to Unbound Christ.
        CLS, Madras,1974.
   "   Lordship of Jesus Christ and Religious Pluralism.
        CLS, Madras, 1981.
SHARPE, E. Not to Destroy but to Fulfil: The Contribution of J.N.Farquhar
        to Protestant Missionary Thought in India before 1914.
        Uppsala, 1965.
   "   The Theology of A.G. Hogg.
        CISRS, Bangalore and CLS,Mdras,1971.
SCHILLEBEECKX, E. Ministry. SCM, London. 1981
SCHREITER, R.J. Constructing Local Theologies.
        SCM, London, 1985. ISBN 334019559
SCHLEIERMACHER, F. The Christian Faith.
        T and T Clark, Edinburgh, 1928.
SCHNACKENBERG, R. The Church in the New Testament. London, 1965.
SEAL, Anil The Emergence of Indian Nationalism.
        CUP, Cambridge, 1971. ISBN 0521062748

SEGUNDO, Juan L. The Community Called Church.
    Gill and Macmillan, 1980. ISBN 717110508
SEN, Keshub Chundra The Brahmo Samaj: Letters and Tracts.
    Strahan and Co, London, 1870.
SENGUPTA, Kanti P. The Christian Missionaries in Bengal, 1793-1833.
    Firma K.L. Mukhopadhyay, Calcutta, 1971
SILCOX, C.E. Church Union in Canada. Charles Edwin, New York, 1933.
SINGH, D.V. Nationalism and Search for Identity in 19th Century
    Protestant Christianity in India. Indian Church History Review.
    Vol.XIV, No2, December 1980, pp105-116.
SMART, Ninian Doctrine and Argument in Indian Philosophy.
    George Allen and Unwin, London, 1964.
SMITH, Anthony D. Theories of Nationalism. Duckworth,
    London, 1971.1983 (reprint). ISBN 071560550/844
SMITH, George Life of Alexander Duff. 2 Vols.
    Hodder and Stoughton, 1879.
SONG, C.S. Third Eye Theology. Lutterworth,
    London, 1980. ISBN 0718824539
Scottish Journal of Theology.
South India Church Man: the Official Magazine of the Church of
    South India.
South Asian Review.
SPEAR, Percival A History of India. Vol.II, Penguin, Harmondsworth, 1968.
SRINIVAS, M.N. Social Change in Modern India. University of
    California Press, California, 1966.
STROUP, G. W. The Promise of Narrative Theology. SCM, London, 1984.
STUHLMUELLER, Carroll and SENIOR, Donald The Biblical Foundations
    for Mission. SCM, London. 1983. ISBN 334001277
SUNDKLER, Bengt The Church of South India. Lutterworth, London, 1965.
SUNDKLER, L. ed. Consensus in Theology. Westminster Press, 1980.
SYKES, Stephen The Identity of Christianity.
    SPCK, London, 1984. ISBN 0281040885.
    "   The Story and Eucharist. Interpretation.
    Vol.37, No4, October, 1983, pp340-52.
SYKES, Stephen ed. Karl Barth: Studies of His Theological Method.
    Clarendon Press, Oxford, 1979. ISBN 0198266499.
SYKES, Norman Old Priest and New Presbyter. CUP, Cambridge, 1957.

TAYLOR, R.W. ed. Religion and Society: First 25 Years. 1953-78.
    CLS, Madras, 1982.
TERESA, Okure Johannine Approach to Mission.
    Mohr, Tubingen, 1988. ISBN 3161450493
THAPAR, Romila The Tradition of Historical Writing in Early India.
    Indian Church History Review. Vol.VI. No.I, June, 1972, pp1-22.
"   Imagined Religious Communities? Ancient History and Modern
    Search for a Hindu Identity. Modern Asian Studies.
    Vol.23, No.2. May, 1989, pp209-231.
"   A History of India. Vol.I, Penguin, Harmondsworth, 1968.
THANGASAMY, D.A. ed. The Theology of Chenchiah. CISRS,
    Bangalore,1966.
THEKKEDATH, Joseph History of Christianity in India:1542-1700. Vol.II
    Theological Publications in India, Bangalore, 1982.
THIEMANN, Ronald F. Revelation and Theology: The Gospel as Narrative
    Promise University of Notre Dame Press, Notre Dame, 1985
THOMAS, P.T. ed. The Theology of Chakkarai. CISRS, Bangalore, 1968.
THOMAS, M.M. Acknowledged Christ of Indian Renaissance.
    CLS, Madras, 1970.
"   Salvation and Humanisation. CLS, Madras, 1971.
"   Some Theological Dialogue. CLS, Madras, 1977.
"   Man and Universe of Faith. CLS, Madras, 1975.
"   Risking Christ For Christ's Sake.
    WCC, Geneva, 1987. ISBN 2825408824.
THOMAS, George   Christian Indians and Indian Nationalism 1885-1950.
    Verlag Peter D Lang, 1979.
THURIAN, Max   The Eucharistic Memorial: Part I The Old Testament.
    Lutterworth, London, 1960.
"   The Eucharistic Memorial Part II The New Testament
    Lutterworth, London, 1961.
THURIAN, Max ed. Churches Respond to Baptism Eucharist and Ministry.
    Vol.I-VI, WCC, Geneva, 1986-88
"   Ecumenical Perspectives on Baptism, Eucharist and Ministry.
    WCC, Geneva, 1985. ISBN O825407585.
TILL, Barry   Churches Search for Unity. Penguin, Harmondsworth, 1972.
TORRANCE, Thomas F. Kingdom and Church: A Study in the Theology of
    the Reformation. Oliver and Boyd, Edinburgh, 1956.
"   Royal Priesthood. Oliver and Boyd, London, 1955.

TORRANCE,Thomas F.The Ground and Grammar of Theology. Christian
    Journal Limited, Belfast, 1980. ISBN 0904302598
  " " ed. The Incarnation: Ecumenical Studies in the Nicene-Constan-
    tinopolitan Creed. Handsel Press, 1981. ISBN 0905312147
TOWNSEND, W.J., WORKMAN, H.B. and EAYRS, George eds. A New
    History of Methodism. Vol. I and II.
    Hodder and Stoughton, London, MCMIX.
TRACY, David Lindbeck's New Program For Theology. The Thomist.
    Vol.49, No.3, July 1985, pp460-72.
VANDUSEN, Henry P. One Great Ground of Hope.
    Lutterworth, London, 1961.
VISCHER, Lukas. ed. A Documentary History of the Faith and Order
    Movement 1927-1963. Bethany Press, St. Louis, Missouri, 1963.
WARD, Marcus The Pilgrim Church. Epworth Press, 1953.
WARD, A.M. Churches Move Together Denholmhouse, 1968.
WALKER, G.S.M. The Churchmanship of Cyprian. Lutterworth,
    London,1968
WALLER, E.H.M. Church Union in South India. SPCK, London, 1929.
WARREN, Max Social History and Christian Mission. SCM, London 1967
WAINWRIGHT, Geoffrey Eucharist and Eschatology.
    Epworth Press, London, 1971. SBN 716201607.
  "   Doxology: The Praise of God in Worship, Doctrine and Life
    Epworth Press, London, 1980. ISBN 716203324.
 " ed. Keeping the Faith. SPCK, London, 1989. ISBN 0281043922
WEBBER, H.R. Asia and Ecumenical Movement. London, 1966.
WEBSTER, John C.B. The Christian Community and Change in 19th
    Century North India. Macmillan, India, 1976. SBN 333901231
WELLS, D.S. Ye are My Witnesses: The Work of the BMS in India.
    BMS Press, Calcutta. 1942.
WHITEHEAD, H. South India Mass Movement. 1924.
  "   Our Mission Policy in India. SPCK, Madras, 1907.
WILSON, B.R. ed. Patterns of Sectarianism. Heinemann, London, 1967.
WCC Baptism Eucharist and Ministry: Faith and Order Paper 111
    WCC,Geneva, 1982. ISBN 2825407097
  "   Baptism Eucharist and Ministry 1982-1990: Report on the
    Process and Responses. WCC, Geneva, 1990. ISBN 2825409847.
ZECHARIAH, M. ed. Ecumenism in India. ISPCK, Delhi, 198 .

advaita 180-182, 184, 202, 204
Anderson, Rufus 15, 331
apologetic 61, 180, 204, 222, 245
Appasamy, A.J. 183-185, 331
baptism 19, 44-46, 82, 92, 94, 98, 109, 110, 113, 118, 122, 124, 132, 149,
        151, 157, 161-164, 166, 176, 195, 235, 249, 264, 293, 300, 312,
        313, 332, 347, 348
baptists 18, 23, 35, 46, 106, 112, 114, 115, 120, 122, 124, 125, 127, 133,
        161, 225, 277, 333
bhakti 182-184, 331
BMS 16, 34, 35, 323, 333, 347
Brass,Paul 332
brethren 3, 82, 90, 94, 97, 106, 107, 109, 124, 125, 127, 130, 133, 134,
        137, 174, 295
caste 4, 7, 9, 15, 44-52, 61-63, 66, 73, 82, 95, 97, 98, 177, 178, 190, 195,
        198, 199, 204, 206, 208, 212, 213, 230, 242, 246, 299, 310,
        311, 313, 314, 318, 336
CBCNI 127, 133, 134, 137
Christ 3, 9, 19, 27, 40-44, 48, 49, 51, 52, 59, 70, 82, 83, 87-90, 94, 97, 98,
        106, 107, 111-114, 116, 118, 119, 121, 122, 125, 127, 130, 133,
        134, 137, 138, 141, 142, 144, 145, 148, 150-159, 161-167, 174,
        176, 180, 184, 188-190, 192-196, 200, 201, 203, 215, 221-223,
        226, 227, 230, 232-234, 236, 238-241, 248, 249, 256, 259, 264,
        265, 267, 269, 271-273, 276, 277, 280, 284, 287, 288, 294, 295,
        296, 299, 301, 302, 304, 307-309, 313, 314, 319, 324, 326, 327,
        328, 331, 336, 337, 342-344, 346
christology 159, 180
church 1, 2, vii, ix, xii, 1-7, 9-14, 16-18, 20, 21, 24, 26, 28-40, 42, 44, 48,
        49, 50-52, 54-56, 59-61, 64-67, 69, 80-87, 90-99, 101-162, 164,
        165, 166-182, 184, 185, 187, 189-196, 198, 199, 201, 202, 205,
        206, 207, 209-213, 220-223, 225-227, 229, 230, 232-252, 254,
        260, 264, 265, 267-271, 273-292, 295, 298, 299, 301-308, 310,
        312, 313-327, 329, 331-347

349

church union 6, 102, 104, 105, 107, 111, 115, 120-124, 131, 139-141,
          143, 144-150, 153, 154, 173, 175-177, 185, 187, 189, 211, 238,
          277, 279, 284, 289, 317-319, 331, 333, 334, 337, 339, 341, 345,
          347
CIPBC 104, 124, 128-131, 133, 135, 137, 147, 175
classical view 254-256, 268, 286
CMS 17, 18, 26, 28, 31, 32, 35, 37, 54, 59, 90, 323
CNI xii, 3, 4, 6-8, 105, 132, 134-137, 139-142, 146, 147, 156, 158-160,
          162, 164-166, 168, 171, 177, 207, 225-227, 229, 241, 244,
          245-248, 251, 260, 264, 271, 273, 274, 279, 284, 287, 289, 290,
          301, 314, 317-320, 322, 323, 329, 334
colonial 9, 12, 59, 71-76, 191, 209, 224, 244, 316, 333
comity 28, 29, 35, 332
community ix, x, 1, 4, 8-11, 20, 33, 37, 39, 46, 51, 52, 56, 57, 60-62, 64,
          66, 67-69, 73, 77, 79, 80, 86, 98, 99, 101, 102, 152, 157, 161,
          163, 176, 186, 187, 191-196, 198-200, 208-210, 212, 213, 220,
          221, 222, 223, 226-229, 231-233, 236, 237, 240-248, 250-252,
          258, 259, 262, 263, 265, 267, 272-276, 278-280, 282, 284, 287,
          290, 292-294, 298-314, 316-321, 333, 335, 337, 343, 345, 347
confession 17, 82, 85, 118, 157, 159, 160, 231, 236, 274, 294, 320, 325
congregationalism 95, 108
cooperation xi, 20, 26-28, 30, 35, 96, 100, 117, 140, 141, 176, 223, 286,
          290
creeds 110, 116, 133, 150, 156-158, 179, 272, 324, 326
CSI 106, 120, 137, 141, 142, 146, 150, 158, 169, 173, 178, 185, 225, 323
culture 10, 25, 41, 45, 69, 71-73, 80, 184-186, 196-198, 200, 201, 207,
          208, 209, 210, 213, 217, 222, 223, 238, 245, 246, 248, 249,
          285, 318, 327, 333, 342
dalit 197, 198, 205, 223, 230, 245, 246, 344
dialogue 43, 143, 197, 198, 200, 206, 227, 245, 257, 263, 264, 307, 320,
          346
disciples of Christ 3, 106, 107, 116, 125, 127, 134, 137, 154, 336
doctrine 34, 83, 85, 88, 110, 112, 133, 146, 147, 154, 156, 157, 160, 161,
          164, 167, 179, 180, 182, 184, 185, 201, 203, 227, 240, 241,
          251, 252-274, 276, 283, 292, 294, 301, 303-305, 311, 315, 318,
          319, 331, 333, 337, 340, 343, 345, 347
early church 132, 157, 168, 229, 232, 237, 239, 243, 250, 284, 301, 319,
          333

ecclesiology 2, xii, 1, 4, 6-8, 148, 205, 207, 225-227, 229, 230, 238, 240,
            251, 253, 268, 274, 292, 312, 314, 317-321, 339, 343
ecumenical theology 207, 331
ecumenism 1, 5, 69, 178, 245, 271, 306, 317, 348
education 21, 24, 34, 36, 39, 44, 45, 55, 68, 83, 86, 279, 286, 289, 316,
            334, 339
ekklesia 152
election 7, 240, 241, 243, 246, 247, 250
elite 24, 68, 73-76, 78, 79, 81, 102, 316
episcopacy 17, 37, 113, 153, 167, 168, 279, 289
equality 53, 55, 58, 61, 85, 202
eschatology 295, 303, 305, 347
eucharist 166, 167, 265, 293, 295, 300-303, 305, 311, 312, 339, 346-348
evangelism 20, 95, 100, 128
exclusivism 220
experience 2, 21, 26, 33, 57, 75, 95, 111, 113, 143, 144, 147, 157, 159,
            160, 163, 183-185, 192, 218, 220-222, 228, 231, 235, 238, 247,
            253, 255-259, 261, 262, 289, 300, 319, 324, 337
fulfilment 42, 43, 89, 90, 120, 123, 141, 143, 230, 232, 235, 237, 249, 328
Hick, John 215, 337, 338
hinduism 7, 19, 20, 42, 43, 49, 62, 87-90, 92, 97, 99, 180, 182, 185, 192,
            194, 196, 204, 208, 215, 242, 244, 251, 260, 321, 331, 336,
            338, 343
holy spirit 110, 112, 113, 122, 132, 133, 138, 152, 158, 159, 162, 163,
            165, 171, 192, 205, 240, 241, 273, 274, 291, 294, 302, 309,
            324, 327
identity ix, xi, xii, 1-9, 14, 20, 46, 59-61, 65, 67, 69, 71, 74, 78-81, 93,
            101, 103, 142, 157, 177-180, 183, 191, 197-200, 204, 205, 207,
            208, 209-211, 213, 214, 221, 223-225, 228-231, 234-239, 241,
            242, 243-247, 250, 251, 254, 258, 259, 262, 273, 277, 278, 284,
            289, 290, 293, 294, 297-301, 304-306, 310, 311, 313-320, 322,
            337, 345, 346
Indian Christian Theology 185, 188, 197, 201, 202, 204, 207, 245, 332
Indian Church 6, 26, 35-37, 40, 60, 65-67, 92, 93, 101-103, 105, 149,
            189, 199, 201, 223, 245, 279, 321, 334, 336, 338, 339, 342,
            345, 346
Indian Nationalism xi, 1, 4, 5, 20, 67, 68, 70, 75-77, 81, 186, 244, 345,
            346

Indian society 1, 7, 9, 11, 23, 45, 51, 63, 64, 66, 74, 79, 99, 102, 195-197,
        207, 209, 212, 213, 221, 222, 226, 242, 244, 284, 311, 320, 323
indigenous 5, 7, 18, 38, 40, 44, 66, 68, 74, 76, 87, 89, 92, 96, 99-102,
        144, 179, 180, 186, 187, 199, 200, 203, 204, 207, 244, 245,
        247, 319, 321, 331, 333
institution 82, 97, 118, 165, 190, 191, 211, 227, 237, 238, 242, 254, 275,
        276, 278, 279, 284, 285, 288, 291, 292, 297, 302, 303, 307,
        309, 311, 315, 318, 319, 322, 334
Israel 227, 229-237, 239, 241, 243, 247, 249-251, 262, 271, 275, 284, 291,
        297, 299, 320
joint council 104, 113-117, 141, 142, 338
Lambeth Conference 104, 108, 120, 129, 146, 170, 172-174, 225, 272,
        339
liberal 36, 41, 42, 44, 187, 188, 251, 262
liberation 64, 71, 163, 193, 194, 197, 198, 205, 206, 307, 317, 328, 337,
        343
liberation theology 205, 206, 337
Lindbeck, George 229, 237, 243, 250, 253, 255-257, 262, 264-266, 340
LMS 17, 41, 93, 114, 323
Lord's Supper 8, 48, 49, 109, 165-167, 227, 235, 298-300, 302, 318, 319,
        321, 340
Lucas, Bernard 44
management 277, 285-288, 291, 292, 307, 344
map xii
mass movement 50-52, 199, 348
methodism 347
ministry 16, 21, 30, 83, 90, 92, 110-114, 116-120, 122-125, 129-134, 137,
        139, 140, 147, 165, 166, 168-177, 225, 265, 277, 280-284, 287,
        291, 292, 293, 302, 306, 307, 312, 320, 334, 340, 344, 347, 348
mission xi, 1, 5-7, 9, 11-20, 24, 26, 28-30, 33, 35-42, 44-52, 56, 59, 60,
        62, 65, 66, 80, 84-86, 90, 93, 95, 96, 101, 107, 109, 125, 127,
        128, 141-144, 153, 155, 168, 179, 185, 187, 192, 207, 221, 223,
        226, 227, 241, 244, 248, 250, 254, 273, 277, 282, 285, 286,
        289, 299, 311, 316-319, 321, 331, 332, 336, 338, 339, 345-348
missionary vii, viii, xi, 2, 5, 11, 13, 15-21, 24-32, 34-46, 49, 50, 52-60,
        63, 67-69, 80-82, 84, 85, 87, 90-96, 98-102, 106, 107, 127, 128,
        137, 166, 167, 186-188, 190, 223, 226, 242, 250, 284, 290, 292,
        306, 323, 331, 333-337, 340-342, 344

missionary societies 17, 27, 31, 34, 95, 98, 190
narrative 65, 227-229, 232, 237, 243, 244, 250, 252, 262, 267, 270, 295,
            299, 300, 311, 318-320, 335-337, 339, 340, 345, 346
national church 5, 56, 61, 66-72, 76, 77, 79-84, 86, 93, 95-102, 109, 121,
            144, 149, 179, 186, 201, 207, 232, 244-247, 283, 290, 310, 314,
            316, 317, 318, 331, 334, 335, 341, 342
nationalism xi, 1, 4, 5, 20, 55, 61, 65, 67-79, 81, 90, 93, 99-101, 176, 179,
            185, 186, 213, 244, 316, 321, 331, 332, 336, 338, 339, 341,
            345, 346
negotiating churches 121, 125, 126, 129-131, 134, 148, 149, 153, 169,
            172, 272, 273, 279
negotiating committee 106, 120, 121, 124, 125, 129-131, 134, 323
NMS 69, 99, 100
open community 191
ordination 31, 48, 49, 117, 118, 120, 123, 130, 165, 167, 171-175, 287,
            305
organic union 3, 27, 141, 151, 177, 225, 238
parity 85, 216, 283, 318
people of God 2, 8, 165, 213, 232-234, 236, 237, 239-241, 243, 244, 246,
            247, 282, 283, 287-289, 291-293, 297, 306, 315, 317, 320, 322,
            326, 334, 340
Plamenatz 71, 72
plan 6, 33, 104, 114-117, 120-124, 126, 129, 131-136, 139-141, 146-148,
            150, 153, 162-167, 170, 172, 173, 175, 182, 234, 334, 338, 340
pluralism 160, 213-217, 221, 222, 241, 320, 335, 338, 344
poor 32, 56, 59, 202, 206, 209, 223, 246, 295, 309, 311, 328
poverty 205, 206, 221, 222, 318
presbyterianism 17, 95
priesthood 113, 276, 280, 287, 306, 340, 347
raj 52, 56-59, 76, 332, 339, 344
Ramanuja 180, 182, 183, 202
reconciliation 213, 215, 222, 225-227, 230, 254, 260, 264, 298, 327
relativism 6, 160, 216, 217, 220, 221, 256
religions x, 25, 40-43, 98, 179, 187, 188, 194-196, 202, 213, 215, 216,
            218, 221, 222, 241, 257, 261, 311, 322, 327, 329, 338, 339
rethinking 149, 185-191, 251, 278, 289, 312, 338
revelation 87, 112, 158, 159, 185, 188, 200, 201, 210, 214, 215, 228, 247,
            254, 255, 256, 259, 324, 346

Roman Catholic 11, 12, 82, 180, 254, 265, 303
RTC 104-108, 110, 112-120, 126, 153, 172, 323, 341
rule theory 256, 260-263, 265, 266, 269, 343
sacraments 110, 113, 122, 132, 151, 167, 177, 272, 283, 300-302, 306
salvation 19, 41, 44, 82, 110, 113, 158, 159, 182, 183, 200, 214-216, 221,
       222, 241, 254, 273, 287, 297, 299, 324, 346
Sankara 180-183, 202
scheme 44, 108, 111, 115, 116, 121, 126, 143-145, 149, 150, 155, 158,
       159, 260, 333, 334
scripture 110, 156, 159, 185, 206, 227, 266, 272, 287, 300, 339
Serampore vii, 15, 16, 19, 21-23, 33, 34, 36, 47, 85, 334
SIUC 69, 144
social reform 22, 23, 52, 60, 79, 80
society vii, 1, 7, 9, 11, 16-23, 25, 26, 30, 32-34, 39, 43, 45, 47, 49-51, 59,
       60, 61, 63, 64, 66, 69, 70, 72, 74, 79, 88, 91, 93, 99, 100, 102,
       107, 109-112, 116, 121, 127, 137, 142, 145, 177, 180, 189, 190,
       192, 194-197, 205, 207, 209-213, 217, 220-223, 226, 242-244,
       246, 248, 251, 277, 278, 281, 283-285, 290, 299, 308, 309, 311,
       318, 320, 323, 331, 333, 335, 336, 340-342, 344, 346
SPG 16, 34, 35, 47, 57
statement of faith xi, 109, 131, 155, 156, 158-161, 271, 273, 274, 319
story xi, 5, 9, 12, 30, 70, 78, 99, 104, 106, 158, 160, 204, 210, 217, 221,
       227, 228, 227-237, 239, 241, 243, 244, 247-253, 259, 261, 262,
       266, 267, 270, 271, 273, 275-277, 284, 291-300, 302, 303, 305,
       314, 315, 317-320, 335, 336, 340, 346
subaltern 74-76, 199, 246, 337
supper 8, 48, 49, 109, 110, 165-167, 227, 235, 294-309, 311-314, 318,
       319, 321, 340, 344
synod 29, 107, 120, 129, 133, 139, 141, 166, 169, 279, 289, 334
translation 20-22, 199
tribal 23, 51, 63, 64, 198, 223, 230, 242, 246, 310, 314, 329, 343
trinity 120, 133, 154, 156, 182, 270, 273, 274, 319, 333, 340
truth 27, 39, 40, 44, 47, 54, 87, 92, 113, 147, 148, 201, 204, 215, 216,
       218, 220, 249, 252, 255, 256, 260-262, 266, 268-270, 288, 304,
       322, 327, 331, 338, 343
UCNI 104, 106-108, 113, 115, 126, 128-130, 133, 135-137, 160, 174, 175
unification 2, 54, 114, 117-120, 122, 123, 125, 129-131, 137, 139, 140,
       169, 170-175, 177, 225, 312

union xi, 2-6, 27, 29, 35, 81, 84, 86, 92, 94, 98, 101-111, 113-118, 120,
121, 122-127, 129-131, 134-141, 143-151, 153-155, 158, 162,
163, 167, 170, 171, 173-177, 182, 184, 185, 187, 189, 211, 225,
231, 238, 260, 277, 279, 284, 289, 313, 317-320, 322, 329, 331,
333, 334, 337-342, 345, 347

uniting xii, 2, 3, 6, 96, 110, 112, 113, 117-119, 122, 123, 125, 129, 131,
133, 137, 140, 142, 148, 155, 156, 158, 160, 169-171, 173, 175,
221, 223, 225-227, 238, 247, 248, 259, 280, 305, 319, 325

unity 1, 2, 7, 13, 28-30, 32, 56, 62, 70, 78, 80, 81, 95, 97, 100, 102, 109,
114, 119, 121, 127, 129-132, 139, 142, 144, 145, 147, 148, 150,
151, 152-156, 158-161, 163, 164, 168, 172, 174-179, 181, 187,
203, 207, 220, 221, 223, 225-227, 230, 232, 234, 235, 238, 239,
248, 249, 259, 260, 272, 273, 275, 299, 304, 305, 317, 325,
328, 332-335, 337, 338, 340, 343, 344, 347

WCC 2, 58, 166, 167, 265, 293, 323, 336, 340, 342, 346-348

STUDIEN ZUR INTERKULTURELLEN GESCHICHTE DES CHRISTENTUMS
ETUDES D'HISTOIRE INTERCULTURELLE DU CHRISTIANISME
STUDIES IN THE INTERCULTURAL HISTORY OF CHRISTIANITY

Begründet von/fondé par/founded by
Hans Jochen Margull †, Hamburg

Herausgegeben von/edité par/edited by

Richard Friedli   Walter J. Hollenweger   Theo Sundermeier
Université de Fribourg   University of Birmingham   Universität Heidelberg

Jan A.B. Jongeneel
Rijksuniversiteit Utrecht

Band   1   Wolfram Weiße: Südafrika und das Antirassismusprogramm. Kirchen im Spannungsfeld einer Rassengesellschaft.

Band   2   Ingo Lembke: Christentum unter den Bedingungen Lateinamerikas. Die katholische Kirche vor den Problemen der Abhängigkeit und Unterentwicklung.

Band   3   Gerd Uwe Kliewer: Das neue Volk der Pfingstler. Religion, Unterentwicklung und sozialer Wandel in Lateinamerika.

Band   4   Joachim Wietzke: Theologie im modernen Indien - Paul David Devanandan.

Band   5   Werner Ustorf: Afrikanische Initiative. Das aktive Leiden des Propheten Simon Kimbangu.

Band   6   Erhard Kamphausen: Anfänge der kirchlichen Unabhängigkeitsbewegung in Südafrika. Geschichte und Theologie der äthiopischen Bewegung. 1880-1910.

Band   7   Lothar Engel: Kolonialismus und Nationalismus im deutschen Protestantismus in Namibia 1907-1945. Beiträge zur Geschichte der deutschen evangelischen Mission und Kirche im ehemaligen Kolonial- und Mandatsgebiet Südwestafrika.

Band   8   Pamela M. Binyon: The Concepts of "Spirit" and "Demon". A Study in the use of different languages describing the same phenomena.

Band   9   Neville Richardson: The World Council of Churches and Race Relations. 1960 to 1969.

Band   10   Jörg Müller: Uppsala II. Erneuerung in der Mission. Eine redaktionsgeschichtliche Studie und Dokumentation zu Sektion II der 4. Vollversammlung des Ökumenischen Rates der Kirchen, Uppsala 1968.

Band   11   Hans Schöpfer: Theologie und Gesellschaft. Interdisziplinäre Grundlagenbibliographie zur Einführung in die befreiungs- und polittheologische Problematik: 1960-1975.

Band   12   Werner Hoerschelmann: Christliche Gurus. Darstellung von Selbstverständnis und Funktion indigenen Christseins durch unabhängige charismatisch geführte Gruppen in Südindien.

Band   13   Claude Schaller: L'Eglise en quête de dialogue. Vergriffen.

Band   14   Theo Tschuy: Hundert Jahre kubanischer Protestantismus (1868-1961). Versuch einer kirchengeschichtlichen Darstellung.

Band   15   Werner Korte: Wir sind die Kirchen der unteren Klassen. Entstehung, Organisation und gesellschaftliche Funktionen unabhängiger Kirchen in Afrika.

Band   16   Arnold Bittlinger: Papst und Pfingstler. Der römisch katholisch-pfingstlerische Dialog und seine ökumenische Relevanz.

Band   17   Ingemar Lindén: The Last Trump. An historico-genetical study of some important chapters in the making and development of the Seventh-day Adventist Church.

Band 18 Zwinglio Dias: Krisen und Aufgaben im brasilianischen Protestantismus. Eine Studie zu den sozialgeschichtlichen Bedingungen und volkspädagogischen Möglichkeiten der Evangelisation.

Band 19 Mary Hall: A quest for the liberated Christian. Examined on the basis of a mission, a man and a movement as agents of liberation.

Band 20 Arturo Blatezky: Sprache des Glaubens in Lateinamerika. Eine Studie zu Selbstverständnis und Methode der "Theologie der Befreiung".

Band 21 Anthony Mookenthottam: Indian Theological Tendencies. Approaches and problems for further research as seen in the works of some leading Indian theologicans.

Band 22 George Thomas: Christian Indians and Indian Nationalism 1885-1950. An Interpretation in Historical and Theological Perspectives.

Band 23 Essiben Madiba: Evangélisation et Colonisation en Afrique: L'Héritage scolaire du Cameroun (1885-1965).

Band 24 Katsumi Takizawa: Reflexionen über die universale Grundlage von Buddhismus und Christentum.

Band 25 S.W. Sykes (editor): England and Germany. Studies in theological diplomacy.

Band 26 James Haire: The Character and Theological Struggle of the Church in Halmahera, Indonesia, 1941-1979.

Band 27 David Ford: Barth and God's Story. Biblical Narrative and the Theological Method of Karl Barth in the Church Dogmatics.

Band 28 Kortright Davis: Mission for Carribean Change. Carribean Development As Theological Enterprice.

Band 29 Origen V. Jathanna: The Decisiveness of the Christ-Event and the Universality of Christianity in a world of Religious Plurality. With Special Reference to Hendrik Kraemer and Alfred George Hogg as well as to William Ernest Hocking and Pandipeddi Chenchiah.

Band 30 Joyce V. Thurman: New Wineskins. A Study of the House Church Movement.

Band 31 John May: Meaning, Consensus and Dialogue in Buddhist-Christian-Communication. A study in the Construction of Meaning.

Band 32 Friedhelm Voges: Das Denken von Thomas Chalmers im kirchen- und sozialgeschichtlichen Kontext.

Band 33 George MacDonald Mulrain: Theology in Folk Culture. The Theological Significance of Haitian Folk Religion.

Band 34 Alan Ford: The Protestant Reformation in Ireland, 1590-1641. 2. unveränderte Auflage.

Band 35 Harold Tonks: Faith, Hope and Decision-Making. The Kingdom of God and Social Policy-Making. The Work of Arthur Rich of Zürich.

Band 36 Bingham Tembe: Integrationismus und Afrikanismus. Zur Rolle der kirchlichen Unabhängigkeitsbewegung in der Auseinandersetzung um die Landfrage und die Bildung der Afrikaner in Südafrika, 1880-1960.

Band 37 Kingsley Lewis: The Moravian Mission in Barbados 1816-1886. A Study of the Historical Context and Theological Significance of a Minority Church Among an Oppressed People.

Band 38 Ulrich M. Dehn: Indische Christen in der gesellschaftlichen Verantwortung. Eine theologische und religionssoziologische Untersuchung politischer Theologie im gegenwärtigen Indien.

Band 39 Walter J. Hollenweger (Ed.): Pentecostal Research in Europe: Problems, Promises and People. Proceedings from the Pentecostal Research Conference at the University of Birmingham (England) April 26th to 29th 1984.

Band 40 P. Solomon Raj: A Christian Folk-Religion in India. A Study of the Small Church Movement in Andhra Pradesh, with a Special Reference to the Bible Mission of Devadas.

Band 41 Karl-Wilhelm Westmeier: Reconciling Heaven and earth: The Transcendental Enthusiasm and Growth of an Urban Protestant Community, Bogota, Colombia.

Band 42 George A. Hood: Mission Accomplished? The English Presbyterian Mission in Lingtung, South China. A Study of the Interplay between Mission Methods and their Historical Context.

Band 43 Emmanuel Yartekwei Lartey: Pastoral Counselling in Inter-Cultural Perspective: A Study of some African (Ghanaian) and Anglo-American viewes on human existence and counselling.

Band 44 Jerry L. Sandidge: Roman Catholic/Pentecostal Dialogue (1977-1982): A Study in Developing Ecumenism.

Band 45 Friedeborg L. Müller: The History of German Lutheran Congregations in England, 1900-1950.

Band 46 Roger B. Edrington: Everyday Men: Living in a Climate of Unbelief.

Band 47 Bongani Mazibuko: Education in Mission/Mission in Education. A Critical Comparative Study of Selected Approaches.

Band 48 Jochanan Hesse (Ed.): Mitten im Tod - vom Leben umfangen. Gedenkschrift für Werner Kohler.

Band 49 Elisabeth A. Kasper: Afrobrasilianische Religion. Der Mensch in der Beziehung zu Natur, Kosmos und Gemeinschaft im Candomblé - eine tiefenpsychologische Studie.

Band 50 Charles Chikezie Agu: Secularization in Igboland. Socio-religious Change and its Challenges to the Church Among the Igbo.

Band 51 Abraham Adu Berinyuu: Pastoral Care to the Sick in Africa. An Approach to Transcultural Pastoral Theology.

Band 52 Boo-Woong Yoo: Korean Pentecostalism. Its History and Theology.

Band 53 Roger H. Hooker: Themes in Hinduism and Christianity. A Comparative Study.

Band 54 Jean-Daniel Plüss: Therapeutic and Prophetic Narratives in Worship. A Hermeneutic Study of Testimonies and Visions. Their Potential Significance for Christian Worship and Secular Society.

Band 55 John Mansford Prior: Church and Marriage in an Indonesian Village. A Study of Customary and Church Marriage among the Ata Lio of Central Flores, Indonesia, as a Paradigm of the Ecclesial Interrelationship between village and Institutional Catholicism.

Band 56 Werner Kohler: Umkehr und Umdenken. Grundzüge einer Theologie der Mission (herausgegeben von Jörg Salaquarda).

Band 57 Martin Maw: Visions of India. Fulfilment Theology, the Aryan Race Theory, and the Work of British Protestant Missionaries in Victorian India.

Band 58 Aasulv Lande: Meiji Protestantism in History and Historiography. A Comparative Study of Japanese and Western Interpretation of Early Protestantism in Japan.

Band 59 Enyi Ben Udoh: Guest Christology. An interpretative view of the christological problem in Africa.

Band 60 Peter Schüttke-Scherle: From Contextual to Ecumenical Theology? A Dialogue between Minjung Theology and 'Theology after Auschwitz'.

Band 61 Michael S. Northcott: The Church and Secularisation. Urban Industrial Mission in North East England.

Band 62 Daniel O'Connor: Gospel, Raj and Swaraj. The Missionary Years of C. F. Andrews 1904-14.

Band 63 Paul D. Matheny: Dogmatics and Ethics. The Theological Realism and Ethics of Karl Barth's Church Dogmatics.

Band 64 Warren Kinne: A People's Church? The Mindanao-Sulu Church Debacle.

Band 65 Jane Collier: The culture of economism. An exploration of barriers to faith-as-praxis.

Band 66 Michael Biehl: Der Fall Sadhu Sundar Singh. Theologie zwischen den Kulturen.

Band 67 Brian C. Castle: Hymns: The Making and Shaping of a Theology for the Whole People of God. A Comparison of the Four Last Things in Some English and Zambian Hymns in Intercultural Perspective.

Band 68 Jan A. B. Jongeneel (Ed.): Experiences of the Spirit. Conference on Pentecostal and Charismatic Research in Europe at Utrecht University 1989 .

Band 69 William S. Campbell: Paul's Gospel in an Intercultural Context. Jew and Gentile in the Letter to the Romans.

Band 70 Lynne Price: Interfaith Encounter and Dialogue. A Methodist Pilgrimage.

Band 71 Merrill Morse: Kosuke Koyama. A model for intercultural theology .

Band 75 Jan A. B. Jongeneel a.o. (Eds.): Pentecost, Mission and Ecumenism. Essays on Intercultural Theology. Festschrift in Honour of Professor Walter J. Hollenweger.

Band 76 Siga Arles: Theological Education for the Mission of the Church in India: 1947-1987. Theological Education in relation to the identification of the Task of Mission and the Development of Ministries in India: 1947-1987; with special reference to the Church of South India.

Band 77 Roswith I.H. Gerloff: A Plea for British Black Theologies. The Black Church Movement in Britain in its transatlanctic cultural and theological interaction with special reference to the Pentecostal Oneness (Apostolic) and Sabbatarian movements. 2 parts.

Band 78 Friday M. Mbon: Brotherhood of the Cross and Star. A New Religious Movement in Nigeria.

Band 79 John Samuel Pobee (ed.): Exploring Afro-christology.

Band 80 Frieder Ludwig: Kirche im kolonialen Kontext. Anglikanische Missionare und afrikanische Propheten im südöstlichen Nigeria.

Band 81 Werner A. Wienecke: Die Bedeutung der Zeit in Afrika. In den traditionellen Religionen und in der missionarischen Verkündigung.

Band 82 Ukachukwu Chris Manus: Christ, the African King. New Testament Christology.

Band 83 At Ipenburg: 'All Good Men'. The Development of Lubwa Mission, Chinsali, Zambia, 1905-1967.

Band 84 Heinrich Schäfer: Protestantismus in Zentralamerika. Christliches Zeugnis im Spannungsfeld von US-amerikanischem Fundamentalismus, Unterdrückung und Wiederbelebung "indianischer" Kultur.

Band 85 Joseph Kufulu Mandunu: Das "Kindoki" im Licht der Sündenbocktheologie. Versuch einer christlichen Bewältigung des Hexenglaubens in Schwarz-Afrika.

Band 86 Peter Fulljames: God and Creation in intercultural perspective. Dialogue between the Theologies of Barth, Dickson, Pobee, Nyamiti and Pannenberg.

Band   87 Stephanie Lehr: "Wir leiden für den Taufschein!" Mission und Kolonialisierung am Beispiel des Landkatechumenates in Nordostzaire.

Band   88 Dhirendra Kumar Sahu: The Church of North India. A Historical and Systematic Theological Inquiry into an Ecumenical Ecclesiology.